ENJOY THE GAME

FOOTBALL

A BLOODY AND MURTHERING PRACTICE

TRACING FOOTBALL'S FAMILY TREE

GRAEME DOBSON

We acknowledge the Traditional Owners of the land on which we publish books, the Quandamooka people, and pay our respects to Elders past, present and emerging.

Published by:
Boolarong Press
38/1631 Wynnum Road
Tingalpa Qld 4173
Australia.
www.boolarongpress.com.au

First published 2024

A catalogue record for this book is available from the National Library of Australia

ISBN: 9781922643995 (paperback)

Cover design by Boolarong Press
Cover images: jamesteohart, Nastco, Lorado, master1305, OSTILL from iStock
Typeset by Boolarong Press in Granjon LT Std 12pt

Printed and bound by Watson Ferguson & Company, Tingalpa, Australia

For my beautiful Barbara,
who remained stoic in the face of far too much random
information about football and other apparently unrelated topics.

Uncomplaining, almost.

If you don't count eye rolls.

As concerning football, I protest unto you that it may rather be called a friendly kind of fight than a play or recreation — a bloody and murthering practise than a fellowly sport or pastime.

The Anatomie of Abuses.
Philip Stubbs, Puritan pamphleteer, 1583

Better than wrestling or running because it exercises every part of the body, takes up little time, and costs nothing. It is profitable training in strategy and could be played with varying degrees of strenuousness … When, for example, people face each other, vigorously attempting to prevent each other from taking the space between, this exercise is a very heavy, vigorous one, involving much use of the hold by the neck, and many wrestling holds.

Claudius Galenus, Roman physician. 130–210 CE.

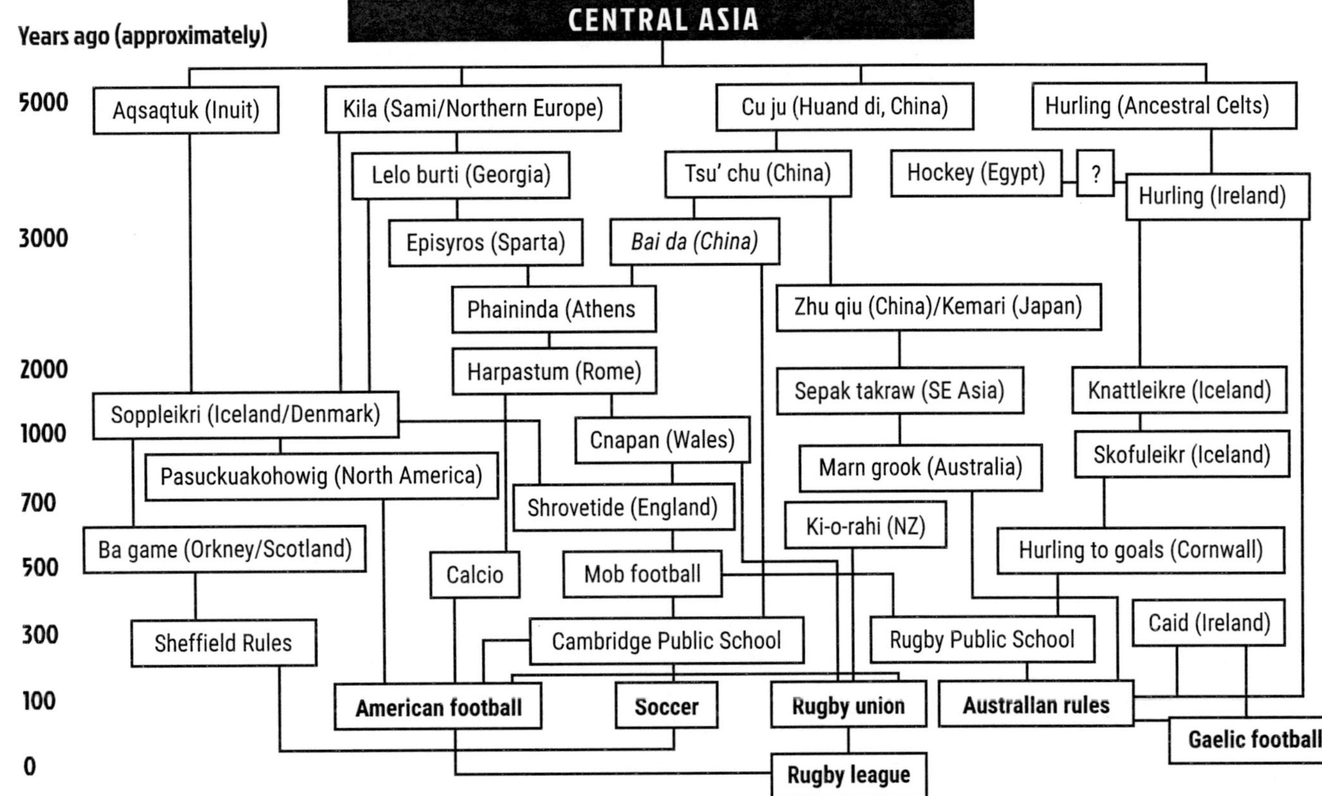

FOOTBALL'S FAMILY TREE
CENTRAL ASIA
Years ago (approximately)
5000
3000
2000
1000
700
500
300
100
0
Aqsaqtuk (Inuit)
Kila (Sami/Northern Europe)
Cu ju (Huand di, China)
Hurling (Ancestral Celts)
Lelo burti (Georgia)
Tsu' chu (China)
Hockey (Egypt)
?
Hurling (Ireland)
Episyros (Sparta)
Bai da (China)
Phaininda (Athens
Zhu qiu (China)/Kemari (Japan)
Harpastum (Rome)
Sepak takraw (SE Asia)
Knattleikre (Iceland)
Soppleikri (Iceland/Denmark)
Cnapan (Wales)
Marn grook (Australia)
Skofuleikr (Iceland)
Pasuckuakohowig (North America)
Shrovetide (England)
Ki-o-rahi (NZ)
Ba game (Orkney/Scotland)
Calcio
Mob football
Hurling to goals (Cornwall)
Sheffield Rules
Cambridge Public School
Rugby Public School
Caid (Ireland)
American football
Soccer
Rugby union
Australlan rules
Gaelic football
Rugby league

FOOTBALL:

Any of several games played between two teams on a usually rectangular field having goalposts or goals at each end and whose object is to get the ball over a goal line, into a goal, or between goalposts by running, passing, or kicking. (Webster Dictionary)

CONTENTS

INTRODUCTION

Like the wild Irish, I'll ne'er think thee dead
Till I can play at football with thy head
John Webster, *The White Devil*, 1612

One Saturday afternoon, after a long morning behind the lawnmower, I sat on the couch to watch a game. To be honest, it wasn't the most exciting game I'd ever watched and my mind wandered. Why, I thought, do people do this? Thousands, hundreds of thousands, millions of men and increasing numbers of women worldwide spend hours in strenuous training just to have eighty or ninety minutes on a field trying to get a ball past an opponent, sometimes with extreme violence and the very real risk of serious injury, broken bones, occasionally a lifetime of paralysis, or even death?

It defies all logic.

At the end of the game nothing has changed in the world, nothing has been produced and no one is better off (except some of the professional players, who make a fortune). Yet hundreds of thousands of people enthusiastically risk life, limb and dignity week in, week out just to play with a ball.

Why?

And if it comes to that, why do they try to do it in so many and varied ways? Why do some pick the ball up and try to carry it through their opponent's line while others try to push it past them with their feet while performing a delicate and confusing dance?

Why are some balls round and some oval?

Why is the beer warm, the pies cold and the queues so bloody long?

While these questions were bubbling up I realised that I was watching the game, but not seeing it. The scores had changed and I had to rewind to see why, then I wondered why I'd done that. Why was it important for me to see every point being scored? It wasn't even my team that scored!

All those questions were interfering with the game and I had to keep rewinding because I was away with the fairies, so after the whistle I did a little digging. Then a little more, then a lot more, and I got drawn down so many deep rabbit holes it's a wonder I ever saw the light of day again.

In the dark, muddy recesses of those holes I unearthed football's ancestors, all the players and all the games that led inexorably to our modern games. Deep in those rabbit holes there were Vikings, Inuit, ancient Greeks, Romans, and in the deepest, darkest hole of all, an ancient, rather vicious Chinese warlord. But, like any family tree, the further I went the more the story got peppered with 'perhapses' and 'maybes' and 'possiblies'. 'Could haves' abound, and unprovable theories are plentiful, because finding the first game was like finding the pebble that started the landslide. And trying to make sense of all that happened all those years ago is like trying to make out players at the other end of a field, in a fog, at night, with only half the lights working.

I found football's family tree, and it's like nothing I'd ever dreamed.

But I never did find out why the beer's warm, the pies are cold and the queues so long. That, I'm afraid, would take a PhD.

*

Before I start, a word of warning. If you're looking for names of individual players or in-depth analysis of individual games, I'm afraid you'll be disappointed. This is a history of football and not a commentary on any particular code; its only concern is their histories, development, and how they relate to each other and their predecessors. I make no apologies for trying to lead the reader through the cultures and histories that nurtured the games, they're all part of the story and without understanding them, even at a basic level, you can't understand how the games reached the point they have.

Oh, and in case you're wondering, I've followed the tradition of genealogists and started with the latest generation and worked my way backwards.

Prologue
STONES AND STOMACHS

Evidence for the first games is virtually impossible to find. Archaeology is really the only option, and that, for something that tends not to leave any solid traces, is a problem.

But there is, perhaps, one exception.

According to archaeologists, football was played in the stone-age when balls were made of, appropriately enough, stone. It seems unlikely, but stone balls that date back nearly 100,000 years have been dug up in Xujiayao in China and, apparently, the best explanation is that they were primitive footballs. The oldest were roughly formed and about the size of a baseball, but as time passed and presumably skills improved, they became smoother and better made. By the time the Han Chinese appeared on the scene about two thousand years ago they were using perfect stone balls to play a game that seems to have been like a modern day game of bowls, but played with the feet.

I don't know if this game still exists somewhere in rural China or if it has any links to the ancient stone balls, but if it does it would have a legitimate claim to be the oldest football code—actually, the oldest sport of any kind—in the world.

It's intriguing that the stone balls were discovered in roughly the same locale where a game involving kicking a purpose made ball was first recorded. It appeared in oral history, or mythology if you prefer, about 5,000 years ago—that's about the same time as Stonehenge and the Pyramids were built. Unfortunately ancient oral history is a lot less substantial than stone structures, and the older oral history gets the more it's regarded as mythology, and eventually the two terms become interchangeable and are dismissed by modern commentators. But almost all myths ultimately have some basis in truth, no matter how abstract.

And in this case it was one of the first stories to be written down when writing was invented a thousand or so years later, which lends it some degree of credibility. And it sounds right, but as you would expect of a 5,000 year old story, the details are sketchy.

In a nutshell, it goes something like this:

A great battle was fought in which Huang di, the Yellow Emperor as he was later known, defeated a great rival. After the battle he had the enemy general's skin mounted for archery practice and his stomach stuffed and given to his troops to use as a football.

Not much to go on, really. Other oral history of the time tells of a great battle Huang di fought against Chi yu on a field called Zhuolu. Huong di won that battle, so there's a good chance that, while Huang di went on to become the first Emperor, Chi yu became the world's first, or at least the first recorded, purpose-made football.

It's probably unlikely that the idea of making a ball out of a stomach and then kicking it simply sprang to Huong di's mind out of the blue. When you think about it, it's quite a sophisticated idea—someone had to know what part of the body was tough and resilient enough to withstand repeated kicking, and how to cut it out so it could be stuffed to make a responsive ball. It's very likely that stomachs, probably sheep's or goat's, had been used to make footballs for a long time before Huang di came along, and he just adopted the idea as an insult to the spirit of his enemy.

Or perhaps he simply wanted to give his enemy a final, emphatic, kick in the guts—although it seems, at least to me, that it would have been easier, more logical and more insulting just to kick his head around. Heads are, after all, ball shaped and there are many examples through history of them being used as footballs. But someone must have known that stomachs make much better balls than heads.

Cutting a stomach out and preparing it for play is a premeditated action to make a responsive and resilient ball for an organised game, and perhaps making a stomach into a football for a celebratory game was a time honoured custom.

Stuffed stomachs were a significant point in the evolution of a functional ball that maybe started with stones and progressed through various round objects, carved wood or cork, heads, stuffed linen bags and eventually leather sewn around a bladder. All went quiet on the football front for a couple of thousand years after Huang di, but people must have been playing it because it turned up as a training exercise called *zhu qui,* or *tsu' chu* in a Chinese military manual called the *zhan guo ce* about 2,500 years ago.

But that was all a very long time ago. For now, as promised, we'll start with the modern games and how they developed and spread around the world.

Part 1
THE LATEST GENERATION

Without a doubt, modern football players have some of the highest IQs on the planet. I confidently base this statement on the number of times match commentators describe players as 'genius', 'brilliant' or 'extraordinary', which is usually several times in a game.

Unless, of course, their assessments are made only in relation to the commentator's own intellectual abilities, which changes things a bit.

Graeme Dobson. Personal observation. 2023 CE

Chapter 1
THE MODERN GAMES

In the 21st century (C) there are six major codes played around the world. They are, in the order that they were codified, which is not necessarily their order of age:

- Australian Rules or AFL (Australian Football League) 1859
- Association Football (Soccer) 1863
- Rugby Union 1871
- Gaelic Football 1885
- Rugby League 1895
- American Football (Gridiron) 1880s onward

Most of the modern codes have birthed spin-off games; their children, so to speak. Some are played by just a few people and some have become global success stories and are well on their way to becoming distinct codes in their own right.

Each code has its clubs, and within every club there is a dedicated, often fanatical, fan base which have sometimes earned reputations for violence, sometimes extreme violence bordering on full scale tribal warfare ('hooligans'). This violence has led to the necessity for some grounds to segregate spectator areas and place security fences around the playing fields to protect players.

These fan bases illustrate the strongly tribal nature of football. In the modern era we are mostly shorn of our ancient tribal identities, but there seems to be an innate need for people to belong to a tribe-like group that they can identify and band together with. Football clubs and religion, more than anything else, fulfil this need. And they reflect tribal structure—they have chiefs (presidents), bureaucracy (officials), the masses (fans) and the warrior class who are pampered, feted by all and sent out to do battle with the enemy.

First Nations tribes in North and Central America took this concept a step further—they used football as a substitute for costly wars to settle inter-tribal disputes.

Modern day fans go to watch matches live, not so much for the game because at games it's often not easy to see the play, but to be a part of it all, to belong. Being at a match as a neutral is not a terribly rewarding experience, no matter how much you enjoy the sport. Actually, fan clubs and fan behaviour are such a major part of all modern football codes that they are worth looking at as a separate issue, but I fear not in this book. I have, however, one observation that I'd like to share.

The more violence there is on the field, the less there is off it. Soccer, the least violent of all the football codes, has a fan base renowned around the world for their violence; whereas fans of rugby, which often features quite extreme on-field violence, rarely foment anything worse than being good-naturedly drunk and disorderly.

Perhaps the Romans, with their extremely violent public games, knew a thing or two about population control.

To the occasional confusion of non-football people, all codes refer to their own game as 'football', or 'footie' in Australia and Aotearoa-New Zealand (Aotearoa-NZ), and bestow often unflattering names on the other codes. To try and avoid confusion, I use only their proper names and reserve the term 'football' for reference to the collective game.

All modern codes grew out of two prototype games, soccer and rugby. Actually, most codes evolved from rugby; soccer stayed true to itself and went on to become the world's favourite sport, so it's to soccer we'll go first.

Chapter 2
ASSOCIATION FOOTBALL (SOCCER)

The Beautiful Game, the World Game.
Watching grass grow, the Most Boring Game Ever Invented.
All depends on your point of view.

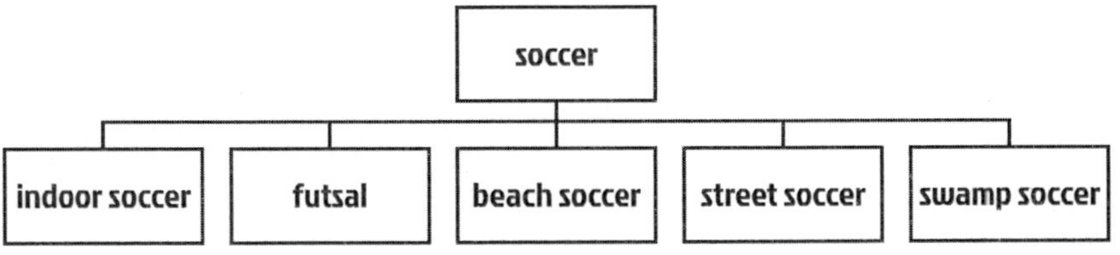

The Mechanics of the Game

The object of the game is to get a round ball into a goal behind the opposition. Each time the ball enters the goal a single point is scored. The size and weight of the ball is fixed by regulation at 68–70 cm (27–28 inch) in circumference, 410–450 gm (14–16 oz) weight, and is inflated to 0.6–1.1 bars (8.7–16.0 psi) at sea level.

Soccer is played on a field of green natural or artificial grass, between 64 and 75 m (246') wide and 100–110 m (328'–360') long (FIFA recommendation is 68 x 105 m, or 223' x 344'). The field is divided crosswise into two equal halves, and centred at each end there is a goal 7.32 m (24') wide X 2.44 (8') high and 1.54 m (5') deep. The top, back and sides of the goals are netted and it's fronted by a rectangular penalty box 24 x 16.5m (79' x 54').

There are two teams of eleven players on the field. Each team is divided into four categories; forwards, midfielders, backs and a goalkeeper. The forwards are responsible for attacking the opposition's goal and scoring. The backs, as the name suggests, stay pretty much in their own half of the field to defend and prevent the ball from reaching the goal, and the midfielders range up and down the field kicking the ball backward and forward in an attempt to set the forwards up in a position to score, or helping the backs with defence. The goal keepers are the only truly specialised positions on the field and the only players permitted to touch the ball with their hands—so long as they do so in their own goal area. The forwards tend to be the most glamorous of the team because they're the ones that score the goals, but the goal keeper has the potential to be either the greatest hero of the team by saving goals or its arch-villain by letting them in, and a goalie's popularity can fluctuate wildly in the course of a match.

Every game is controlled by four officials. The main one is the referee, who runs with the players on the field to control the game and enforce the rules. The referee is assisted by two linespersons who patrol the sidelines to signal when the ball is out, and also help the referee if they see a play infringement that's been missed. A fourth official remains more or less static on the sideline to supervise player substitutions and monitor their equipment.

Each match has two 45 minute halves, the time is kept on the field by the referee who keeps track of stoppages and adds them at the end of each half (referee's or stoppage time). In tournament play, if the game is drawn at the end of 90 minutes plus stoppage time, an extra 15 minutes are played each way. If, at the end of extra time, the scores are still tied, the game is decided by penalty kicks where each team takes turns at kicking (shooting) for goal from a penalty mark located 11 m (36') out from the mid-point between the goalposts. Five players from each team are allowed one kick each in a one-on-one contest with the goal keeper. The team with the most successful kicks wins.

It goes without saying that penalty kicks put huge pressure on goal keepers because the outcome of the match rests on them. Soccer is a low scoring game, so every miss a goal keeper makes is significant. It's the only football code that puts such pressure on an individual player.

In the course of the game penalty kicks are also awarded against a team that commits foul play in the opposition's penalty box, which results in a one-on-one contest with the goal keeper. Fouls elsewhere on the field are, depending on the seriousness of the offense, punished by a free kick, a yellow card or, if particularly serious, a red card. The yellow card in soccer is a warning and the player stays on the field, but a second yellow results in the player being 'red carded' and sent off. Red-carded players cannot return to the match nor be substituted so their teams have to play out the rest of the game with ten players. Awarding penalties is entirely at the discretion of the referee, and any arguing can also result in a card. A player can also be red-carded for:

- Violent actions against the referee or other players
- Unsportsmanlike behaviour
- Delaying the game
- Entering or leaving the game without informing the referee
- Using their hands to stop a goal
- Or even using bad language!

Which appears to mean that if a player swears within the hearing of a particularly delicate eared referee they can be sent off. I wonder how often that one's enforced.

Soccer is the only strictly non-contact football code, and most foul play revolves around players making contact with opposition players in scenarios ranging from a slight push to kicking their legs out from under them. Unfortunately, the foul play rules encourage acting, or 'putting on a Hollywood', where a player pretends that they've been badly fouled or injured in order to secure a penalty, especially in the penalty box where good acting can change the course of the game.

Soccer is also a no-hands game and penalties are awarded against any player that touches or handles the ball, regardless of whether it's accidental or on purpose. The only exception is the goal keepers, but they can be penalised if they:

- Hold the ball for more than 6 seconds.
- Touch the ball with their hands after a teammate has kicked the ball to them.

- Touch the ball with their hands directly after a throw-in by a teammate.

Or, presumably, any of the other offenses listed above.

The game is organised into clubs, which are, in turn, organised into leagues. Currently there are about 210 soccer leagues in the world, ranging from small and local to major national and international. The larger clubs are multimillion, in some cases multibillion dollar enterprises and their top players command huge fees unmatched by any other code except, perhaps, for American football.

History of Soccer

Soccer was born in the Freemasons' Tavern in London on 26th October, 1863, when a collection of representatives from schools and clubs met to form the Football Association (FA). The name 'soccer' comes from an English abbreviation of 'association'—they took the **'soc'** out of it and added **'er'** to make **'soccer'** (it's an English thing). Today it's the most popular football code in the world and is counted as the number one sport in over 225 countries.

Its success was, at least in part, due to the new, highly responsive ball. Originally it was made of a leather-encased pig's bladder and varied in size and shape, depending mostly on the size of the pig. The bladder used to be blown up by mouth using a pipe stem, which was both physically demanding and dangerous. Mrs Lindon discovered this when she died of a lung disease she caught from blowing up bladders for her husband. As a result of her death Mr Lindon, a shoe-maker who'd turned his hand to making leather balls, began using newly invented vulcanised rubber for bladders and, because rubber was a lot more difficult to inflate, he also invented a pump—shame, for Mrs Lindon's sake, that he didn't think of them a bit earlier.

Over the years the shape of the leather panels enclosing the bladder changed as manufacturers strived to make a perfect sphere. Eventually a design using a series of 20 hexagonal and 12 pentagonal panels was found to be the most effective and provided the most consistent performance (the origins of this design are a bit murky, but I'll look at that later). In the 1960s synthetic leather began to be used in place of natural leather because it didn't absorb water so retained its weight and playing characteristics, and within 20 years had completely replaced cow-hide.

The original rules were published by the FA on the 8th of December, 1863, under the heading 'The Laws of Football' and the first game was played less than three weeks later.

It was a draw.

The laws laid down on that day are:

1. The maximum length of the ground shall be 200 yards, the maximum breadth shall be 100 yards, the length and breadth shall be marked off with flags; and the goal shall be defined by two upright posts, eight yards apart, without any tape or bar across them.

2. A toss for goals shall take place, and the game shall be commenced by a place kick from the centre of the ground by the side losing the toss for goals; the other side shall not approach within 10 yards of the ball until it is kicked off.

3. After a goal is won, the losing side shall be entitled to kick off, and the two sides shall change goals after each goal is won.

4. A goal shall be won when the ball passes between the goal-posts or over the space between the goal-posts (at whatever height), not being thrown, knocked on, or carried.

5. When the ball is in touch, the first player who touches it shall throw it from the point on the boundary line where it left the ground in a direction at right angles with the boundary line, and the ball shall not be in play until it has touched the ground.

6. When a player has kicked the ball, any one of the same side who is nearer to the opponent's goal line is out of play, and may not touch the ball himself, nor in any way whatever prevent any other player from doing so, until he is in play; but no player is out of play when the ball is kicked off from behind the goal line.

7. In case the ball goes behind the goal line, if a player on the side to whom the goal belongs first touches the ball, one of his side shall he entitled to a free kick from the goal line at the point opposite the place where the ball shall be touched. If a player of the opposite side first touches the ball, one of his side shall be entitled to a free kick at the goal only from a point 15 yards outside the goal line, opposite the place where the ball is touched, the opposing side standing within their goal line until he has had his kick.

8. If a player makes a fair catch, he shall be entitled to a free kick, providing he claims it by making a mark with his heel at once; and in order to take such kick he may go back as far as he pleases, and no player on the opposite side shall advance beyond his mark until he has kicked.

9. No player shall run with the ball.

10. Neither tripping nor hacking shall be allowed, and no player shall use his hands to hold or push his adversary.

11. A player shall not be allowed to throw the ball or pass it to another with his hands.

12. No player shall be allowed to take the ball from the ground with his hands under any pretence whatever while it is in play.

13. No player shall be allowed to wear projecting nails, iron plates, or gutta-percha on the soles or heels of his boots.

But the London based FA didn't have it all to themselves. In the north of England the Sheffield Football Club devised its own rules in 1858 and formed the Sheffield Football Association in 1867, incorporating teams from across Northern England, Scotland and the English Midlands. Teams from the north and south played several games against each other, but, as could be expected, the different rules caused arguments until, finally, in 1877 the rules were combined with compromises on both sides. Among the rules that Sheffield brought to the new game were the header, where players could play the ball with their head, the corner which restarted play with a kick from the corner closest to where the ball had gone out of play over the goal line, and the free kick following a foul.

The history of soccer games in the north of England also had one major influence on the modern game that can't be ignored—professionalism. Being mostly working class, northern players needed an income to survive. Unlike their southern counterparts who were generally well heeled public school graduates, if a northern player skipped work to travel and play for his team he and his family suffered. When you consider that most, if not all, major fixtures were held in the south, this became a serious factor. And it wasn't just lost wages that had to be counted, travel itself was expensive and players had to be compensated if clubs were to survive.

But the richer southern clubs disagreed. Professionalism was anathema to them, going completely against their public school ethics. It came to a head in 1884 when Preston North End was accused of employing professional players and expelled from the FA. It was later established that the club had arranged sinecures for players that allowed them to play full time—essentially professional players without the title. All the northern clubs supported Preston and threatened to start a rival league. The FA caved in 1885 and professionalism was legalised. A new league of professional teams was formed in 1888 with eleven founding members, mostly from the North and the Midlands. The era of public school dominance of soccer ended and the sport became mostly the preserve of the working man.

After the professional league was formed in the UK in 1888 soccer, more or less in its modern form, was established as the premier working class sport in the UK and was ready to ride to the rest of the world on the coat tails of the British industrial revolution, colonialism and railways.

Across the sea soccer was introduced to Ireland in 1878 by Belfast merchant, John McAlery. John went to Edinburgh for his honeymoon, saw the game played there and so enjoyed it that he organised an exhibition match to be played in Ulster between Scottish teams Queens Park and Caledonians.

Ireland, however, was a difficult place for English sport to gain traction.

Northern Ireland regarded (and, in some eyes, still regards) itself as British, because many of its people are descended from English and Scottish Protestants brought over several hundred years ago during the 'plantation' period, when the English attempted to displace the native Irish Catholics. The plantation movement did not spread far beyond the north, but it left a legacy of religious and ethnic division and outright hatred of an intensity seldom seen anywhere else in the world. Hundreds of years later it still bubbles just below the surface. So Northern Ireland became a fertile ground for the English game of soccer, but the Irish Catholics had a deep suspicion of anything English and uptake was slow in the rest of the island. It was being played in Dublin in 1885, probably by English troops and local upper classes, and from there gradually spread, but the Football Association of Ireland wasn't formed until 1921, the same year the first League of Ireland was introduced with eight teams. The Irish national team appeared in the 1924 Olympics.

But the Irish remained wary of the English game and at home tended to stick with Gaelic football and their native game, hurley. Irish soccer players had to go to England if they wanted to advance, and as a result the Irish public preferred to follow their stars in the English football clubs. The local, home grown clubs became essentially feeders for the English and Scottish behemoths. Today soccer is a major, if not the major participation sport in Ireland, but spectators still prefer to travel to the UK to watch games, and even at home soccer lags behind hurley, Gaelic football and, in some places, rugby.

The great soccer diaspora
Europe

It's not impossible, but it'd be tedious, repetitive and time consuming to detail how soccer spread to each country. Instead I'll look at the major European players, those countries that have gone on to become the 'power-houses' of Europe'. Each of these—Germany, The Netherlands, Italy, Spain and France—have a slightly different story to tell, but together they give a pretty good picture of how association football spread.

The Industrial Revolution in Britain brought, obviously, industry, and with it innovation and engineering expertise that was in heavy demand overseas. British companies picked up lucrative contracts throughout Europe and sent British crews to work on them. The rapid expansion of expat British communities abroad included both public school educated 'gentlemen' and working men—contract workers, technicians, sailors and traders who were in demand all across Europe.

The public school men set up clubs to play cricket, football (whether association or rugby is uncertain, probably both), sip gin and tonics and moan about the locals; while the workers organised games of soccer, played cricket, drank beer and probably did their best with the local ladies. It was probably the working men that left the greatest legacy—in both football and the gene pool.

So it was British expats, ably assisted by returning European students, teachers and traders who'd spent long enough in Britain to pick up the game, who spread soccer across Europe.

In Spain the first football game was played in 1873 by either British miners working at a Rio Tinto copper mine at Huelva, who formed the 'Rio Tinto Football Club' club; or by British workers for a telegraph company in Vigo who called their team 'The Exiles'. Meanwhile returning students who had been introduced to the game in England began to teach their compatriots and the first Spanish club, the 'Cricket and Football Club of Madrid', was established in 1879 under the sponsorship of, no less, the king of Spain, Alfonso XII.

In Italy it was Edoardo Bosia, an Italian textile merchant who'd spent time in England, who is credited with introducing the game to his native Turin in 1887. He subsequently helped sponsor it throughout the country, attracting the attention of the rich and noble who had the resources to speed its spread. Six years later, in 1893, the Genoa Cricket and Football Club was formed by expat British residents, but they didn't start playing soccer in earnest for another three years. The Italians themselves didn't take up the game en masse until the first decades of the 20th C, mostly because the country was slow to industrialise, and back then it was industry or the military that drove soccer's development. The advent of Mussolini in the 1930s changed that and the game flourished under the fascists, who idealised it as a fitness regime. But initially they had a problem—soccer was regarded as an 'English game', and they were dead against anything foreign. Oddly, they were very keen on rugby which they saw as a modern interpretation of an ancient Roman game, *harpastum*, and they promoted it as part of their propaganda. When rugby proved resistant to being used for propaganda they invented their own game, *voluta,* which was based on home grown harpastum and a medieval Italian game *calcio Fiorentino*. Voluta flourished briefly, but it was on a hiding to nothing because soccer's popularity endured among the masses. In 1933, Mussolini gave up, voluta was abandoned and the government swung its support behind soccer.

Most of Europe took to soccer with enthusiasm, except, apparently, for Germany. Around 1874 two German schoolteachers, named August Hermann and Konrad Koch are credited with introducing the game there. At the time physical education was not part of the German school's curriculum and August, a passionate physical education instructor, was determined to get it accepted. He went on a tour of public schools in England, was introduced to the game of soccer and brought a ball home with him and, with the help of Konrad Koch, began the uphill battle to introduce the game. In 1878 they founded the first football club in Germany, Deutscher FV Hannover.

But, curiously, it wasn't soccer that they were playing, because they were playing with an oval ball, and some German clubs continued to play with an oval ball right up to the turn of the century.

This suggests that it was not soccer but rugby that August introduced and history has become a little confused on the issue. It's an understandable mistake. Given that soccer grew to be so important and influential in Germany while rugby virtually disappeared, it's reasonable for modern day commentators to assume football in the early days meant soccer.

Another curiosity of early German football was the public hostility to it. Players were harassed, abused and denied space to play. Why this was is a bit of a mystery, perhaps it was because people resented the English influence, or perhaps they begrudged the time taken from work and Sunday worship, or perhaps it was actually the roughness of rugby that they didn't like—many other countries, including America and Australia, were turned off rugby for that reason. Soccer, or whatever it was, pushed on and clubs formed into leagues and the game, presumably now with a round ball, began to establish itself. It was given the final push, first toward acceptance, then popularity, when there was a series of exchange games with English clubs round the turn of the century.

A meeting of 86 clubs established the Deutscher Fussball Bund (German Football Association) in 1901, and by the time WWI arrived soccer had gained enough strength for German soldiers to play friendly games against British soldiers during Xmas truces in 1914 and '15. Instead of just laying back and enjoying a rare bit of quiet, the troops fraternised, sang carols, exchanged gifts—and organised spontaneous games of soccer with the enemy.

Then they went back to killing each other so the détente had no lasting effect, but for just a brief moment the world regained a touch of sanity.

After the first war Germany went on to become a European soccer powerhouse. As in Italy, the advent of the fascists in the '30s saw soccer become even stronger when the regime sought to exploit it to promote its policies.

In other European countries soccer history gets even more muddied. For example The Netherlands has a story that soccer was introduced by a sporting guru called Pim Mulier in 1889—when he was just 14 years old. But a 2020 PhD thesis by Jan Luitzen says that football was actually introduced in 1864 by English teachers at the prestigious Protestant Christian boarding school, Noorthey, and spread when the students left the school and returned to their various homes. It's quite possible that the boys from the posh school actually played rugby, but in any case they were elite members of society so how well they passed it on to the working class is unclear.

The story of Pim Mulier may, however, have some basis in fact. Pim founded a cricket club called Root en Zwart with three friends in 1881 (when he was 16, not 14, but still pretty young) to play—reasonably enough—cricket. A year later they began playing rugby, then soccer a year or two after that. It's more than likely that he started playing rugby which he'd learned from Noorthey before discovering soccer. Why they changed is unknown, but it's possible German antipathy to rugby extended across Northern Europe. Or perhaps it was just that rugby was seen as too elitist for a working class game.

The first French soccer club was started in 1862 by English gentlemen living in Paris. The French were, apparently, 'amazed', although I find it hard to believe that anything the English did could amaze a Parisienne. Other pockets of English expats organised a few clubs and played a few games, and sailors are credited with introducing it to workers at Le Havre in 1872, but it didn't catch on with the French. They were suspicious of its bourgeoisie origins and it was viewed as possibly contradictory to their 'Republican principles'. At that time France was a conservative, mostly agricultural society and the bulk of people lived in comparatively isolated villages with little access to new ideas, little appetite for travel, nor much spare time to play. So, despite the first national team being established in 1904, soccer received very little attention from most of the French.

Their first match was a 3 – 3 draw against Belgium, but a 15 – 0 drubbing by Britain in 1906 can't have done much for the sport.

Oddly enough, it was the First World War that finally got them into the game.

In the trenches French and English fought alongside each other, living cheek-by-jowl in the mud and misery. Football clubs across Britain were major contributors to the war effort, urging their members to join up with the result that, in at least one case, an entire team enlisted together. So it was inevitable that balls were kicked about whenever possible, and the French could not help but become involved.

The British army adopted the view that soccer was good for its soldiers; apart from diverting them from the sheer horror of their lives, it promoted cooperation, and discipline while helping with morale, alleviated boredom and diverted the men from the brothels, wine sinks and other debauchery on offer (they weren't the first to recognise the military benefits of football, that had happened over two thousand years earlier—but we'll get to that later. Much, much, later).

French troops soon learned the game and challenge matches between them and the British kicked off, which soon developed into formal tournaments such as the *Cordiale Cup* and the *Coupe des Alliées* with prizes of cigarettes, food and drink on offer. The French military hierarchy also recognised the benefits of soccer for its troops and began actively encouraging play, going so far as to send footballs to the front.

After the war the troops went home and the French soldiers took soccer with them. As roughly 65% were workers they enthusiastically introduced it to their brothers and before long it was a major phenomenon (once again, this was not the first time that a returning army has turned football into a major national sport, but, once again, we'll get to that). The French Football Federation was established in 1919 and the first championship held in 1920. France went on to quickly become a force in the sport and played a major part in organising the first World Cup in 1930.

Eastern Europe at the turn of the 20th C was dominated by the Ottoman Empire, ruled from Istanbul. The Ottomans had an interesting, and often fractious relationship with the British Empire but, like the rest of the world, they were avid for British industrial technology. And with British technology came British workers, and with British workers came soccer. The first recorded match on Ottoman territory was played in 1875 in what is now Thessaloniki, in modern Greece, between mixed teams of Armenians, Greeks and English. By 1895 the game had spread to

Istanbul and from there to the rest of the Empire, which at the time was a very long way—from the Balkans right across most of the Middle East. After WWI the Middle East was occupied by British and French military, both armies that encouraged their troops to play soccer, but I've got no idea how much fraternising and interplay there was with the locals. Not much, I suspect.

And a similar story came from the north, in Russia. At the time the Russian Empire was vast, extending from the Baltic Sea through Central Asia to the Pacific Ocean. Despite fraught relations with the British Empire, the Russians also wanted British technology and products and a sizable expat British community grew in the capital, St Petersburg. Inevitably, they organised soccer matches amongst themselves, then the Russians started playing and the first match between the British and Russians was played in 1897 (the Brits won 6 – 0). Despite this rather humiliating outcome soccer spread rapidly through the Tsar's empire, a football league was formed and a national team was playing by 1910. It started well enough, but as the empire crumbled and chaos became the norm the team's fortunes slumped. Then revolution and wars put official soccer very much on the back-burner, but the game survived, undoubtedly played by soldiers from all sides, and began rebuilding at a national league level in 1936.

Within thirty years of merging the British Northern and Southern leagues and the writing of compromise rules, the game had spread across Europe.

And not just Europe—British expats carried it to the rest of the world, which was just as much in need of British technology as Europe.

South and Central America

The game was introduced to that other great powerhouse of modern soccer, South America, by British railway workers in Buenos Aires, Argentina, in 1867. That was the same year as the Sheffield Football Association was formed so it would have been a very early form of the game, possibly even with an oval ball, which may be why uptake was slow and sporadic. At that time British contractors were building railways across the country, and each railway company set up its own soccer team (a number of them are still going), but the game's early development must have been a disjointed affair. The idea of the game undoubtedly appealed, but without a comprehensive set of rules matches would not have been easy.

Soccer got a boost in the 1880s when a Glaswegian schoolteacher at an English-language school in Buenos Aires began teaching it as part of the curriculum. In 1891 the first Argentinian Football League was formed (by another couple of Scottish teachers) and launched the first official competition between just five clubs. It was the first football league anywhere outside Britain.

It lasted just one season.

Three years later soccer was introduced to Brazil by Charles Miller, the son of an aristocratic Brazilian mother and a Scottish railway worker. At the tender age of ten he was packed off to boarding school in England where he learned to play and, on his return in 1894 founded Brazil's first club.

South American soccer remained somewhat chaotic because there was no consistent set of rules, and it was not until an English team toured in 1904 that rules began to be standardised. The tourists, Southampton FC, were popular and a massive turnout watched the Englishmen play—including the President and his War Secretary. By that time soccer had been incorporated into the Argentinian Army, possibly the first to do so in the modern era.

Southampton FC also visited Paraguay where William Paats, a Dutch born physical instructor, had introduced soccer to his students and set up the first Paraguayan club in 1902. Southampton made a strong impression on the locals wherever they played and were able to pass on a lot of playing tips, and they must have enjoyed the experience because a year later Nottingham Forest toured and raised the local standards again and led to the restructuring of South American soccer into a professional sport.

Then, in 1906, a South African team toured and, although they won most of their matches in Brazil, Paraguay and Argentina easily, one Argentinian club managed to beat them. This was the first time a South American side had defeated an international team and it marked a turning point for the sport.

Soccer's introduction into Central America and north into Mexico followed a very similar pattern—British (or occasionally other European) contract workers brought their sport of choice, soccer, with them, and, like other highly infectious organisms brought in by Europeans, passed it on to the locals.

During the Spanish occupation of Mexico the vast silver and gold mines at Mineral del Monte produced huge amounts of silver, which the Spanish shipped across the Pacific to their base in the Philippines to fuel their trade with China (the Chinese valued silver above all else, and the Spanish lusted after luxury oriental goods). But in the later stages of the Spanish occupation the mines became flooded and the new state of Mexico didn't have the technology to drain them.

Enter British technology and Cornish miners.

The Spanish had enslaved thousands of local tribesmen to work the mines, but conditions were appalling and thousands died, leaving a badly depleted workforce and a very natural reluctance in the local population to have anything to do with mining. So the British contractors imported hundreds of Cornish miners, a people with a very long history in the mining business, to fill the void.

And, of course, they brought soccer with them (and probably rugby, the Cornish were very keen rugby players, but that doesn't seem to have caught on in Mexico) and spread it to the locals, leading to the first Mexican team, C.F. Pachuca, being formed in 1901. C.F. Pachuca remains one of the oldest teams in the Americas and is still in the top division of the professional league. Mexican soccer got a major boost 30 odd years later when there was an influx of Spanish refugees from the Spanish civil war, and it's never looked back since.

Today Latin American soccer has an unrivalled status verging on the religious, with at least 90% of Latin Americans actively supporting one team or another. In fact, Latin Americans are so passionate about their soccer that two of them—El Salvador and Honduras—even went to war over a disputed result in a 1969 soccer championship. Before it was over 2,000 people had been killed, El Salvador had been badly bombed and Honduran troops had occupied a large slice of El Salvadorian territory.

Actually, it wasn't the match that caused the war, that was just the last straw in a long list of grievances and border disputes, but it certainly says something about fanaticism when something as simple, and, supposedly, innocent as a soccer game can set off a major international incident.

Africa

Across the Atlantic in Africa soccer was also gaining huge popularity, but the impetus was a little different than Latin America or Europe. Africa's lot was to be the cornucopia of Europe, and the Europeans fell over each other to get at its riches. Over just a few centuries European nations carved virtually the whole continent up among themselves and exploited its massive reserves of minerals, agricultural products—and people. Never before, not even at the peak of the Roman Empire, had the world seen such concentrated exploitation and misery imposed on one place. The Africans were, for the most part, powerless to resist and their lives were reduced to poverty, subservience and slavery on a massive scale.

But imposing subjugation and exploitation on that level required vast administrative and military forces. By the time soccer made its appearance at end of the 19th C the continent had been firmly divided between the colonial powers, borders fixed and virtual armies of clerks, engineers and technicians, and literal armies of soldiers—mostly recruited form the working classes—flooded across the land. And with the working classes came soccer. It's very doubtful that they played with the indigenous people—that would have been below them—but the locals watched and learned and began making their own games. Cohorts of missionaries spread across the continent and took soccer with them as a part of their 'civilising' campaign, and it caught on with the masses of Africa and acted, at least in part, as a way to let out frustration and temporarily alleviate misery.

Actually the missionaries were acting in accordance with a long established colonial technique—ban native sports and replace them with those played by the colonial masters. Like banning language and insisting that colonised people speak the language of the colonists, introducing games like soccer was a form of mass cultural destruction and subversion.

Very much the same as the colonial experience across the rest of the world but, as we will see, the results varied considerably.

The first game was reportedly played in South Africa in 1862 between civil servants and soldiers—a year before the first London rules had been laid down. It's impossible to say what that game would have looked like, but it would almost certainly have been between the lower ranks of both the army and civil service, many of whom were drawn from the northern English cities, so it was probably Sheffield Rules (I'm making an assumption here—the officers and higher rank public servants were mostly drawn from the more affluent south and the other ranks mostly came from the northern riff-raff).

The first soccer club in Africa was the Pietermaritzburg County Football Association, established in South Africa in 1880. At about the same time teams and clubs were being formed across North Africa from Algiers to Egypt and the game spread rapidly to Central Africa. It was an ad hoc affair because the continent was a collection of European colonies, each with their own laws and who jealously guarding their borders and resources; which in turn overlay the millennia old laws and cultures of the native populations. But by the mid-20thC resistance and independence movements were making themselves heard and felt, and a feature of this was the re-emergence of a nascent African identity, and with it came the Confederation of African Football in 1957.

Teams from that continent have been competing successfully on the world stage on an equal footing ever since, and African players have found very lucrative positions playing for rich European clubs.

More power to them—they deserve all they can get.

Southern an South-East Asia

The story was similarly in South and SE Asia. Soccer was spread to the masses by the armies and servants of the British East India Company, the Dutch East India Company (*Verenigde Oostindische Compagnie*, or VOC), France, Spain and, to a lesser extent, Germany. Soccer began in SE Asia, as in so many other places, as a diversion for the colonials and a way of keeping their troops occupied over long periods of boring garrison duty. Despite having different colonial masters, the process was similar and India may be taken as an example of how things happened across the region.

The first club to be established in India was the Calcutta F.C. in 1872, followed by a heap of regiment-based clubs scattered across the sub-continent and Sri Lanka over the next few decades, but few of them had native input or players. The Indian Football Association was formed in 1893 without a single Indian on the board. But as soccer gradually spread to the local population, Indian players became accepted and Indian teams, probably mostly native troops, played regimental sides with mixed success. Slowly it gained momentum until it became one of the premier sports in India, but it had mixed success internationally and began to lose popularity. By the 1960s it was overtaken by that other great British sporting export—cricket—as India's number one passion.

The story is similar in Indochina where the French introduced the sport into Vietnam in 1896. It spread through the region in the subsequent years, mostly at a local level, but a seemingly endless series of wars in the mid-20th C restricted its development. It was not until the end of the American war in 1975 that Vietnam and the neighbouring countries were free to develop soccer to its full potential, and since then it's gone ahead in leaps and bounds.

Indonesia and Malaysia share a similar story, with soccer introduced in the early years of the 20th C to Indonesia by Dutch colonials and Malaysia by the English. In both countries, particularly Indonesia, it has gone on to be a major sport that commands large and often fanatical followings.

Outside of Europe, association football was introduced to almost every country through colonialism of one sort or another. Colonialism was rampant in the 19th C, with huge empires being formed by every European nation, from the British in the west to the Russians in the east. Europe itself was comparatively resource poor, a fact that drove them to venture out into the world in search of plunder and raw material to fuel their burgeoning industries. And what they found when they did venture out was that the rest of the world was:

a) Much richer than them
b) Militarily, much weaker than them.

The Europeans had been developing fearsome arsenals and honing their military skills through centuries of internal and interminable wars, and when they realised their military superiority the world became their oyster. No one and nothing was safe. Unfortunately they also mistook military superiority for cultural superiority, and between their arrogance, the destruction wrought by their military machines and the zealotry of their missionaries, entire cultures were subverted and destroyed. Not to mention entire peoples.

Soccer was introduced to the world at the height of colonialism, at a period where most of the conquering was done and the Europeans were concentrating on consolidating and 'civilising' their conquests. European workers, mostly English working class, were streaming out across the world and soldiers, for the most part no longer engaged in battling local populations, but instead living beside them, needed to combat boredom.

It was the perfect storm for soccer—literally thousands of teachers and huge populations in dire need of something to take their minds off their lot in life.

And, as I think I mentioned before, here was also the cultural factor. Ban native sports and language and get a people playing your sport and speaking your language, and your more than half way to dominating them.

And there was a lot of dominating to do because, throughout the world, the number of countries that were not colonised can be counted on your fingers, and of those almost all were subject to serious interference bordering on colonisation.

In SE Asia the only country to escape was Thailand. It managed it in two ways. The first was by rapidly modernising as soon as the threat became obvious—the French were threatening from the east and the British from the west and south.

The first thing they did to modernise was to revamp education and adopt an English style system, along with imported English administrators and teachers. Many of the aristocracy, including the royal family, sent their children to Europe, mostly England, for education. The most progressive of the kings, Vajiravudh, was educated in England from the age of twelve, first by private tuition followed by Sandhurst Military College and then Oxford. By the time he took the throne in 1910 he was a thorough English gentleman with all the tools to convince The West that he was a friend and ally on something approaching an equal footing, or at least as equal as a non-European could hope to be.

And, having been extensively exposed to soccer in England, he saw the sport as an ideal recreation for young Thais and was more than happy to lend his support to the mostly English teachers who taught it as part of the Thai curriculum. As a result of his sponsorship soccer began in Thailand as the preserve of the rich and noble, and soccer only gradually seeped down to the masses.

At the time the army was dominated by German advisors who, perhaps mirroring prevalent German disapproval at home, saw it as a waste of time and refused to let the army have anything to do with it. This opposition presumably stopped when Thailand sent an expeditionary force to join the Allies in WWI.

But the main reason for Thailand's evasion of colonisation was colonial practicality. The French and British agreed that Thailand should remain independent as a neutral 'Buffer State' between them to reduce the risk of accidental incidents.

Thailand shared the 'Buffer State' status with two other countries that I know of—Afghanistan and Iran—who acted as buffers between the British in the south and the Russians in the north, but in neither of those was friendship a factor. When they totally destroyed a British army, the Afghanis made it very clear (and still do) that they could resist foreign interference. They destroyed the British troops with such total finality that only one man was left to carry news of the defeat to his headquarters. After that the great powers decided that it would be prudent to leave them alone militarily.

But while the Afghanis won the battle, they lost out in the subsequent treaty they signed with the British. While Russia extended its influence into the north of the country, the British took control of Afghanistan's international and diplomatic decisions, and the country became a British protectorate. Under British influence the Emir started a program of modernisation that saw an influx of British workers—and the inevitable introduction of soccer. And cricket, of course.

The same happened in Iran (then known as Persia) with the Russians entrenched in the north and the British in the south, but Iran had oil and in the rush to exploit it hundreds of British oil and support workers flooded the country.

In both countries soccer was viewed by religious leaders as being an 'infidel game' and discouraged, but on this occasion the people seem to have taken little notice and the game flourished. By the time the religious extremists took control they'd bowed to the inevitable and dropped their opposition, and the game flourished.

North of the Himalayas, Central Asia was dominated by, first, the Russian Empire and then the Soviet Union which introduced soccer throughout. But the culture and the region's wide spaces and tiny populations made the uptake sporadic.

Back in SE Asia, Thailand's cosy relationship with the European powers was brought to an abrupt end in WWII when another imperial power, Japan, entered the scene and expelled the Europeans from Asia. Ever pragmatic, the Thais avoided colonisation again by becoming a Japanese ally and acting as a staging post for invasions of Burma and Malaysia (then Malaya). Curiously, although Britain and its allies declared war on Thailand, America never did, and after the war vetoed punitive action against the Thais. Once more the Thais managed to steer a safe course through some very turbulent waters and became a staunch ally of America in its fight against Communism.

Northern Asia

Northern Asia—China, Korea and Japan—were three of the other countries that avoided European colonisation. Korea was, however, always the meat in the sandwich between Japan, China and Russia. After centuries of battling one or the other for its independence, at the turn of the 20th C the Koreans made the fatal mistake of siding with Russia in the Russo – Japanese war. The world, especially Korea, were shocked when Japan won decisively and following the 1905 treaty it officially became a Japanese colony.

But the Japanese victory was not an accident or a quirk of history. After realising in the mid-19th C that it would be unable to defend itself militarily against America or any of the major European powers, Japan began a rapid and highly successful modernisation program modelled on, and with the support of, the English. It developed its armed forces to the point that it could challenge to be a world power and emphasised this by, first clearing the Germans out of Asia and the Pacific, then sending its navy to support the allies in WWI. It was awarded the Victory medal for its contributions, but its successes set it upon a collision course with the rapidly expanding Americans, who had their eyes on a Pacific empire of their own.

And we all know how that worked out.

The Japanese left a major legacy—they very firmly destroyed the European's aura of military invincibility. In the years that followed one country after another fought their way to independence until the Age of Empire was no more and only continued a tenuous existence in the minds of some Europeans, mostly English.

But I seem to have got well away from soccer—again.

Soccer came to Japan in the usual way, with impromptu matches between British sailors in Kobe in 1871 about the same time games were organised by English teachers and their pupils in Tokyo. Two years later a match was played at the Tokyo Bay Naval Academy, and the first official game was in 1888 between the Kobe Regatta and Athletic Club and the Yokohama Country and Athletic Club. Those two clubs still play each other.

Despite their affinity for the English and all things English, the Japanese people never really took to soccer. Perhaps it was because it was too much like the courtly ancient Japanese game of *kemari* (we'll get to that later, too). Or perhaps it just didn't fit well with the Japanese psych at the time, but for whatever reason soccer remained a minor sport up to the late 20th C when it at last gained some traction.

Across the sea, China wasn't colonised either, apart from odd bits like Hong Kong and Macau, and various concessions where colonial merchants lived and were guarded by various colonial troops. China had been badly caught short militarily by the Europeans, Americans and Japanese but, unlike the Japanese and Thais, had done little about it. They were ancient, rich, and believed very strongly in their own power, and didn't see a need for Western ideas or technology. That was a mistake and the colonial powers ran rampant across the country. The ancient Celestial Kingdom was looted, raped, its capital sacked, its people massacred or turned en mass into opium addicts and its economy all but destroyed by brutal trade concessions imposed on it. China was not colonised because it was too big and too complex, but it suffered what it has come to call the 'century of humiliation'.

China has a long memory and those hundred years may yet come back to bite the powers that inflicted it.

As for soccer, it became entrenched in British Hong Kong and Portuguese Macau and was undoubtedly played by European troops on the mainland, but it was not taken up to any great extent by the people, although China did compete internationally in 1913, and in the 1920s and '30s its national team was one of Asia's best. But in the mid-20th C invasion, chaos and revolution again engulfed the country and Chinese soccer suffered a setback from which it has yet to fully recover.

Soccer spread to the colonised countries, which was most of the world, through the British working classes—the technicians, miners, engineers, sailors and soldiers—and for the very few countries in the world that retained their independence (including Ethiopia and Tonga, six, I think), it was introduced by the upper classes through education and imported teachers. Eventually the colonials were thrown out of almost everywhere and the populations, whether native or hybrid, have sought to establish their own national identities in the modern world. For many of them soccer became central to that identity, it is the one colonial legacy that has truly lived on while others were neglected, scorned and discarded.

But what of those places where the colonials came and stayed, where European populations became the overwhelming majority, took over entirely and created new countries and new identities. How did soccer fare in Australasia and North America beyond Mexico?

By the time soccer was codified and began to spread around the world America, Canada, Australia and Aotearoa-NZ were established, settled, English speaking nations with their own colonial ambitions. They all began as British colonies (let's not get bogged down in the French Canadian thing, by the time soccer rolled around it was a more-or-less united country). Except for the United States which had been an independent country for more than a century, they were all still tied to Britain when soccer began its spread, only leaving the British Empire in the wake of WWII when the Empire was no longer financially viable.

North America

The US and Canada were historically heavily intertwined and, except for Ireland and a couple of Caribbean Islands, their histories go back way further than any other British colony. By the time soccer arrived, they had their own established and mostly European social structures and were far less susceptible to foreign influence. But they did have large scale European immigration, and the migrants brought soccer with them.

In the United States, British companies set up textile factories along the NE seaboard, around New Jersey and Massachusetts, in the late 19th C and staffed them with imported skilled British workers who, naturally enough, brought their favourite sport with them. The American Football Association (AFA) was founded to coordinate the East Coast industry-based soccer leagues and started a competition for the American Cup. Further west, in Missouri, the Catholic Church brought soccer into its recreational programs and the St Louis League (later the St Louis Soccer League) was formed in 1886 and, gradually, the sport spread to other centres, including on the West Coast.

But it was plagued by dissention from the start. In 1894 the owners of Major League Baseball teams attempted to set up a professional soccer league to generate income from their expensive pitches in the winter when there was no baseball. The AFA objected and banned its players from participating and the idea died very rapidly. An economic downturn about the same time saw many of the teams hit hard times. Competition for the American Cup was suspended and interest in the game faltered, until it was reinvigorated in 1905 by a touring English team.

In 1911 the American Amateur Football Association (AAFA) was set up in opposition to the AFA and an alternative competition—the American Amateur Football Association Cup—was established. Both associations applied to join FIFA, but were told to go away and decide which one was going to represent America. Thus started the first of the American football wars.

The AAFA evolved into the United States Football Association (USFA), which eventually gained the ascendancy and FIFA accreditation over the AFA, which went into decline and finally died in 1924.

In the meantime the professional American Soccer League was formed in 1921 by the merger of a number of mostly East Coast teams under the auspices of the USFA. This was an attempt to provide a single professional league, but by the late 1920s the second great soccer war had broken out with bitter disputes over who was in charge and how the game should be managed. By this time, despite the early setbacks, many of the clubs were owned by Major League Baseball Clubs who wanted it organised in the same way as baseball and stacked their clubs with European professionals. That led to charges from FIFA that they were poaching players that were already on contract to European clubs. After a lot of increasingly vitriolic infighting and accusations of corruption, the public, understandably, became disenchanted with the whole thing. Finally the Great Depression put American soccer out of its misery and it became relegated to an 'immigrant sport' played mostly by ethnic communities. It was not fully revived in the wider community until the 1960s when it made a somewhat shaky comeback, but the US has never been considered as top flight soccer nation.

North of the border, in Canada, the first identifiable game of soccer was played in Toronto in 1876 and led to the formation of the Dominion Football Association in 1877. This was followed by the Western Football Association in Ontario which promoted the sport throughout the east and sent teams south of the border to New Jersey, where they played American teams from the American Football Association. Over the next few years, from the late 1890s to the 1920s, most other provinces formed their own associations and the sport developed peacefully.

In the aftermath of WWI a large influx of British migrants vitalised the sport, but their numbers were such that it became a sport that was played by British immigrants rather than native born Canadians. Never-the-less soccer developed strongly, right up until WWII put a brake on it and much of the infrastructure was lost or badly compromised. After the war a new influx of migrants, this time from all over Europe revitalised the game and introduced new passion. But they also brought old rivalries and ethnic dislikes that coloured the sport and saw many Canadian-born followers turn away.

By the 1960s the country had largely accepted multiculturalism and the game began to reflect the wider society more accurately. Its popularity rose along with the number of registered players, until today it's by far the most popular participation sport in the country. That's mostly amateur participation however, as opposed to the professional spectator-oriented sports of ice hockey and Canadian football, which both rate well above soccer in number of fans, if not in the number of players.

Australasia

Like America and Canada, Australia and Aotearoa-NZ were both British colonies with some shared colonial experiences, but on the whole they were quite different from the northern colonies (although Australia and North America have some uncomfortable parallels, but that's another book entirely!).

Australasia experienced British migration throughout the 19th C, but mostly before soccer was invented. In Australia you'd think the mass deportation of convicts from England would have brought the game, but the last of them arrived in January 1868—just five years after the first rules of soccer were written down and well before it became popular. The convicts and the troops that guarded them played some sort of football, but it wasn't soccer as we know it.

Nor would the free colonists in Australia, who were generally drawn from the middle to slightly upper classes attracted by the uninhabited, and therefore free, land and, of course, the convict slave-labour to work it. Many of these would have been public school educated and would have brought the style of football that their particular school had played—soccer-like or rugby-like or something in the middle—and the games underwent similar, but separate, evolution to that which occurred in England.

Football in Australia, both soccer and rugby, grew more as an offshoot to cricket than anything else. Cricket is probably Australia's oldest non-Indigenous sport and was first recorded in the Sydney in 1803, just fifteen years after the first fleet arrived in New South Wales (NSW). By the time soccer was even dreamt of, cricket was so well established that there had been inter-colonial matches going on for 20 years. In the late 19th C the cricket clubs had the land, the organisation, and the players looking for a way to keep fit in the off-season. Actually, that's not strictly true—the cricket clubs had the land, but they were mostly very reluctant to allow a mob of scruffy footballers to wreck it during the off-season and the footballers had to make do with whatever bits of flattish cleared land they could find.

It must be remembered that Australia in the 19th C was a very different place to today. For a start, it wasn't actually Australia, but a collection of six colonies, each with its own government and identity. Distances were vast and land travel was dangerous, inconvenient and impossible for most, so the only real means of communication was by sea, which was slow and expensive. So football tended to evolve locally, independently, and strange, hybrid games cropped up all over the place.

The first actual football match was played in 1870 between the Melbourne Football Club and the Police, but, as I said, it would have been a hybrid affair and a precursor to the modern game of Australian Rules football.

The first official football match played was in 1880 between King's School, who played by the rugby rules, and the newly establish Wanderers Football Club, who presumably played by Association rules. Clearly a compromise must have been reached so it's unlikely that the resulting game would have been recognisable today. Football advanced quite quickly after that and by 1875 was interesting enough that a Victorian paper called 'The Footballer' recorded a match near Brisbane in Queensland (Qld), between the Brisbane Football Club and the warders and inmates of the Woogaroo Lunatic Asylum. Rules of the game had to be agreed on before kick-off, the most important of which was that the ball could not be handled.

The first actual soccer club in Australia was (and is) the Wanderers Football Club in Sydney. They played their first recorded match against King's School on the 14th of August, 1880, at Parramatta in NSW. It was followed two years later by the establishment of the first official body for the administration of the sport, the New South Wales English Football Association (NSWEFA). The person behind its formation was John Walker Fletcher, a Londoner who was educated at elite English schools and graduated from Oxford, where he excelled at sport. In Australia he became the first secretary of the Paddington Cricket Club and also secretary for the newly formed Wanderers. In 1882 he formed the NSWEFA with the word 'English' differentiating it from Rugby, which was already popular in NSW and Qld, and Australian Rules, which was popular in Victoria. It was one of the first football associations outside Britain.

Not surprisingly John Fletcher is regarded as the Father of Australian Soccer.

In Victoria the sport was also on the move. In 1884 a meeting was called in Young and Jackson's pub to form a club called the 'Anglo-Australian' to test the waters and see if soccer could be established there. Also in 1884, newly arrived Arthur Gibbs established the Anglo-Australian Football Association and captained the Victorian team against NSW in a series of games from 1884 to 1886. He remained very active in his promotion of the sport in Australia until his bank transferred him to Aotearoa-NZ in 1890. After he retired to England in 1909 he continued to promote Australian soccer for years to come.

Across the Australian colonies, football associations were being formed to promote the game, but they all had an uphill battle against rugby in the east and a developing Australian Rules Football in the rest of the continent. Ten years after Australia officially became a united country in 1901, the Commonwealth Football Association was created as an overall governing body. Ten years later in 1921, the name was changed to the Australian Soccer Association, presumably to differentiate itself from the other codes which had already cornered the name 'football'.

Like Canada, the influx of British migrants after WWI gave soccer a huge boost, but it remained largely a migrant game that struggled to find acceptance in the local population. After WWII, from the late 1940s onward, European migration accelerated and with it the development of the sport. It still remained largely a migrant game, but now there were a lot more migrants with a lot more varied backgrounds, and soccer was one of the very few things that united them. Soccer clubs were formed across the continent, usually originating in community centres where new migrants could go and speak their own language, be among their own countrymen and learn from older migrants the ways of their new world. They also tended to spark patriotic passions that often spilled onto the soccer field with sometimes unfortunate results. Sadly these sporadic outbursts of passion and violence turned native born Australians off the sport and it is only in recent years that it's become popular.

Across the Tasman Sea in Aotearoa-NZ it was a similar story. Early migrants had established a settled population by the time soccer was invented, and although new migrants brought the game with them, it had an uphill task. In the early days players often switched regularly between soccer, rugby and the newly evolving Australian rules, and matches were more often than not hybrid mish-mashes of them all. Even the shape of the ball was variable from the round soccer ball to the oval rugby one, probably depending on what was available on the day.

This uncertainty as to the code they played extended right to the top. In 1888–89 the New Zealand Native Rugby Team toured Australia and Britain, and their matches included nine played under Australian and two under Association (soccer) rules.

The first football club in Aotearoa-NZ was the Canterbury Association Football Club in Christchurch, on the South Island, which played its first game in April 1882. It played under Association rules but oddly, its first games were against rugby playing Christ's College and other local rugby clubs. Auckland, in the North Island, was not far behind with the Devonport Club being founded in 1886 (it's the oldest surviving soccer club in the country) and a year later the city boasted 13 clubs.

The New Zealand Football Association was established in 1891 and embarked on its first international matches 15 years later. As with the other colonies, post WWI British migration boosted the sport's profile and by the 1920s there were 460 clubs and 6,000 players, third behind rugby and cricket. But the country didn't experience the mass European migrations that in Canada and Australia brought new blood and vigour to the game. It gradually slipped in popularity and participation and remained largely a game for British migrants—Aotearoa-NZ born players kept their preference for rugby.

Today soccer's high international profile has led to its regaining some of its popularity and it's often seen as a safer sport for developing players, but no matter what some enthusiastic supporters may think, it has no hope of challenging rugby as the national sport.

Women in soccer

Today there seems to be an impression that women have only recently, or comparatively recently, taken up the sport of soccer.

Nothing could be further from the truth! Women's soccer dates back almost to the founding of the game, but it's always been at the mercy of overwhelmingly misogynistic football associations across the world, and the story of women's soccer in Britain is echoed in almost all countries that play the game—which is virtually everywhere. So, if we look at the women's game in England we can assume that it's pretty much the same, with minor variations, across the board.

By 1880 British women across the UK were playing soccer by the FA rules, and the first international women's match ever recorded was played in 1881 in Edinburgh between English and

Scottish based teams. Although the women endured a severe and unrelentingly negative backlash from the public and the press, they defiantly kept playing. One of the first teams was Edinburgh based Mrs Graham's XI, whose players had to resort to false names to avoid being targeted off the field. It was an odd thing—they were almost universally derided but their matches attracted huge crowds. Perhaps people, especially men, were happy to pay their sixpence to watch what they seemed to regard as a 'freak show', and to be able to shout abuse to their hearts content, secure in the knowledge that their peers would agree with them.

There was the universal view that, if a women played badly it was confirmation that women could not play football, but if she played well then she must be a man in women's clothing. Except for Mrs Graham who, by all accounts, played very well but was of such stunning appearance that her gender was never called into question.

The women suffered continuous abuse and often violent pitch invasions, and many of them must have been traumatised, but they kept playing—either through love of the game or sheer bloody-minded defiance.

Go girls!

In 1894, thirteen years after Mrs Graham's XI, the British Ladies Football Club was founded by Nettie Honeyball and Lady Florence Dixie.

Nettie was one of those players that had seen the need to change her name (I can't find her real name), but despite playing under an assumed name she didn't shrink from publicity. In 1895 she appeared in the Daily Sketch, one of the few papers of the time that was even marginally supportive of female soccer, in an interview together with a photo.

In that interview she said;

There is nothing farcical about the British Ladies Football Club. I founded the association late last year, with the fixed resolve of proving to the world that women are not the 'ornamental and useless' creatures men have pictured. I must confess my convictions on all matters, where the sexes are so widely divided,

> *are all on the side of emancipation, and I look forward to a time when ladies may sit in Parliament and have a voice in the direction of affairs, especially those which concern them the most.*[1]

Those were fighting words, shocking in their day, as was her dressing in men's football playing clothes for the photo, but they had a purpose. Nettie was entrepreneurial and saw ladies football as a money making proposition, and such publicity stirred the public into coming to the matches either out of curiosity or to harangue (it was a tactic adopted almost a hundred years later by Mohamed Ali, who used his words—a lot of words—to stir up conservative crowds who happily paid big money in the hope of seeing him get beaten up).

Miss Nettie J. Honeyball, one of the world's first feminine footballers. *The Daily Sketch*, 1895. *(British newspaper Archive)*

Technology was allowing the press more and more scope, and changing work patterns meant that the working man had more time for leisure activities—including attending football matches—than ever before. And if they attended matches they would also read about them in the paper, and girls playing men's games was definitely something that men would read about. It worked for Nettie and the ladies, and they drew huge crowds, close to 10,000 people went to their first match in London, and they all payed at the gate as they went in. And the

1 Gemma Clarke. 'Meet Britain's First Woman Soccer Player, Nettie J. Honeyball'; The Founding of the British Ladies Football Club Was Met with Violent Resistance.' June 6, 2019

press had a field day, covering the British Ladies Football Club's first match with such quotes as;

> *It must be clear to everyone that girls are totally unfit for the rough work of the football field. As a means of exercise in a back yard garden it is not to be recommended; as a public entertainment it is to be deplored.* (The Sketch)

Others expressed concern that '*lewd fellows of the baser sort watched with improper eyes*', but undeterred, Nettie took her team on a national tour, which drew even more adverse press from the provincial papers, such as this from the Blackburn Times.

> *Woman in her place is a charming creature [but] the idea of donning foot-ball shirts, knickers, and shin-guards, and trying to ape the man is somewhat disturbing to one's peace of mind. . . . Let them look to their hop-scotch and skipping-ropes, and leave cricket and football to the boys.*

To be fair, the papers were only reflecting the values and mores of Victorian society, which had a very specific place for middle class women; in the home and, discretely, in a man's, preferably her husband's bed. She had no place on a football field playing a man's game, wearing men's clothing and probably doing who-knows-what off the field. And, to add insult to injury, they were middle class women (for all her progressive views, Nettie was not interested in playing with the lower sort of people) playing a working class man's game!

It was outrageous, and the public lapped it up.

And while Nettie got on with playing and promoting football among the middle class ladies, her co-founder, Lady Florence Dixie, was using football to pursue her own political agenda. Florence was an artist, writer, war correspondent and a serious activist of her day who went out pretty hard on things like family planning, equal rights for women—including the right to wear men's clothing if they wished—and women's suffrage. She was heavily into sport, not surprising as her father and brother were the 8th and 9th Marquis' of Queensberry (of boxing fame). Her politics got her into trouble more than once, most notably surviving an attempted assassination by two men disguised as women. She was saved, first by the whalebone in her corset turning the knife point, then by her very large St. Bernard dog. The charges were never proven and no one was convicted. Ironically, if she had been wearing the men's clothes that she campaigned for, she would, in all probability, have died.

Lady Dixie and Nettie promoted women's soccer with such success that they well deserve the title of mothers of the women's game.

Anyway, back to the game. By the end of Nettie's national tour the novelty had waned and the crowds had dropped off, so as a promotion, a tour of Scotland was organised which included games against men's teams. This got the interest back, but it proved a step too far. In the first match one of the women got a black eye during play, possibly in the course of play but probably not, which sparked a pitch invasion by men outraged at the idea that women would attempt to compete with men in a men's sport. The game was called off and the women had to fight their way off the field.

A week or so later the team was attacked by a large mob as they went to their hotel in Glasgow and several were injured. After that the violence escalated and the FA responded by banning their teams from playing the women. Eventually it all got too hard, too dangerous, and Nettie's grand experiment was over.

For now.

It's interesting to see how history repeats itself. Nearly 1,000 years earlier the Chinese (spoiler alert—sorry) had had a huge, well organised, professional football league with organised gambling and official fan clubs. They played with round balls made of pieces of hexangular shaped leather sewn together around an inflated pig's bladder to make a standardised ball weighing 600 gm (21 ounces). Women played on the men's teams, but when all-female teams were fielded there was a backlash. The women were accused of being prostitutes and their teams sponsored by brothels to drum up business, and it all went downhill from there.

But back to the modern game. After the trauma of the late 19th C, the women's game went into the doldrums at the start of the 20th C. Women kept playing, they just maintained a lower profile.

The First World War changed that. The men went away to the trenches and the women stepped up to fill their roles in factory and field. Men's soccer was also suspended, so the women stepped up to that, too, staging matches to raise funds for the war effort. In 1917 female munitions workers began a tournament called the 'Tyne Wear & Tees Alfred Wood Munition Girls Cup', also known as the 'Munitionettes Cup'. Also in 1917 an English women's football team played an Irish women's team in front of 20,000 spectators, and then after the war, in 1920 they played against French and Scottish teams. In the same year a match between the Dick Kerr Ladies and the St Helen Ladies at Everton attracted a crowd of 53,000, respectable even by today's standards, and another 10,000 were turned away.

It was all too much for the men who'd recently come home to find their womenfolk successfully filling male roles, and worse, enjoying it. The men were not impressed and very quickly began putting the genie back in the bottle to restore the natural order of how it was before the war. Rumours that the women were being paid to play enraged the men even further and in 1921 the conservative Football Association banned women from playing on any of their grounds or having access to any of their facilities.

Although the rugby union was happy to allow them to play on its grounds, the FA ban remained in place for 50 years, until 1970, and all but destroyed the British women's game.

Similar things were happening all over the soccer world. In France a thriving women's league was playing until it got banned in 1933 and not reinstated until 1970. In Germany, where even the idea of men playing football was slow to be accepted, women playing was even slower and didn't happen until the 1920s, and was not properly organised until 1933. Then it got banned from 1955 until 1970 on the grounds that women were, basically, too fragile and would hurt themselves. And when the women's game was eventually reinstated they could only play in warm weather and studs on boots were banned.

Far be it for me to comment on the frailty (or not) of German women, but it seems to me to be a fairly spurious excuse for a ban.

In Italy the first women's team was formed in 1933, but within a year the national soccer authorities had come down on it and prevented all official competition, although there doesn't seem to have been an outright ban as there was in other places. The women's game stumbled along with another two teams being formed in 1946, and in 1950 the Italian Football Women's Association was founded in Naples. That, however only lasted for nine years and the game didn't really get going until the Italian Women's Federation was formed in 1968 and, despite periodic outbursts of misogyny ('a bunch of lesbians', said Felice Belloli from the Italian National Amateur League in 2015) the Italian women have gone from strength to strength since.

Spanish women seem to have had the hardest time of all in Europe. Although women were playing the game as long ago as 1910, women were officially banned from playing in the 1930s right through to 1975 and the Royal Spanish Football Federation (RSFF) didn't recognise the women's game until 1980. When asked in 1971 about women playing, the RSFF president said that he wasn't against women's sport, but he didn't consider it feminine from an aesthetic point of view and the women aren't favoured by wearing trousers and shirts—a dress appropriate to the region would suit them better.

Today the Spanish FA spends millions on developing the women's game, which resulted in them taking out the 2023 Women's World Cup.

How times have changed.

The story of women's soccer appears to follow the same pattern across the world. In South America it began with a bang in most countries, only to find obstacles placed in its way and being sidelined by the men. In Brazil it was banned outright by the military regime between 1941 and 1979, but most other South

Americans simply ignored the ladies while at the same time making it as difficult as they could for them.

It was seen as an affront to Latin American machismo, just as it was an assault on male bastions in Europe.

The women had it no easier in the USA where the game's development lagged well behind the rest of the world. A brief 'golden age' in the 1920s was sparked by a tour by the English team, Dick Kerr Ladies, but when the Ladies arrived there were no established American women's teams to play, so they played the top men. At the end of their tour they'd recorded three wins, two draws and two losses, an admirable record against top class male athletes. But perhaps a little too good because it was a challenge to male egos. For most of the 20th C women's soccer in the US bubbled along in a very low key manner, flying under the radar mostly in women's colleges. In 1951 the first women's league was established in St Louis with four teams, but it only lasted two seasons. Then, in 1972, new legislation made gender equality mandatory in education, including in college athletics, and the women were able to gain ground—slowly at first, momentum gathered until today the US women are one of the world's top teams and the American game claims one of the highest participation rates in the world.

It was a similar story in Canada, and in Australia (and probably most other colonies) the pattern followed the English example. The games had a brief flowering in the 1920s, especially in Queensland where the Queensland Women's Ladies Soccer Football Association games drew crowds of up 10,000 spectators (a lot of people back then). Then the English FA intervened against the ladies in England and the reverberations were felt around the Empire. In line with the English, colonial football administrators promoted selective medical opinions that said that women were not suited to the game, public opinion turned against them and it was not until the 70s that it began to regain some momentum.

Sad, really, that egos, machismo and misogyny combined so strongly that it managed to deny a healthy sport from half the population for 50 odd years. Men must have been very insecure back in the day. Today, in case anyone's missed it, women's soccer is hugely popular worldwide with participation and a fan base rivalling the men's game.

The recent Soccer Women's World Cup in Australia and Aotearoa-NZ saw massive crowds of spectators gather from around the world to support the women's teams. The tournament was a huge success and bodes well for the future. I just hope that history will not repeat again, that men have moved on, attitudes have genuinely changed, and the women's game is here to stay.

Now the big challenge is the massive gender pay gap…

Soccer's children

For the most part soccer's children reflect the local physical and social conditions where they were conceived, for instance beach soccer was invented on the tropical beaches of Rio de Janeiro. People had been playing games on beaches, including informally kicking balls around, ever since beach culture came into existence in the early 20th C, and in densely populated cities like Rio the beach is the only open space that many of the poorer residents have to play ball games. But playing on sand is very different to playing on manicured grass, so it was inevitable that a beach version of the game became established in its own right, with its own rules and a momentum that's taken it far from its humble beginnings.

Beach soccer became so popular that it formed a professional league recognised (and governed) by FIFA. It played its first pro tournament in Rio in 1992 and has since developed to the point where there is now a Beach Soccer World Cup, last played in Moscow in 2021. No, Moscow doesn't sound a very likely venue for a sport called 'beach soccer', but with increase in popularity it's moved off the beach into arenas, sometimes even indoors, where the playing surface is covered with at least 40 cm (16') of sand.

Official FIFA rules state that the playing area must be between 35 and 37 m (115' – 121') long and 26 to 28 m (85' – 92') wide. The area is marked out by 10 cm wide lines, but the half way and penalty areas are imaginary lines marked by flags. Goals 2.2 m (7') high and 5.5 m (18') wide are centred at each end. The ball is the same size as a normal soccer ball, but slightly lighter and pumped to a lower pressure to make it easier to control on sand. Each team fields five players, including a goalkeeper, with unlimited substitutions allowed. There are two referees on the field with a third umpire and timekeeper on the sideline.

Matches are played in three 12 minute periods with a three minute break between. The clock's stopped for injuries, goals, fouls and time wasting. The game cannot end in a draw, if scores are tied at the end of the third period an extra three minutes play is added, after which, if there is still no result, the outcome is decided by penalty kicks.

But those are just the FIFA rules, and they're not exactly adhered to in all competitions. For instance I've seen games advertised with six players aside playing over two 18 minute halves. I think that, despite all attempts to make it into a serious game, beach soccer will always remain a fun kick-around for most people.

Futsal (from the Spanish *futbal sala,* or room football) is another of soccer's stronger offspring. Like beach soccer, futsal was invented in South America back in the 1930s when a coach named Juan Carlos Ceriani—there seems to be some debate about whether he was Argentinian or Uruguayan—started training his players indoors when it was wet, and the idea quickly grew into a full blown game. Juan borrowed rules from several other team sports to create a game played with a standard soccer ball by five a-side teams on a wooden-floored handball court (25–42 m x 16–25 m or 82' – 138' x 52' – 82') or a basketball court (28 × 15 m or 92' x 49'). A netted goal measuring 3m (10') wide, 2m (6.5') high and 1 m (3.3') deep is set in the middle of the shorter boundaries.

There are three referees, one on court to control the game, a second to assist the first, and a third on the sidelines to keep track of fouls etc. There's also a timekeeper—which means that the number of officials is almost equal to the number of players on each team. Matches have two 20 minute periods with a 15 minute break between halves, although matches may be extended somewhat because the time clock is stopped for dead balls, and each team's allotted one minute time out per half.

Futsal was picked up by the YMCA as a keep-fit exercise and spread throughout South America as clubs recognised the advantage of it being able to be played at any time of the year with minimal infrastructure, which made it ideal for keeping their players fit in the off-season—a bit like cricketers using soccer to keep their players fit in winter.

Although it's now played around the world, futsal doesn't seem to have caught on in a big way outside of South America, but on its home turf it's big—an international between Argentina and Brazil in 2014 attracted a crowd of over 56,000.

Indoor football, a comparatively recently invented North American version of futsal, is also known as mini-football. As with futsal, the game's origins were weather related; soccer players moved indoors when the weather got too cold and the snow got too deep to play outside, and the game evolved to suit the conditions. It's played by teams of six a-side in a large room—originally gymnasiums were used, but later, when it became popular elsewhere, in walled basketball courts or outdoors in a walled enclosure—with a synthetic grass or carpeted surface. The main feature that differentiates indoor football from any other soccer derivative is that there is no 'out of bounds' and the players are permitted to bounce the ball off the walls like squash, which makes it a much faster game than its parent.

Indoor football is played mainly in North America, but it's gained a following around the world. Unlike futsal, FIFA does not recognise or sanction mini-football, so it's governed at international level by the World Mini-football Federation which organises World Cups for men, women and under 21s.

Street football, soccer's wild child, is really the original beach soccer without sand. In essence it's just a fun, disorganised, kick-around that can be seen in the often-rare open spaces anywhere in the world, but most commonly in slums and refugee camps. At some point more affluent people tried to formalise it with rules and umpires and all the other trappings of civilisation—like they did with beach soccer—even going so far as to organise a world championship in Berlin in 2006.

But for the vast majority, street football remains, obstinately, pure fun. It's often not even played with a proper ball, at least not a soccer ball, but uses whatever is available. In some places, particularly refugee camps, balls are made out of accumulations of garbage, probably mostly plastic bags bound together. Many of the world's greatest soccer players learned their skills playing street football with unpredictable, makeshift balls.

In fact street football is probably primarily responsible for soccer's original spread around the world—people saw European soldiers and workers playing soccer and emulated them with whatever they had at hand, and quickly honed skills beyond their erstwhile masters.

More power to street football!

Swamp soccer is possibly the oddest of the children, although I shouldn't say that, in case some swamp player is offended. It's thought to have originated in Finland where it developed as a form of endurance training for athletes and the military—playing football in mud would be bloody hard work!—but in recent times it's been gaining traction in other Scandinavian countries as well as in some of the wetter parts of the world, such as, Russia, Europe (particularly Scotland) and even Brazil. There are now about 300 clubs scattered around the world and in 2009 a world cup in Scotland, which has become a stronghold for the sport, attracted 100 teams from 25 countries.

The game is played in two 13 minute halves by two, six player teams on a mud pitch approximately 60 x 35 m (197' x 115'). There are 12 players in each squad so that players can be subbed in and out as often as needed, there's no off-side rule and penalty kicks, corner kicks and throw-ins are taken with a drop kick. One of the quirkier rules states that boots cannot be changed during the game.

That it originated as a form of military endurance training suggests that it has strong links to much older traditions and

I suspect that swamp football may not be wholly, or even partly, descended from soccer. Finland is in a part of the world that has a very long tradition of ancient types of football—but more on that later.

There are undoubtedly many other lesser known children of soccer played in various parts of the world and I apologise to the followers of those games for not including them here, but it's time to move on to soccer's siblings.

Chapter 3
RUGBY

The Game Played in Heaven,
Thugby,
or a simple case of one man trying to push two men up three men's arses.
All depends ...

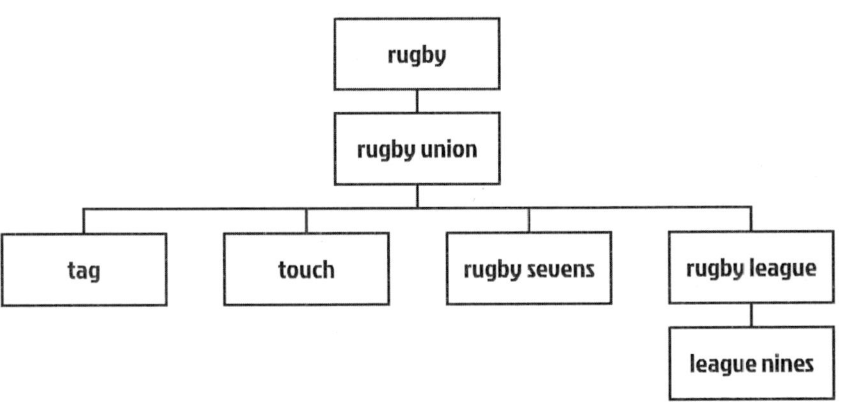

Rugby, or 'rugger' as the English sometimes call it (like changing 'association' to 'soccer') was officially born in 1871, although the game itself had been around in one form or another for years before that. The name 'rugby' comes directly from the place it was said to have been invented—Rugby Public School in Warwickshire, England. Founded in 1567 as a free grammar school for local boys. Rugby is one of the oldest independent schools in Britain, which probably explains why it developed and held to its own very distinctive style of football while other influential schools and clubs were pushing for a universal soccer-type game.

As with all other schools of that time, Rugby played its own unique football game involving mass participation of pretty much the whole school, literally hundreds of boys on the field at the same time. The juniors lined up on the goal lines to defend while the seniors tried to get close enough to kick the ball over the goal and score. There were few rules, but at Rugby at the time one of them was that the round ball could not be carried—it could be caught, and then a free kick was given, but nobody could actually pick it up—and there was no tackling, just a lot of indiscriminate kicking.

The original game resembled soccer much more than modern rugby until, at some time in the early 1800s, carrying the ball was allowed. There is a story, now one of the games legends, that in 1823 a boy named William Webb Ellis caught the ball and ran toward the opposite goal—and got away with it. Despite its almost sacred modern status, this story is, at best, somewhat dubious. When they were interviewed later in the 19th C, none of the Rugby old boys who survived from Ellis' time could remember anything about this event, although one did recall someone by that name who tended to take 'unfair advantages on the field.

However it came about, running with the ball became legal in 1841-2, provided the ball was caught '*on the bound*' (I'm uncertain of the meaning of this, but I think it possibly means on the edge, or outside of the ruck where the players were 'bound' together, alternatively, it may have meant that the ball was caught in the air from a kick or a pass), not picked up off the ground, the player was on side, and that he touched down over the goal line himself and didn't pass the ball to another player. I suspect the 'not picking it up off the ground' actually referred to picking the ball up in the ruck, something that remains against the rules today.

At that time the game was, basically, a huge, ongoing brawl with a great melee of older, larger boys trying to kick the ball through a crowd of younger, mostly smaller boys to their goal. Or heel it back to their fast runners (called 'dodgers') who waited behind and to the side of the pack for the ball to emerge, caught it and tried to dodge their way through the massed juniors who waited for them on their goal line. If the ball went out of bounds it had to be immediately thrown back in by the first boy (or last, not sure, sorry) to touch it—from this we get the modern rugby term 'touch', meaning the side-line.

The goal posts were 'H'-shaped, as in the modern game, and scoring was by kicking the ball over the cross bar. This was usually achieved by a field goal similar to today's game, but if anyone managed to get through and touch the ball down across the line they were able to kick it back to a team-mate who, if he caught it cleanly, was given a free kick at goal.

Rugby football was first tentatively codified in 1845, albeit very sketchily, by boys at Rugby School who actually played it, not the masters. While they might have enjoyed watching the game and encouraged the boys to play, the masters left the actual mode of play and the rules entirely up to the boys. Seems to have been all very egalitarian, except the boys who wrote the rules were appointed by the masters and the rules they laid down were far from comprehensive and intended only to be used within the school. Because the game was only played at Rugby, they assumed that everyone at the school new the rules, so they instead dealt with such things as 'what happens if the ball ends up in the trees' and 'what to do about delicate boys who forge sick notes to get out of playing'.

Sketchy rules or not, rugby spread throughout the English school system and was introduced to Scotland by boys moving into the Scottish schools from Northern England. The first major Scottish institution to take it up was Edinburgh Academy in 1854, a uniform set of rules for the Scottish game was drawn up in 1868 by the Edinburgh Academic Football Club and, with the agreement of the other clubs and schools, was published in a booklet known as the 'Green Book'. In a fine show of independence, no mention was made in the booklet of the word 'rugby'. The Scottish Football Union was formed in 1873, but the word 'rugby' was not used in Scotland until 1924.

Rugby was introduced to Ireland in 1867 when an Anglo-Irish student called Charles Barrington, who'd been at a public school in England, started at Trinity College in Dublin and was surprised to find that they played football without rules of any kind, so he set about introducing some order. In 1868 he and the club secretary drew up a comprehensive list of rugby-like rules, which included a prohibition on hacking, or deliberately kicking shins. This was a big change, previously it was a major part of the game and at Trinity they took it to extremes when, at the end of a match the ball was dispensed with and all the players stood in a huddle for five minutes and kicked the shit our of each other's shins.

It was called a 'Hallelujah'.

In December 1870 Edwin Ash published a letter calling for those who play the rugby-type game to meet to form a proper code of practice. The letter was probably written in response to a public backlash against the sport after a player was killed in a practice match, and it drew representatives from 22 clubs to a meeting on the 26th of January, 1871, at the Pall Mall Restaurant in London. At the meeting a draft of the rules was agreed on and the Rugby Football Union (RFU) was established. Three Rugby School old boys, all lawyers (even then lawyers were involved in the game) drew up the laws which were approved in June that same year.

As to be expected from lawyers, those rules (they called them laws) were very long, comprehensive and tedious, but I've included them here—all 59 of them—because they form the basis for modern rugby and all its derivatives—which are all the modern codes except soccer. Each code interpreted the rules to suit their players and consequently they've diverged considerably, but you can still see traces of these rules in all of them (although you have to look very hard in Aussie rules).

1. A drop kick, or drop, is made by letting the ball fall from the hands, and kicking it the very instant it rises.

2. A place kick, or place, is made by kicking the ball after it has been placed in a nick made in the ground for the purpose of keeping it at rest.

3. A punt is made by letting the ball fall from the hands and kicking it before it touches the ground.

4. Each goal shall be composed of two upright posts, exceeding 11ft in height from the ground, and placed 18ft 6in apart, with a cross bar 10ft from the ground.

5. A goal can only be obtained by kicking the ball from the field of play direct (i.e., without touching the dress or person of any player of either side), over the cross bar of the opponent's goal, whether it touch such cross bar or the posts or not; but if the ball goes directly over either of the goal posts it is called a poster, and is not a goal.

6. A goal may be obtained by any kind of kick except a punt.

7. A match shall be decided by a majority of goals only.

8. The ball is dead when it rests absolutely motionless on the ground.

9. A touch-down is when a player putting his hand upon the ball on the ground in touch or in goal stops it so that it remains dead or fairly so.

10. A tackle is when the holder of the ball is held by one or more players of the opposite side.

11. A scrummage takes place when the holder of the ball being in the field of play puts it down on the ground in front of him, and all who have closed round on their respective sides endeavour to push their opponents back, and by kicking the ball to drive it in the direction of the opposite goal-line.

12. A player may take up the ball whenever it is rolling or bounding, except in a scrummage.

13. It is not lawful to take up the ball when dead (except in order to bring it out after it has been touched down in touch or in goal) for any purpose whatever; whenever the ball shall have been so unlawfully taken up, it shall at once be brought back to where it was so taken up, and there put down.

14. In a scrummage it is not lawful to touch the ball with the hand under any circumstances whatever.

15. It is lawful for any player who has the ball to run with it, and if he does so it is called a run. If a player runs with the ball until he gets behind his opponent's goal-line and there touches it down, it is called a run in.

16. It is lawful to run in anywhere across the goal-line.

17. The goal-line is in goal, and the touch-line is in touch.

18. In the event of any player holding or running with the ball being tackled and the ball fairly held, he must at once cry down, and there put it down.

19. A maul in goal is when the holder of the ball is tackled inside goal-line, or being tackled immediately outside is carried or pushed across it, and he or the opposite side, or both, endeavour to touch the ball down. In all cases the ball when so touched down shall belong to the players of the side who first had possession of it before the maul commenced, unless the opposite side have gained entire possession of it.

20. In case of a maul in goal those players only who are touching the ball with their hands when it crosses the goal-line may continue in the maul in goal, and when a player has once released his hold of the ball after it is inside the goal-line he may not again join in the maul, and if he attempts to do so may be dragged out by the opposite side. But if a player when running in is tackled inside the goal-line, then only the player who first tackled him, or if two or more tackle him simultaneously they only may join in the maul.

21. Touch in goal (see plan).—Immediately the ball, whether in the hands of a player (except for the purpose of a punt-out, see Rule 29) or not, goes into touch in goal it is at once dead and out of the game, and is brought out as provided by Rules 41 and 42.

22. Every player is on sid but is put off side if he enters a scrummage from his opponents› side, or being in a scrummage gets in front of the ball, or when the ball has been kicked, touched, or is being run with by any of his own side behind him (that is, between himself and his own goal-line).

23. Every player when off side is out of the game and shall not touch the ball in any case whatever, either in or out of touch or goal, or in any way interrupt or obstruct any player, until he is again on side.

24. A player being off side is put on side when the ball has been run five yards with or kicked by or has touched the dress or

Plan of the Field

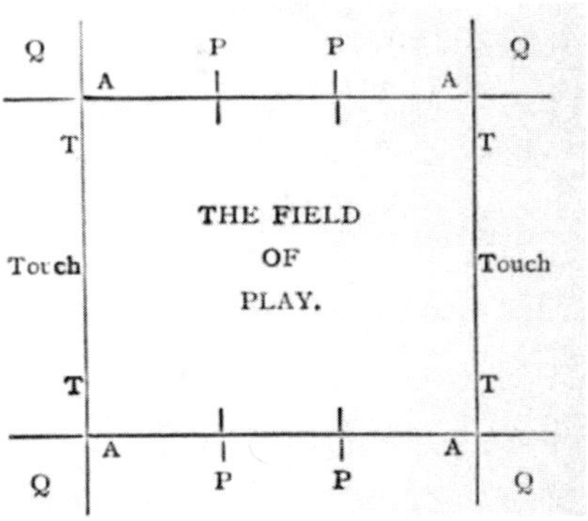

Q P P Q
A A
T T
THE FIELD OF PLAY.
Touch Touch
T T
A A
Q P P Q

AA. AA. Goal Lines. **PP. PP. Goal Posts.**

TT. TT. Touch Lines. **QQ. QQ. Touch In Goal.**

The Touch-lines and Goal-lines should be cut out of the Turf.

person of any player of the opposite side, or when one of his own side has run in front of him either with the ball or having kicked it when behind him.

25. When a player has the ball none of his opponents who at the time are off side may commence or attempt to run, tackle, or otherwise interrupt such player until he has run five yards.

26. Throwing Back.—It is lawful for any player who has the ball to throw it back towards his own goal, or to pass it back to any player of his own side, who is at the time behind him in accordance with the rules of on side.

27 Knocking on—i.e., deliberately hitting the ball with the hand — and throwing forward—i. e., throwing the ball in the direction of the opponent's goal-line, are not lawful. If the ball be either knocked on or thrown forward, the captain of the opposite side may, unless a fair catch has been made, as provided by the next rule, require to have it brought back to the spot where it was so knocked or throw on, and there put down.

28. A fair catch is a catch made direct from a kick or a throw forward or a knock on by one of the opposite side, or from a punt out or a punt on (see Rules 29 and 30), provided the catcher makes a mark with his heel at the spot where he has made the catch, and no other of his own side touch the ball. (See Rules 43 and 44.)

29. A punt out is a punt made after a touch-down by a player from behind his opponents› goal-line, and from touch-in-goal, if necessary, towards his own side, who must stand outside the goal-line and endeavour to make a fair catch, or to get the ball and run in or drop a goal. (See Rules 49 and 51.)

30. A punt on is a punt made in a manner similar to a punt out, and from touch if necessary, by a player who has made a fair catch from a punt out or another punt on.

31. Touch (see plan).— If the ball goes into touch the first player on his side who touches it down must bring it to the spot where it crossed the touch-line, or if a player when running with the ball cross or put any part of either foot across the touch-line he must return with the ball to the spot where the line was so crossed, and thence return it to the field of play in one of the modes provided by the following rule.

32. He must then himself, or by one of his own side, either bound it out in the field of play, and then run with it, kick it, or throw it back to his own side, or (2) throw it out at right angles to the touch-line, or (3) walk out with it at right angles to the touch-line any distance not less than five or more than fifteen yards, and there put it down, first declaring how far he intends to walk out.

33. If two or more players holding the ball are pushed into touch the ball shall belong in touch to the player who first had hold of it when in the field of play and has not released his hold of it.

34. If the ball when thrown out of touch be not thrown out at right angles to the touch-line, the captain of either side may at once claim to have it thrown out again.

35. A catch made when the ball is thrown out of touch is not a fair catch.

36. Kick off is a place-kick from the centre of the field of play and cannot count as a goal. The opposite side must stand at least ten yards in front of the ball until it has been kicked.

37. The ball shall be kicked off at the commencement of the game, after a goal has been obtained.

38. The sides shall change goals as often as and whenever a goal is obtained, unless it has been otherwise agreed by the captains before the commencement of the match.

39. The captains of the respective sides shall toss up before the commencement of the match; the winner of the toss shall have the option of choice of goals or the kick-off.

40. Whenever a goal shall have been obtained the side which has lost the goal shall then kick-off.

41. Kick-out is a drop-kick by one of the players of the side which has had to touch the ball down in their own goal, or into whose touch in goal the ball has gone (Rule 21), and is the mode of bringing the ball again into play, and cannot count as a goal.

42. Kick-out must be a drop-kick, and from not more than twenty-five yards outside the kicker's goal-line; if the ball when kicked out pitch in touch it must be taken back and kicked out again. The kicker's side must be behind the ball when kicked out.

43. A player who has made and claimed a fair catch shall thereupon either take a drop-kick or a punt, or place the ball for a place-kick.

44. After a fair catch has been made the opposite side may come up to the catcher's mark, and (except in cases under Rule 50) the catcher's side retiring, the ball shall be kicked from such mark or from a spot any distance behind it.

45. A player may touch the ball down in his own goal at any time.

46. A side having touched the ball down in their opponents' goal, shall try at goal either by a place-kick or a punt out.

47. If a try at goal be made by a place-kick a player of the side which has touched the ball down shall bring it up to the goal-line (subject to Rule 48) in a straight line from and opposite to the spot where the ball was touched down, and there make a mark on the goal-line, and thence walk straight out with it at right angles to the goal-line such distance as he thinks proper, and there place it for another of his side to kick. The kicker's side must be behind the ball when it is kicked, and the opposite side must remain behind their goal-line until the ball has been placed on the ground. (See Rules 54 and 55.)

48. If the ball has been touched down between the goal-posts, it may be brought out in a straight line from either of such posts, but if brought out from between them the opposite side may charge at once. (See Rule 54.)

49. If the try at goal be by a punt out (see Rule 29), a player of the side which has touched the ball down shall bring it straight up to the goal-line opposite to the spot where it was touched down, and there make a mark on the goal-line, and then punt out from touch in goal, if necessary, or from any part behind the goal-line not nearer to the goal-post than such mark, beyond which mark it is not lawful for the opposite side, who must keep behind their goal-line, to pass until the ball has been kicked. (See Rules 54 and 55.)

50. If a fair catch be made from a punt out or a punt on, the catcher may either proceed as provided by Rules 43 and 44, or himself take a punt on, in which case the mark made on making the fair catch shall be regarded (for the purpose of determining as well the position of the player who makes the punt on as of the other players of both sides) as the mark made on the goal-line in the case of a punt out.

51. A catch made in touch from a punt out or a punt on is not a fair catch. The ball must then be taken or thrown out of touch as provided by Rule 32; but if the catch be made in touch in goal the ball is at once dead, and must be kicked out as provided by Rule 21.

52. When the ball has been touched down in the opponents' goal, none of the side in whose goal it has been so touched down shall touch it or in any way displace it or interfere with the player of the other side who may be taking it up or out.

53. The ball is dead whenever a goal has been obtained, but if a try at goal be not successful, the kick shall be considered as only only an ordinary kick in the course of the game.

54. Charging — i.e., rushing forward to kick the ball or tackle a player — is lawful for the opposite side in all cases of a place-kick after a fair catch or upon a try at goal, immediately the ball touches or is placed in the ground; and in cases of a drop-kick or punt after a fair catch, as soon as the player having the ball commences to run or offers to kick, or the ball has touched the ground; but he may always draw back, and unless he has dropped the ball or actually touched it with his foot, they must again retire to his mark (see Rule 56). The opposite side in the case of a punt out or a punt on, and the kicker's side in all cases, may not charge until the ball has been kicked.

55. If a player having the ball when about to punt it out goes outside the goal line, or when about to punt on advances nearer to his own goal-line than his mark made on making the fair catch, or if after the ball has been touched down in the opponents› goal or a fair catch has been made, more than one player of the side which has so touched it down or made the fair catch touch the ball before it is again kicked, the opposite side may charge at once.

56. In cases of a fair catch the opposite side may come up to and stand anywhere on or behind a line drawn through the mark made by the player who has made the catch, and parallel to their own goal-line; but in the case of a fair catch from a punt out or a punt on they may not advance further in the direction of the touch-line nearest to such mark than a line drawn through such mark to their goal-line, and parallel to such touch-line. In all cases (except a punt out and a punt on) the kicker›s side must be behind the ball when it is kicked, but may not charge until it has been kicked.

57. No hacking or hacking over or tripping up shall be allowed under any circumstances.

58. No one wearing projecting nails, iron plates, or gutta percha on any part of his boots or shoes shall be allowed to play in a match.

59. The captains of the respective sides shall be the sole arbiters of all disputes.[1]

It's probable that the Trinity College rules, especially the ban on hacking, had an influence because Rule 57 bans the practice. Up until then hacking was considered a vital part of rugby and was the major cause of the rift with soccer—perhaps if someone had relented a bit sooner there would have been no separation of codes and the modern football landscape would be very different.

Today there are two codes that have kept the name 'rugby'—rugby union and rugby league. Rugby league came about in very much the same way as professional soccer, in an argument over payments between the working class men in the north of England and the elites in the south. Rugby had spread quickly through the mines and factories of the north and was well established there by the time it was codified in 1871, but the northerners faced the same problem as they had with soccer—working men couldn't afford to take time off work to train or play, let alone travel to matches.

But, whereas soccer's southern based FA caved in to demands that players be allowed to receive payment, the RFU dug in and the dispute became quite acrimonious with comments like 'if men couldn't afford to play, then they shouldn't play at all'. The

1 https://en.wikisource.org/wiki/Laws_of_the_Rugby_Football_Union_(1871)

southerners wanted to keep rugby a sport for the elite and the northern working men wanted to be able to play on an equal footing, and neither side was willing to compromise.

The dispute came to a head in 1895 when the breakaway Northern Rugby Football Union (NRFU) was formed in Huddersfield with the specific aim of allowing players to receive compensation for lost wages. Within a couple of years this had extended to actually being paid to play, so long as it wasn't their sole income.

Over the next 30 years the NRFU went from strength to strength and in 1922 differentiated itself from the amateur sport by changing its name to the Rugby Football League.

So now there were officially two rugby codes, union and league, and they would spend the next century, and probably the next one too, bickering and competing for the hearts and minds of rugby fans. They've evolved differently and need different explanations, so, first, as the oldest and biggest, rugby union.

Chapter 4
RUGBY UNION

The mechanics of the Game

Today rugby union is the second most popular code of football in the world, with more than 3.2 million registered and over six million unregistered players across about 120 countries.

It's a full contact sport played by two opposing teams of 15 players aside, each team divided into two groups; eight forwards, seven backs one of which is called a half-back. Play is controlled by one referee, two line umpires and, more recently, with advice from a video umpire. It is played over two 40 minutes halves, with a 10–15 minute break between. After the break the teams change ends to nullify any advantages from playing with the wind or sun behind them.

The game is played on a rectangular field of natural grass. The playing area is between 68–70 m (223' – 229') wide and 94–100 m (308' – 328') between goal lines, plus an area behind the goal line (the in-goal) that can vary from 6–22 m (20' – 72') wide. A half-way line divides the field in half lengthwise, and each half is further divided by a line 22 m out from each goal line. The side lines (called 'touch lines') are not in the field of play—if the ball or ball player touches the side line they are considered out of play.

An 'H' shaped set of goal posts are positioned centrally on each goal line, the posts are 5.6 m (18') apart, with a minimum height of 3.4 m (11') and are connected by a cross bar 3 m (10') from the ground.

The object of a game of rugby is to either put an oval ball down behind or on the opponent's goal line, or kick it over their goal's crossbar. Touching the ball down is called a 'try' and worth five points. After each try the scoring team is permitted an unhindered attempt to 'convert' the try (a 'conversion) by kicking the ball over the opponents cross-bar for a further two points. The kick is taken from anywhere on a line perpendicular to the point where the try was scored and may be either a place kick—the ball is placed on a mound or kicking tee on the ground and the kicker employs a run-up to the kick—or a drop kick where the ball is dropped point down onto the ground and kicked fractionally after it rebounds.

The terms 'try' and 'conversion' date back to rugby's origins. Initially no points were awarded for touching the ball down in the in-goal, instead the person touching down kicked the ball back onto the field and if one of his own players caught it cleanly he was allowed a free kick at goal. In other words, if a team managed to get the ball over the line they were allowed to try to convert their efforts into a point. It wasn't until 1886 that a point was awarded for actually scoring a try, and points awarded for a try have gradually increased over the years to reflect the difficulty of actually getting over the line in the first place.

Points may also be scored by kicking the ball over the cross bar from anywhere on the field during the course of play. This can be from a fixed penalty being awarded for foul play by the opponents or from a drop goal, each worth three points. A penalty is taken with a place or drop kick taken from the point where the foul was committed. A drop goal is taken during play from anywhere on the field, although due to the degree of difficulty it's usually from close to and directly in front of the goal.

Goal kicking rules hark back to the original rules where 'rule 6' states that:

A goal may be obtained by any kind of kick except a punt.

In other words a goal can only be scored if the ball is kicked from the ground—a punt is when the ball is dropped or placed directly onto the foot.

Originally rugby balls were the same as soccer balls—roughly round and made of leather encased pig's bladders, and they varied in size depending on the size of the pig and the maker's inclinations.

Rubber bladders were invented in 1862, but phasing out pig's bladders took a while, so balls remained somewhat misshapen for some time. During that time rugby players discovered that, while soccer players needed a predictable round ball, a more oval shaped ball was much easier to handle. Responding to this, Lindon (the shoe-maker whose wife's death prompted him to invent rubber bladders) invented the rugby ball with the oval rubber bladder insert—or so he claimed, but he never patented any of his ideas and by the 1880s there were several ball manufacturers using his rubber bladder and ball designs. His main opposition seems to have been William Gilbert, one of Lindon's former employees who took his bosses ideas with him when he left (an underhand practice not unknown in any age) and made a fortune out of rugby balls. His name still appears on them today.

The fact that an oval ball is easier to handle appears to have been lost on some commentators of the time, with one asking:

> '*Was the oval ball an accident from want of skill in the worker in leather in Rugby, who like the tailors then persuaded his victims that it was the true artistic shape?*'[1]

The distinctive rugby ball was not officially adopted until 1892, although then it was rounder. Over the years it's stretched and flattened until the modern standard became oval shaped, between 280–300 mm (11" – 11.8") long, 580–620 mm (22.9" – 24.4") around the middle and made up of four equal sized panels, pumped to a pressure of 65.7–68.7 kilopascals (9.5–10 psi) and weighing 410–460 grams (14.4–16.2 ounces).

As I said earlier, rugby teams are divided into groups of eight forwards (the pack), six backs and one half-back. This broadly reflects the original formation of teams back when it was still a free-for-all in Rugby school grounds. The forward's task is to challenge for the ball, then to either carry it over, or through, the opposition, or pass it to the faster and more elusive backs. This is

1 The Field, 1863

very physically demanding and makes rugby probably the most violent, albeit controlled violence, sport played today.

Rugby union employs two set-piece plays, both involve direct physical competition for the ball and are, therefore, the exclusive preserve of the forwards.

First, the lineout.

When the ball goes into touch it is thrown back into the field of play along a line perpendicular to the point where it crossed the sideline, as per 'rule 31' of the 1871 rules. Originally this rule called for the last player to touch the ball to throw it in, but in the modern game that's done by the opposition. Each pack of forwards lines up on their own side of the line along which the ball will be thrown and one of their number—usually the hooker, we'll get to that—throws the ball in and the two packs compete for it.

Alternatively, in accordance with 'rule 32' a player may throw (described as 'bound' in the rule) the ball in to another member of his team, or throw it up so he can catch it himself and then either run with it or throw it to a member of his team. Today this rule has evolved to include a 'quick throw-in' and can be taken from anywhere on the attacker's side of the point where the ball went out.

Then there's the scrum.

The scrum is unique in sport, an enigma to most non-rugby people and therefore needs some explanation. It's also a fine example of the rapid evolution of the sport.

It's also the origin of the descriptor 'one man trying to push two men up three men's arses'.

There are two principle rules in a game of rugby. First is the off-side rule which states that any player in front of the ball is off side and can't be involved in the play, infringements of this rule result in a penalty. The second is passing, throwing or knocking the ball forward, whether accidentally or not. Infringing this rule results in a scrum where the forward packs bind together in crouched 3-4-1 man formations and engage each other head on.

Originally there was no scrum in rugby, just a free-for-all ruck in which the object was to kick the ball through the

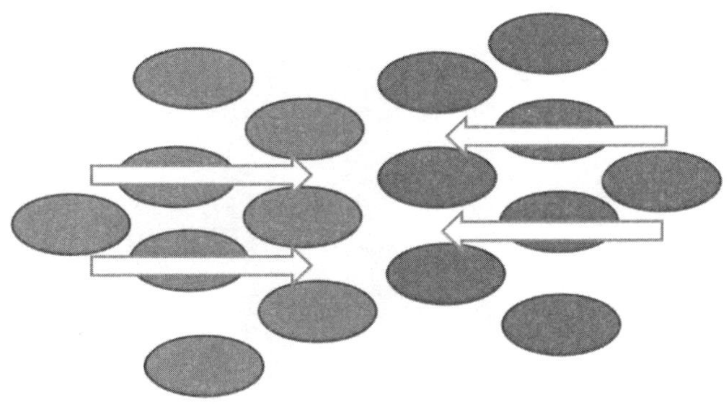

The rugby union 3-4-1 rugby union scrum formation

opposition toward the goal line. In the late 19th C this tactic changed to rucking the ball back and distributing it to the backs, then came a formal scrum, but there were no specialised positions and players simply packed down as they arrived. Then an Aotearoa-NZ Maori team arrived in Britain in 1888 with the first organised scrum, although it didn't look much like the modern formation—that was invented by the South Africans in 1906 and, with minor tweaking, has remained a feature of the game ever since.

For most of the 20th C the scrum involved pushing against the opposition just enough to maintain position while the ball is placed on the ground equidistant between the packs by the team infringed against. It was the job of the 'hooker', the player in the middle of the front row, to compete to hook the ball with his feet so that it travelled back through his pack where, once clear of the scrum, it could be passed out to the backs. It was, and is, absolutely forbidden to handle the ball in a scrum. The feeding team always had a considerable advantage because their hooker was always placed closer to the feed. Scrums were not particularly dangerous because the emphasis was on creating a stable platform for the hooker to do his job rather than dominating the opposition.

That changed in the 1990s when the Aotearoa-NZ national team, the All Blacks, began putting on a major push in the scrum at the same time as the ball was put in and forcing the opposition back off the ball. It wasn't long before other teams copied them. Scrums became a battle of power and referees began allowing the ball to be placed under the feeding team's feet—probably because, with the forces at play inside the scrum it was impractical and dangerous for the hooker to shift his weight to attempt to hook the ball. Hookers became all but redundant and began simply adding their weight to the push.

Forwards are always big people and in a men's game the pack weights are often around 900+ kilograms each, which means that when they engage there are forces close to a tonne pushing against each other and the risk of injury, especially to neck and spine, is high. To lessen the risk, forwards are specialised and highly trained positions, and rule changes such as the referee's four part engagement instructions of 'crouch, touch, pause, engage' slows the initial contact, allows players to set their positions, prevents the front rows from crashing together and limits the impact. Never-the-less, scrum collapses are common and in the resultant jumble of huge bodies it's a testament to their training and fitness that there aren't more injuries.

There are also 'rucks' and 'mauls', which occur in general play and are very much throw-backs to the original game. A ruck normally follows a tackle and once the ball carrier and the ball are on the ground both the tackled and the tackler must roll away from the ball, freeing it to be contested by the forwards who pile in and try to heel it back to their own side. Under no circumstances can they handle the ball in a ruck.

A maul happens when a player with the ball is held up off the ground by the opposing team and players from his own team attempt to help by either forcing him through the opposition, getting the ball free and passed to the backs, or getting the carrier to the ground so that a ruck can be formed.

I apologise to the non-rugby fans who may have been somewhat bored by the above detail, but it's necessary because they both differentiate rugby union from its derivatives and link them together.

But enough of the mechanics of the game—if you need more, look them up. It's time to get to the history, how the game spread and developed.

History of rugby union

Europe

Just as with soccer, rugby spread rapidly and was enthusiastically taken up throughout the UK, especially northern England, in the late 19th C. But from the start it was an elitist sport in its home country, England, it was dominated by the rich at public schools and universities and they resisted all attempts at professionalism. This was to become a problem for the English game.

And like soccer, rugby was born as an amateur sport. But, unlike soccer, it was determined to stay that way even in the face of the breakaway professional league in the north. It wasn't for another hundred years, in 1995, when Kerry Packer tried to set up a rival professional competition under the name World Rugby Championship, that there was enough momentum for change. Rupert Murdoch's News Corp had just finalised a $50 million deal that gave it 10 years of exclusive television rights to the Southern Hemisphere's Tri-nations Super 12 competition, which set a precedent for big money in the game. Added to this there was active recruitment of players lured by big money in rugby league. The only way to ward off the twin threats of Packer's split and rugby league's poaching raids was to professionalise. It was a wise move because since turning professional rugby union's popularity has increased dramatically and the sport has gone from strength to strength.

But I'm getting ahead of myself.

The first ever official international rugby match was played by 20-a-side teams between England and Scotland in Edinburgh in March, 1871. The English wore white with a red rose on their shirts, the Scots wore a thistle on a brown shirt. Scotland scored two tries and converted one of them, England scored one try but failed to convert it. By the rules of the day Scotland won 1 – 0.

The game was re-introduced to Ireland as an elite sport, played by the rich and aristocratic establishments like Trinity College in Dublin, and by elite clubs in Cork and Belfast. The first Irish international was played against England in 1874, which the Irish lost 5 – 0. The game bubbled along until it turned professional in 1995 and more players were attracted to it as a viable profession. Today Ireland is regularly at the top of Northern Hemisphere rugby—and more and more at the top of world rugby.

Outside England, Scotland and Ireland, the game was becoming much more egalitarian as the 19th C turned into the 20th.

In Wales it was largely introduced by miners and other workers returning from the industrial centres of Northern England. It was enthusiastically embraced by the working classes and organised as town or work-place (they were often the same thing) clubs and became a focus for local pride. By the late 19th C rugby had become a focal point of Welsh nationalism and a part of the Welsh identity. The Welsh Rugby Union was formed in 1881 and Wales began competing in the Home Championship with England, Scotland and Ireland. It was so highly competitive that it rose to be a dominant force in the late 19th and much of the 20th C.

There was probably a very good reason for comparatively small Wales and neighbouring Cornwall to be good at rugby. The Welsh had a tradition sport called *cnapan*, and the Cornish had two games, both called *hurling* (or hurlain)—one hurling-to-goals and the other hurling-to-country. All of these games require very skilled ball handling and certainly gave their players a strong head start when pitted against teams that just stayed more-or-less static and kicked the crap out of each other. These traditional sports are probably also why the Welsh and Cornish working men took so readily to the game and why, in that small corner of Britain, it was not regarded as an elite sport.

But more on that later.

In the 1980s the fabric of Welsh society was altered by the closure of many of the coal mines and the subsequent damage to the mining towns. These were the engine rooms of Welsh rugby and the closures had an impact that has seen it decline slightly, but Wales remains a rugby powerhouse.

Across the water in France, rugby was introduced to Paris by British residents who formed the Le Havre Athletique in 1872. Initially they seemed to have played some sort of hybrid rugby/soccer game, but in 1877 a group of British businessmen formed the English Taylors Rugby Football Club to play actual rugby. It was followed in fairly quick succession by the establishment of French clubs and the first rugby club championship was played in 1892. The game spread to the south-west of the country where it became entrenched as a major sport and introduced to the 1900 Paris Summer Olympics, where France won the gold medal. In 1910 France began competing officially in the British Home Nations tournament, turning it into the Five Nations, which it would remain for all but 13 years of the 20th C. That hiatus came about because French rugby was not elitist and its attitude toward professionalism was much more relaxed than the English, which didn't go down well in the Home Nations and in 1932 they cut their ties with the French, refusing to play with them again until 1945.

Today France is regularly at or near the top of the international rugby table and its professional unions attract top flight players from around the world. It regularly recruits players from across Europe, giving developing rugby nations valuable experience and, just as importantly, money. The French system has probably done more to promote healthy international competition than any other national Rugby Federation.

Elsewhere in Europe rugby's uptake lagged behind soccer's, and Northern Europeans appear to have largely shied away from it. Actually, as I said previously, it may have been introduced to Germany by August Hermann and Konrad Koch in 1874 and when the first club, Deutscher FV Hannover, was founded in 1878 it was actually a rugby club. There is still confusion about it, but the fact that they played with an oval ball and Germany went on to enter a rugby team in the 1900 Olympics strongly suggests that it was rugby. Ultimately rugby lost out to the round ball game across most of Europe and today is only a minor sport, at best, across most of the north—although since the advent of professionalism it has gained traction rapidly and some countries have developed a small, but thriving and growing rugby community.

Then there's the vast sprawl of Russia. Rugby's introduction to Russia and the old Soviet Republics was not as straight forward as most other places. Rugby and soccer were introduced at the end of the 19th C. The first rugby match was organised by a Scotsman around 1880, but the Tsar's police thought the violence on the rugby field would encourage violence in the general public so they 'discouraged' it. They didn't actually ban it, however, it did sputter along in soccer's shadow until after the revolution when it began to gain traction, but still lagged far behind soccer. Today Russia itself has more than 15,000 registered players and is, or was before its Ukrainian venture, making gains on the world stage. But it must be remembered that for most of the 20th C it wasn't just Russia, it was the Soviet Union which incorporated several republics where rugby fared better, especially in the north, in the old Novgorod Republic (where it replaced a traditional rugby-like game called *kila*) and Siberia, and Kazakhstan and Georgia in the south where it replaced *lelo burti*, another traditional rugby-like game.

Today virtually all players from their national teams, together with many other Eastern Europeans like the Romanians, play most of their season in France. This has allowed them to develop their game much more rapidly than they could have by just playing in their domestic competitions and turned both Georgia and Kazakhstan into successful rugby playing nations, with Georgia, in particular, rapidly climbing the international ladder.

In Europe the other nation that has taken up rugby with enthusiasm is Italy, albeit somewhat belatedly. British businessmen brought rugby to Genoa in the 1890s, but it was the French and northern Italy's closeness to the heartland of French rugby that was the real spur for Italians to take up the game. In the far northern Italian region of the Po valley, workers returning from Southern France brought rugby with them and it became a local working-class sport. In 1910 French students introduced it to

Milan University and the first match with an Italian representative team was played in July 1911 between a Milanese and a French fifteen. In 1928 the Italian Rugby Federation (Federazione Italiana Rugby) was formed.

The game continued to develop and internationals were played with countries like Romania, Spain and Germany, but then Europe began to descend into chaos. Mussolini saw rugby as a reincarnation of an ancient Roman harpastum and promoted it to encourage Italian unity and values, but when the sport's authorities resisted the fascist's influence he withdrew his support in favour of a type of hand-ball, and rugby faded from prominence. After the war it was revived by occupying allied troops and developed rapidly, gained backing from large companies and was able to attract big name players from around the world. By 2000 it had developed enough to join the Five Nations competition, changing it to the Six Nations.

North America

Outside Europe, rugby was taken up to various degrees around the world. In Canada and the US it had a comparatively brief flowering and enjoyed a considerable following in the 'Ivy League' universities, before it was modified in the late 1800s to make 'gridiron' (American football, we'll get to that). In 1905 rugby enjoyed a revival on the West Coast, from California to British Columbia in Canada, when gridiron was banned following a public outcry about its perceived physical risks. At about the same time rugby got a further boost on both the east and west coasts when an Aotearoa-NZ team toured and exposed the American public to some very high class exhibition games. After that Southern Hemisphere teams often stopped off on their way home from Europe to play exhibition matches, as did Northern Hemisphere teams going the other way. Even today the West Coast of the US and Canada remains the main rugby playing region of the continent, except for Utah which has a concentration of Mormon Polynesians.

Rugby union suffered the same problem there as it did in its home country—amateur vs professional. Americans were, and still are, very keen on professional sport. Gridiron quickly became professional, but American rugby union stubbornly retained its amateur status until 2016, by which time gridiron had long established its pre-eminent position. American rugby teams competed very successful in the 1920 and 1924 Olympics, but rugby was dropped as an Olympic sport and after that its development was slow. Since turning professional it's had a major revival and once again both America and Canada are competing very well at the top international level.

Japan

In Asia the only country to seriously take up rugby was Japan. Japan's introduction to football happened in the aftermath of mid-19th C European and American diplomatic efforts to open the country up to trade with the West. When the Japanese refused to let them in the West, in a common diplomatic manoeuvre of the time, sent warships to shell them into agreement.

That laid the foundations for the WWII war in the Pacific, but that's another book entirely.

By the late 19th C British sailors and long term residents were playing rugby in the Japanese treaty ports, but the Japanese themselves were rarely involved. That changed at the turn of the 20th C when two teachers at Keio University, Clark and Tanaka, began teaching rugby union to their students. Both men were born in Japan and been educated at Cambridge, where they had become involved with the sport. When they returned home they introduced it to encourage the 'boys' to do something constructive outdoors instead of just hanging about.

Rugby took off in universities across the country—they still remain strongholds for the game—and it was given a further push by the Japanese-British alliance in the first 20 years of the 20th C. By the 1920s Japanese rugby had more than 60,000 registered players, but despite the popularity of the game no international sides visited until the 1930s when the Canadians were brought over as part of a trade delegation. The lack of tourists may have been because Japan is out of the way and would have been expensive to get to, but teams had been criss-crossing the world for decades, so the motive was more likely racist.

Just as an aside, following its success in the 1905 war with Russia, Japan colonised Korea and took rugby with them, but it doesn't seem to have caught on with the Korean public. During the Korean War in the 1950s Commonwealth troops reinvigorated the game there, but it became, and remains, mostly the preserve of the Korean Army.

Much of Japanese rugby's success can be attributed to strong imperial support and their active promotion, which continued into WWII despite the government's coolness to it because they viewed it as too foreign. To get around this, it was rebranded *tokyu*, or 'fighting ball'. But the war took many of the players and destroyed most of the infrastructure, and it had pretty much died by 1943. Surprisingly it bounced back very rapidly and large corporations began to promote it among their workers in an attempt to lift morale. Many of the top teams today are corporate based and huge money attracts top flight international players, some of whom stay long enough to get Japanese residency and qualify for the national team. At the same time top Japanese players have been playing in senior competitions around the world, all to the benefit of Japanese rugby.

The Japanese have gone some way to overcoming their overall size handicap by speed, quick thinking and discipline—they play as hard as any team but always within the rules and there is very little 'thuggery' involved in their game.

That's about it for the Northern Hemisphere, it's time to look south.

South America

Like soccer, rugby was introduced to South America by British migrants in the late 19th C and it was taken up, to varying degrees, across the continent. But the main uptake was in Argentina, which became the only Spanish speaking nation represented on the International Rugby Board. Although still lagging far behind soccer, rugby's rapidly making ground. The professional era has seen many of its players able to gain experience with the major rugby-playing nations, especially France, and import considerable expertise.

The Argentine national team, Los Pumas, has had a chequered history on the international stage, but has recorded several outstanding results. An annual competition against other Southern Hemisphere countries saw an overall improvement in play and, although the COVID pandemic stopped the competition, it was a quarter-finalist in the 2023 World Cup.

Africa

On the African continent rugby, like soccer, was introduced by mostly British and French workers and soldiers. In the African colonies, it was initially played almost exclusively within the expat communities and from there extended to the non-white populations. The mid-20th C struggles for independence in countries such as Kenya saw the mass exodus of whites and the general collapse of the game. It slowly gained ground in several African countries over the past few decades, although the difficulties of distance, political upheavals and logistics have seriously hampered its recovery. Today it's organised into the Confederation of African Rugby, which includes countries such as Kenya, Tanzania, the Seychelles, Madagascar, Tunisia, Morocco, Senegal and the Ivory Coast.

The stand-out exception is South Africa, a modern day powerhouse of the game. Like the rest of Africa, the British—many of them miners from the rugby stronghold of Cornwall—brought rugby to South Africa in the late 19th C. The mostly big and tough local Boers found it very much to their liking and enthusiastically adopted it, and in 1889 the South African Rugby Board was formed, the same year as the first nation-wide tournament was held. The Boer wars did nothing to hamper rugby's spread, British forces took it to the interior and games against Boer prisoners-of-war further popularised it.

Although being one of the world's pre-eminent teams, South African rugby has been dogged by racism and controversy for most of its existence. In its early days, it was played extensively by the native and Asian populations, but lack of backing, segregation laws and finally official apartheid discouraged non-white participation and they mostly turned to soccer. For the first half of the 20th C most of the rugby playing world were, officially and unofficially, racist to some degree so the overt racism of South African rugby raised few international eyebrows and the national team, the Springboks, were highly regarded everywhere. Even when non-white players were excluded from visiting teams there was little comment, and in practice this really only affected the Aotearoa-NZ team.

But from the 1950s onward the anti-white sentiment in Africa and the open rebellions in many colonies began to make the world aware of African, particularly South African, repression. The Sharpeville Massacre in 1960 when police opened fire on a crowd of unarmed protesters, killing 69 and wounding 180, and the Soweto Riots in 1975 in which upward of 200 protesting school children were killed, turned the world against South Africa. And South African rugby in particular, was targeted as it was seen as a vehicle for apartheid.

An Aotearoa-NZ tour in 1967 was cancelled because South Africa would not allow Maori in the team, but went ahead three years later when the South Africans changed their minds and decided that Maori were 'honorary whites'.

They might have meant it as a complement, but what an insult to a proud people!

In 1976, soon after Soweto, an Aotearoa-NZ team toured amid huge protests at home and led to international condemnation and a boycott of the 1976 Olympics in protest against Aotearoa-NZ's participation. The following year the Commonwealth countries signed the Gleneagles Agreement discouraging playing against the Springbok. After a disastrous 1981 tour of Aotearoa-NZ went ahead amid protests, pitch invasions and even aerial flour bombing of players, the IRB banned all contact with South Africa so long as it retained its apartheid policy.

In the early 1990s apartheid fell apart and the world welcomed back a revitalised and racially mixed Springboks, which quickly re-established itself on the world stage and has gone on to win four world cups.

The Antipodes

The history of the other great rugby region of the Southern Hemisphere—Aotearoa-NZ, Australia and Oceania—are intricately linked, but to get a good overview they should all be looked at individually.

Aotearoa-NZ

Rugby union was introduce to Aotearoa-NZ by Charles Monro in the small South Island town of Nelson in 1870. Monro was born to wealthy parents and sent to Christs College Finchley, in England, where he learned the game and on his return introducing it to his home town. The rest of the colony wasted no time getting on board and within a few years it had spread nation-wide, with clubs and regional unions being formed in all the major centres. But the county's rugged terrain caused difficulties with communications, which meant that the national body, the New Zealand Rugby Football Union, wasn't established until 1892. In the meantime the regional unions remained isolated and pretty-much went their own way.

Or perhaps the regions were just enjoying doing their own thing and resisted an over-arching body telling them what to do—that would be well within keeping of a national trait that has persisted strongly to the present day.

Despite this lack of an organising body, Aotearoa-NZ was quick to get involved in international rugby. In 1882 a NSW side (not Australian, the colonies were still independent then) toured, two years later an Aotearoa-NZ team returned the visit, and a British Isles team visited in 1888. Then a rather odd thing for the times happened. In 1888–89 a 'New Zealand Native's team' toured Australia and Britain.

At the time there seems to have been a British fascination with Maori. This was probably with Polynesians in general, because of their association with notions of the 'exotic' and 'romantic' South Seas, but they found Maori, in particular, fascinating because several prominent chiefs had visited NSW and England and public interest had been well and truly piqued. Noticing this, a couple of entrepreneurs decided to cash in by using private funds to organise a Maori team. That the 'Native's Team' wasn't all Maori—it even included a native born Englishman—didn't seem to matter, the tour was a huge success. The team was the first from the colonies to tour Britain, it was also the first to wear the black uniform and perform the haka before games. All up, they played 108 rugby matches, sometimes up to three a week, and ended with 78 wins, six draws and 23 losses. They lost seven of the nine Australian rules matches and both of the soccer games, and their biggest success was a 13 - 4 win against an Irish national side.

The British public seem to have taken to them fairly well, the establishment less so, especially as their visitors were obviously making money in a very strictly amateur sport. They also regarded them as 'unsportsmanlike' after three of their number left the field during the match against England in protest at the English referee. He was also the English Rugby Football Union secretary and awarded three dodgy tries to the home team. The 'natives' apologised afterward, but the atmosphere remained hostile at an official level and the team left England without any official send off. Perhaps the upper class English rugby hierarchy did not enjoy the sight of their best teams being beaten by 'natives'.

On the way home the Maori played several games in Australia, including several AFL matches, before finishing with a tour of their home country.

In 1893 the first official Aotearoa-NZ team toured the Australian colonies, and eight years later, in 1905, toured the

British Isles, France and the US. The Europe/US tour opened with a 55 – 4 win over one of the top clubs in England and went on to record a stunning 34 wins from 35 matches, including against the host nations. Their only defeat was a narrow 3 – 0 loss at the hands of the Welsh.

The success was put down mainly to organisation and co-ordination. Building on the 'Natives' innovations, their scrum used fixed positions with each player a specialist, as opposed to the opposition's random approach of players packing down in the order they arrived. The line-out also became specialised with close communication between the player throwing the ball in and the man intended to receive it. The forwards supported the backs and were prepared to run with the ball when needed, unlike their opponents who saw their forward's role as simply securing the ball, feeding it to the backs and letting them deal with it.

There was also an issue with fitness. The visitors practised continuously and had the advantage that in their home country, games were played in 45 minute halves as opposed to 35 in the Northern hemisphere. It may be indicative that the only game they lost was to Wales, the only place in the UK where the game was not dominated by the elite but played by the working class—mostly miners—whose strength, fitness and stamina could match the visitors. At the other end of the scale were the Scottish who were conservative, even for the day, and held strongly to the elitist attitude. They also believed that rugby was for the players and spectators were incidental. That attitude was financially disastrous for them when they declined to contribute 500 pound to the tour expenses. Instead, because they didn't value spectators and didn't expect many, they offered the gate takings. Instead of receiving the 500 pound they'd asked for, the NZRU raked in more than 1700 pound. The Scots lost the match, lost the money, and failed to invite their visitors to their after-match dinner.

Actually, the great 1905 team was the first to be called the All Blacks. The teams black playing strip as worn by the 1888 Maori had been confirmed by the NZRFU back when it was formed in 1892, and it captured the British imagination. After their first games 55 – 4 rout of one of the top English teams, the Exeter Express and Echo wrote '*The All Blacks, as they are styled by reason of their sable and unrelieved costume*', and the name's stuck ever since. Today it's one of the world's most recognisable sporting brands.

And following the example set by the 'native's' tour, they performed a haka before each game, much to the enthralment of the European and American public, and that particular tradition has also endured into the present day.

The success of the 1905 squad made rugby into the favourite sport in Aotearoa-NZ, and it grew into a national passion. The sport's place in the national psych was set in stone when the All Blacks toured Britain, France and Canada in 1924 and won all 32 games they played. That team came to be known as the 'Invincibles' and its success placed the All Blacks at, or near, the top of international rankings, a position it's held ever since. Aotearoa-NZ rugby has kept its status as a world trend setter in rugby—despite not infrequent disagreements with the Northern Unions over rule interpretation.

The contribution of Maori can't be overstated, because right from their first overseas tour in 1888-9, they have been at the forefront of rugby development. The reasons appear to be manifold. The first is obvious—they're big, strong, athletic, and often display explosive power, all of which makes them ideal for the game. But how they got involved to the extent they did, and as early as they did while native people elsewhere in the world were either ignored or excluded, is interesting.

The answer lies in the county's unique history. When the British first arrived in the early 19th C Maori at first welcomed them as trading partners, but when the English began to encroach onto their land they strongly resisted and scored some significant military victories in the process. The upshot of that was that the British and Maori signed a treaty in 1840 that would, in theory, allow the one to colonise and the other to retain traditional rights, including land ownership. But the treaty was more than a little duplicitous because the Maori translation of the English text was not entirely accurate. The result was, inevitably, conflict. But a number of Maori sided with the British and fought alongside them and it was during these campaigns that they learned to play rugby with the British troops. The first, or at least the first recorded, Maori player was Wirihana, who played in 1872. After the wars the children of the Maori elite—generally those that had fought for the British, but also some that opposed them—were given scholarships to some of the best schools in the country where they played rugby as a part of the school activities. Those schools were the breeding ground for many of Aotearoa-NZ's rugby elites, and even today commentators will refer to a player as a product of this or that school.

There is another theory on how Maori, and Polynesians from other islands, especially Fiji, got so heavily involved. Maori were, are, a naturally competitive people and back in the day this manifested itself in warfare, at which they excelled. But after the land wars a diversion was needed to channel that natural aggression, and rugby became an ideal substitute for war. It was certainly not a first, football of one sort or another had been used as a substitute for war in many cultures (for example First Nations people in America had called their game the 'little war', but that's another thing that we'll get to later).

It stands in stark contrast to soccer which, if you remember, started a war.

There was also a traditional Maori game called ki-o-rahi, which greatly resembled rugby in its ball handling and general playing skills. Oddly, although it is making a comeback now, this game was not well known, even in Aotearoa-NZ, in the 20th C and only survived in little remote communities. This may have had something to do with the early missionaries looking askance at all traditional native activities, suspicious that they had religious overtones that had to be supressed, but it's more likely that it was simply overwhelmed by rugby.

It's more than possible that, like Welsh cnapan, ki-o-rahi's ball handling skills and organisation (something distinctly lacking in European rugby at the time) were a fundamental influence on

Aotearoa-NZ's success, and that it consequently changed world rugby.

Pacific Islands

These nations have made contributions to world rugby way out of proportion to their tiny size, so they deserve a mention here.

More than anywhere else in the world, the introduction of rugby into the Pacific exemplifies the principle of replacing existing culture with that of the colonists to reinforce domination—or, as sport sociologist Howard Nixon put it;

> *When sport is introduced to a colonized people, it may reinforce the colonial relationship, with the culture of the conqueror imposed on the culture of the colonized.*[2]

In the Pacific, the island nations that became associated with Britain in one way or another— Aotearoa-NZ, Fiji, Tonga, Samoa and the Cook Islands—adopted rugby with a passion not seen anywhere else—except, perhaps, for Wales. They're all Polynesian (well, technically Fiji is Melanesian, but they share many the same characteristics), which means they share common attributes of size, strength, explosive physical power and a penchant for warfare. But they all came to play rugby in a different way.

Fiji

The Fijians were noted warriors, a trait that the first Europeans found unsettling, and they had games that were designed to prepare the young men—and possibly women—for war. We don't know if any of those were ball sports, but they must have incorporated tactics to make the players fast thinking and skilled at attack and evasion. There may have even been something

2 Howard Nixon and James H. Frey, A Sociology of Sport (Wadsworth Publishing Company, 1996

similar to ki-o-rahi, but we don't know what they were because once they got established, the missionaries succeeded in outlawing and eradicating them all. They were good at that, if it was non-European and fun it was pagan and had to be stamped out and replaced with civilised activities, like cricket and rugby.

The Fijians took to rugby like giant ducks to water, possibly because it resembled their traditional games.

In 1874 Fiji became a British colony and British police and armed forces began to appear in the country, and it wasn't long before they began playing rugby against the locals. The first recorded matches between Fijian and European soldiers of the Native Constabulary go back to the 1880s, and it wasn't long before the sport's popularity spread. But integration received a setback with the introduction of the huge sugar plantations, the importation of Indian labour in the latter half of the 19th C and the stratification of Fijian society, with the ex-patriots (mostly New Zealanders and Australians) on top, the land owning Fijians in the middle and Indian labourers firmly on the bottom. The first rugby clubs were formed in the early 20th C, but they were almost entirely white—the whites played their game and the Fijians played theirs, and the Indians worked.

The Fiji Rugby Union (FRU) was established in 1913 and, in that same year, the All Blacks called in for a game on their way home from a tour of California. Although the 'Fijian' team was all European, the Fijians were inspired—possibly by the presence of Maori in the All Blacks—and wasted no time in organising their own competition and their own union, the Fiji Rugby Native Union (FRNU). As elsewhere, the process was greatly helped by the return of aristocratic boys who had been sent off to school, usually in Aotearoa-NZ, where they inevitably got involved in the game and enthusiastically spread it on their return.

In 1924 Native teams began playing against other Pacific teams, including provincial and University Aotearoa-NZ teams and the sport was boosted by its official introduction into the school curriculum. In 1939 the Fijians toured Aotearoa-NZ and their success brought Fijian rugby to centre-stage on the international scene. That first tour was followed by more tours of Aotearoa-NZ, Australia and Europe during the '50s, '60s and '70s.

Today Fiji is a major power in the international rugby world (it made the quarter finals of the 2023 World Cup) and holds a place that, like its Pacific neighbours belies its comparatively miniscule size and population. Rugby union was the national sport, but in the latter years of the 20th C it adopted one of rugby's children, rugby sevens, as its national code and quickly reached the very top.

Tonga

Tongan society has been cohesive, highly organised and very heavily stratified for at least 1,000 years. They had a very highly developed and very influential religious system which resisted early missionary's attempts at conversion, but the Christians persisted and were finally successful in 1826. This, and other European activities, destabilised Tongan society to the extent that they went through twenty years of civil war before order was restored and, to avoid European annexation, Tonga declared itself a Constitutional Monarchy under the staunchly Christian King Siaosi (George) Tupou.

Under the new king, aristocratic families were encouraged to send their sons to Newington College in Sydney, Australia, which was run by the Reverend Dr James Egan Moulton, a staunch rugby man who had spent many years in Tonga and was a friend of King Tupoa. At the request of the king, Moulton also set up the Tupoa College in Tonga in 1866, which promoted rugby among its students. All of which meant that by the turn of the century there was a generation of aristocratic Tongans steeped in the sport.

Never-the-less, rugby was slow to get established. Perhaps this was because, despite close ties to and a treaty with Britain signed 1900 to keep other Europeans at bay, Tonga never actually became a British colony. Whatever the reason, the Tongan Rugby Union (TRU) was not formed until 1923, and even then games were pretty much limited to its neighbouring islands. After WWII

Tongans began migrating, primarily to Aotearoa-NZ, where they were exposed to rugby on a grand scale. Inevitably, on their return they raised the standard of the local game and Tongan rugby went from strength to strength. In 1969 they played a Maori team and in 1987 joined the International Rugby Board and received development funds that allowed them to compete in the first Rugby World Cup that same year.

Tongan rugby had come of age, but political strife in the nation and accusations of impropriety within the TRU in the late 20th and early 21st Cs has put an unfortunate brake on its development.

Samoa

Samoa's history of European contact differs markedly from both Tonga and Fiji. Missionaries began their activities in the 1830s and slowly spread Christianity through the islands. In the mid-19th C the main centre, Apia, became a Pacific base for European traders, and as a result became a focus for European, particularly British, German and American interests. Unlike Tonga, which had (to European eyes) an acceptable monarchy, Samoa was essentially tribal and therefore ripe for colonisation. The great powers began to vie for rights and in the process promoted inter-tribal conflict, and eventually full scale civil war. Each competing colonial nation supported a faction with arms, and occasionally man-power, to further their own interests.

Ultimately this turned into an international crisis when the three competing powers sent warships into Apia Bay in 1889. Perhaps the old Samoan gods intervened because as soon as they had gathered a cyclone hit that sank all but one of them and ended the crisis. Soon after Britain, Germany and America signed an agreement guaranteeing Samoan neutrality under an approved king.

But that couldn't last, of course, and the treaty was annulled after the death of the king and renewed infighting began over the succession. In a deal, in which the Samoans had no say, the country was divided between America, which got the eastern islands (still held by them and known as American Samoa), and Germany got the rest on condition that it gave up claims to several other Pacific nations, including Tonga.

Understandably, the Samoans were not happy.

German occupation precluded the introduction of rugby—it wasn't German and therefore not culturally appropriate. But that situation didn't last long either. In the opening days of WWI New Zealand troops took control of Western Samoa and set up a military administration. The Samoans weren't happy about that either, but despite their objections the Aotearoa-NZ administration was confirmed by the League of Nations. In 1920 Aotearoa-NZ based missionaries brought rugby to Samoa, the Apia Rugby Union (ARU) was founded in 1924 (although it was linked to the NZRFU) and Samoa's first international was played against Fiji. Despite its obvious links to the colonists, rugby was eagerly taken up throughout Western Samoa and inter-village games thrived alongside the simmering resentment of a warrior nation. It was very likely a case of the authorities encouraging the game as a way to channel resentment and frustration into an acceptable form; perhaps a lesson learnt from earlier Maori experience.

But if it was a diversionary tactic, it didn't entirely work. Resentment against an arrogant administration boiled over in 1929 when eleven unarmed protestors were shot and killed by troops, an event still known as 'Black Saturday' in Samoa. Tensions and resentments remained high into the 1930s when a more moderate and sympathetic government was elected in Aotearoa-NZ. The presence of American troops during WWII improved the Samoan economy, and after the war Western Samoa became a UN Trust Territory, although still under NZ administration. But it was a long haul to complete independence, which wasn't gained until 1962.

Throughout all the turmoil of their colonial years Samoan rugby had thrived and the Samoan Rugby Union (SRU) was set up to replace the old ARU in 1957. The SRU was (and still is) closely linked to chiefs and Government and the national team is regarded as a representative of the Government, and is expected to perform appropriately. So far they've lived up to expectations and acquired a reputation as well-mannered giant killers, especially after they beat Wales in 1991.

After that the team was named '*Manu Samoa*', which roughly translates to 'divine warrior'

The Cook Islands

The Cook Islands are a collection of 15 small islands spread across 240 sq. km of ocean between Samoa and Tahiti. Their traditions are closer to those of Tahiti, Hawaii and Rapa Nui than they are to the islands to their west, in so far as they emphasise sensuality. This presented the missionaries with a challenge when they first landed in 1821, but somehow they managed to impose their values and largely outlawed sinful things; like drumming, singing and dancing.

The Islanders suffered badly from Peruvian slavers in the mid-19th C—something like 75% of some island populations were taken—before the British interceded in 1888, ostensibly to stem such predations, but more likely to stop the French from including them in French Polynesia. In 1901 they were included within the New Zealand Dominion until a vote in the Cook Islands assembly in 1962 opted for self-government, which was implemented in 1965 with Aotearoa-NZ remaining responsible for its foreign policy and defence. It wasn't until 1980 that a formal border was set between the Cook Islands and American Samoa and the Americans gave up claims to several of its islands, and in 1990 the border was fixed with French Polynesia.

Today the Cook Islands, together with nearby Niue, New Zealand and its territories of Tokelau and the Ross Dependency make up the Realm of New Zealand.

With a history like that, it's not surprising that the Cook Islanders have taken to rugby with great gusto, but there seems to be very little information about how it was introduced or why. I suspect that it just came with the New Zealanders and was reinforced by Cook Islanders going to school in Aotearoa-NZ.

However it happened, they have developed a reputation in the sport far beyond their tiny size.

The day that rugby turned professional was a red-letter day in the Pacific. They had a large number of players that were very good at the game, but who mostly came from poor backgrounds. Getting paid to do what they enjoyed and were good at was far too good an opportunity to miss, and they left the islands in big numbers to play in Aotearoa-NZ, Australia, Europe and, more recently, Japan. Like nowhere else in the world, young Polynesians see a future in rugby. Many of them quickly rise very high and end up playing in the top teams, including national teams like the Australian Wallabies, the All Blacks, and the Irish, English, French and Japanese national teams. So successful have they been that I doubt that, outside of Africa, there is a top team in the world that does not include a Polynesian or two.

Although emigration in the late 20th C means that many of today's players were born outside of their home Islands, their culture remains very family focused and many of them send sizable chunks of their extravagant salaries back and make a significant contribution to the Island economies.

Australia

I think it's fair to say that Australia's relationship with rugby union has been somewhat chequered. The first games, which may or may not have resembled rugby as it was being played back in England, were played in the mid-1800s. They were brutal, unruly affairs usually played between soldiers on garrison duty in Sydney and visiting ship's crews. In fact they were so brutal that in 1864 a member of the NSW legislature introduced a bill to have the game banned, saying that it was '*a vicious display of brutish fist-fighting*'. Other members commented along the lines that 'something was needed for the troops to let off steam' and the bill failed to get up, but it did reflect the attitude of a considerable section of the Australian, not just NSW, public. Many parents saw it as dangerous and one current paper, the Guardian, even described it as *'the undertaker's friend'* and commenting that rugby games led to *'a small lot in the nearest bone yard'*[3].

The antipathy to the game may have had something to do with a clash of codes which began around that time. Back then Australia was a collection of six independent colonies; New South Wales, Queensland, Victoria, Tasmania, South Australia and Western Australia. In Victoria a new code, Australian Rules football (Australian football league, or AFL) was developing that was nominally non-contact, although players managed to get a fair amount of 'accidental' contact into the play. We'll get to that game shortly, but for now it's enough to say that it was developed partly in response to a general unease with the level of violence in rugby. Australian rules was adopted across the continent, with the exception of the eastern states of NSW and Queensland, which held out for rugby despite determined efforts by the AFL. Actually, Queensland was a part of the colony of NSW until it was granted separation by Queen Victoria in 1859 and the two remained closely linked until federation in 1901, so it was really only NSW that held out.

The holdout could have been caused simply by NSW – Victorian rivalry (if it's Victorian, we're not having it!), but whatever the reason the east coast stuck with rugby to the present day.

The first rugby club in Australia was formed at the Sydney University in 1864 and the first union, the Southern Rugby Football Union, was established in Sydney in 1874. Initially there were only five clubs in the union, but by the turn of the century it had grown to 79 with both senior and junior leagues, and in 1892 the New South Wales Rugby Union (NSWRU) was formed to administer the growing competition. Sydney's public schools were heavily involved in the first unions, along with Goulburn and Camden country clubs, and they tried to clean the game up to overcome that public perception of brutality.

Boarding schools favoured rugby because most of the teachers were graduates of English public schools where it was played, and

3 Rugby au: https://australia.rugby/about/about-us/history

when the boys went home they took the game with them. Actually, it's a bit misleading talking about the 'boys' from the country, because there was a tendency among the pastoralists not to get their sons educated until they were well into their late teens, so they were essentially near grown men, hardened by hard work and well able to look after themselves on the rugby field—as many a complaisant city man found out.

But, like in most of Britain, the heavy involvement of private schools earned Australian rugby union a reputation as an elite game, something which has clung to it to this day. Perhaps it was a deserved reputation as, over the years, a number of its players went on to become prominent politicians, lawyers and judges.

Across NSW's northern border in Queensland the Northern Rugby Union was formed in 1882 with four foundation clubs. That became the Queensland Rugby Union (QRU) in 1892 and the Queenslanders immediately set out to get a team together to play NSW. They had considerable success, winning far more than they lost.

In 1888 Australian rugby received a boost when they were visited by a British touring team. This wasn't the first tour—NSW toured Aotearoa-NZ in 1882 and the New Zealanders returned the visit in 1884, then the Maori stopped over in their grand 1888 tour. The British team's tour was a success in Australia, but back home in England it added fuel to a bitter argument over payments because, although the British players had all signed statutory declarations to the contrary, they were being paid.

This was an issue that was soon to boil over in Australian rugby, as well.

The resounding successes of touring Aotearoa-NZ teams culminated in a tour by the all-conquering 'Originals' on their way to make their indelible mark on the Northern Hemisphere. The New Zealanders won all their matches, including the first true international played by newly-minted Australia) which they won by 22 – 3. The impact of this tour and the high quality, entertaining rugby on display saw a major boost in Australian rugby's popularity, but it was held back by a lack of dedicated playing fields. Until then a field had to be hired for each fixture and this was a drain on revenues, so the NSWRU bought a race-track in Sydney with a natural amphitheatre and within easy reach of its public, and turned it into a rugby pitch.

The players were unhappy. The Union was set to make good profits, but the players were banned from getting any sort of compensation, even when they were injured and forced to take time off work and lost wages.

In 1908 the first Australian team, dubbed the Wallabies, followed Aotearoa-NZ and South Africa on a tour of Britain and North America. Despite the resounding successes of the previous two, they were not expected to do well, but they confounded their critics by winning 25 out of their 31 matches, including a win over England and a loss to Wales. They didn't play against either Ireland or Scotland—the Scots were suspicious of the Australian's amateur status, and they were still unhappy about the loss of revenue they'd suffered when they unwisely granted the gate takings to the All Blacks a couple of years earlier.

Back home, however, all was not well. Players were in revolt over the non-payment issue and many opted to form a break-away professional league. The new league succeeded in attracting many of union's star players and the amateur code went backwards, reaching a state very close to bankruptcy. Then WWI intervened and rugby union suspended all matches for the duration and went into a nose dive, but league continued playing and went from strength to strength. After the war both the QRU and NSWRU tried to revive the code, but the Spanish flu epidemic restricted their ability to meet, and it wasn't until the late 1920's that the game began to get back on its feet. Once again it was the elite schools and universities that were instrumental—with quite a lot of help from the NZRU, who sent teams regularly to maintain the game's profile in Australia.

After the 1930s things improved dramatically. Successful Wallaby tours went to all the old rugby union playing nations, and the new ones, like Fiji, visited Australia. In 1948 the Australian Rugby Football Union was formed to administer the sport on a national level. The sport received a further boost in the 1950s when licensed clubs were introduced, allowing clubs to become financially independent, although players remained nominally amateur until the mid-1990s.

From about the 1980s Australian rugby received an unexpected bonus with the introduction of large numbers of migrants, especially from the Pacific Islands, New Zealand and South Africa, and these migrants, particularly the large number of South Africans that settled in Western Australia, saw rugby at last make some inroads into staunch AFL states—although increased inter-state mobility of Australians has seen a reciprocal uptake of AFL in the eastern states.

Women in rugby union

Like in soccer, women began playing rugby almost from its inception. The story goes that the first woman to play officially (they'd undoubtedly been playing unofficially for years) was in Northern Ireland in 1887 when a school called Portora Royal School included Emily Valentine in their first rugby team. Surely the inclusion of one woman in an all-boys team went against every Victorian ethic? In fact I doubt it would even happen today—and especially not in very conservative Northern Irish society. And, propriety aside, where did a male-only school find a girl?

Well, it seems that Emily's father was the Assistant Headmaster who, due to the age of the actual Head Master, ran the school. Presumably due to his position, Emily was allowed to attend the school along with her brothers, and between them they were responsible for organising the schools rugby team. She undoubtedly grew up playing and was thought good enough to be included in the school team, apparently on the wing. What the other students and staff thought of the idea is not recorded, but she scored a try so justified her inclusion.

So much for Victorian and Northern Irish rectitude.

But occurrences of 19th C women in rugby are few and far between, and most went unrecorded, or under-recorded. It's possible that some of the exhibition woman's soccer games played in the 1880s were actually rugby, or rugby-like, but reporting was much more concentrated on the fact that it was women playing than the style of the game. What we can be sure of is that, if the public reacted strongly to women playing the comparatively gentle non-contact sport of soccer, the reaction to them playing a violent contact sport like rugby must have been pretty bad.

The first attempt to officially organise an unequivocal women's rugby team was in Aotearoa-NZ in 1891. Echoing the ways soccer and rugby were originally established, Nita Webbe (not sure if her name was a nom-de-plume referencing Webb Ellis, but I think it was probably just coincidence) placed an advertisement in newspapers across the country that read:

> *Wanted, 20 Young Ladies (with parent's consent) to PRACTISE FOOTBALL, preparatory to playing Auckland Ladies. Apply, with photos.*

By then rugby was already popular in the country and women probably played with their siblings and friends, and unofficially in local games. But Nita's ad brought a strong reaction, especially from the conservative press, and her scheme never went ahead. It's difficult to know whether this was because of outrage at women invading a male domain, a perceived affront to femininity, or because Nita's intention was to set up a professional women's team for profit. I think it was probably the last and seen as a blatant attack on the integrity of the amateur ethos of the sport.

And what was 'Auckland Ladies'—were they a team already in existence?

The '*apply, with photos*' bit is also suspect and makes me wonder if she only wanted attractive girls in order to attract more men to the games to watch pretty women, rather than football? It has many similarities to soccer's Nettie Honeyball and the ancient Chinese football league. I'm not for a moment suggesting that either Nettie or Nita had anything to do with prostitutes (or the ancient Chinese girls, for that matter), I'm just comparing reactions. On a slightly baser level, it's possible that the photos were intended to exclude Maori girls. Maori had a somewhat different view of femininity than Europeans and girls getting involved in the rough and tumble of the rugby pitch would not have been a problem for them, therefore it's very likely that Maori women became involved in rugby in greater numbers than Europeans, but dark skinned girls may not have fitted with Nita's plans.

Whatever, Nita's scheme failed to get off the ground and women's rugby languished out of sight for another 20 odd years, and in Ireland it didn't reappear until 1990.

There were a few women's games recorded in Britain and France in the years leading up to WWI, but they barely got a mention. In 1917 the Welsh ladies played a match between Cardiff Ladies and Newport Ladies, and there was the odd report of games in the 1920s and '30s in Britain, North America and Aotearoa-NZ. During this period a modified game for women appeared in France—it was played between teams of ten, had restricted tackling rules and was supported by at least some of the male hierarchy, but for some reason it died out prior to WWII.

The apparent lack of women's games is probably due not so much to a lack of players as to gross under-reporting, at least over the war years. During both wars women took over many of the men's jobs and from what we understand, revelled in them, so it would be surprising if they hadn't taken over their games as well. It was reported that the men who remained told them to go and play soccer, not rugby, because soccer was more 'feminine'. When the wars ended and the men came home the women were very quickly put back in their place and the work given back to the men. Teams that had sprung up in workplaces ceased to exist overnight because of a lessened ability to organise and, in many cases, lack of support or active opposition from their menfolk.

We can safely chalk up another try to male chauvinism.

Women didn't play again, or at least weren't reported as playing, until the 1960s and 70s when women's numbers increased in universities and female students tested their new found freedom on the sporting field, some even organising teams to challenge their male counterparts. When those women left university they took women's rugby out into the world. There it was fostered by the movement toward women's freedoms and equality, and gradually it gained acceptance until today, it's a world game, possibly as widespread as the men's game. Teams from countries that are comparative minnows in the male theatre, like Kazakhstan and Tunisia, field highly competitive ladies teams.

And they play just as hard and skilfully as the men, and the body contact is just as brutal.

And, to the best of my knowledge, no uterus's have yet fallen out.

Chapter 5
RUGBY LEAGUE

Rugby league is the other truly international form of rugby played today. There are league players in more than 70 countries, although it's still a minor sport in most of them.

As I said earlier, rugby league was adopted in the north of England in 1895 when the South England based RFU refused to allow players to be paid, or even compensated for financial loss, and refused to allow its clubs to compete with northern clubs.

With the RFU refusing to play with them, it was inevitable that the original NRFU began to tinker with the rules because, at that time, rugby union was all about the players and spectators were a bothersome incidental. Except for the aficionados, it wasn't much of a spectacle watching a tight bunch of players moving slowly up and down a field, with the ball only occasionally seen when it broke free and was passed to the backs.

But the new profession league had the added cost of paying its players, so it needed to make money. The only way to do this was to attract paying customers, and the only way to do that was present them with something interesting to watch. They had to create a spectator sport. They had to open the game up, which meant changing some of the rules.

The new break-away rules were a bit of a problem because there was no cohesion among the nations that adopted the professional game and they all tended to make up their own, which meant that before every international series a meeting had to be held to fix the rules for that tour. Internationally agreed laws didn't come in until 1948 when the International Rugby League Board (IRLB) was formed. But in the meantime many rule changes were made that applied, more or less, everywhere.

They kept the game as a full contact sport and left the basic structures in place—the field, the ball, goal lines, posts, methods of scoring and rules like 'off side' and not passing or throwing the ball forward. They even left the nomenclature, like the 'touch line' and 'tries', instead they looked for the bottle-necks that turned spectators away, like the set piece line-outs and scrums, and the interminable rucks and mauls.

The first thing they did was do away with the lineout. The original rule 32 said that, after a ball had gone out, the player must either

> *bound it out in the field of play, and then run with it, kick it, or throw it back to his own side, or (2) throw it out at right angles to the touch-line, or (3) walk out with it at right angles to the touch-line any distance not less than five or more than fifteen yards, and there put it down, first declaring how far he intends to walk out.*

Union chose option two and made it into a set piece line-out (with occasional use of option one, now known as a 'quick throw-in'), whereas league went with option three, but instead of any declaration they restarted the game with a modified scrum.

The rugby league scrum is another diversion from union, and the result was probably one of the most pointless activities in any sport anywhere. Firstly they dropped two players from it, which reduced the team sizes to 13 men each. Then the scrum went from contested, as in union, to uncontested where the forwards pack down, but neither push nor compete for the ball. The half-back of

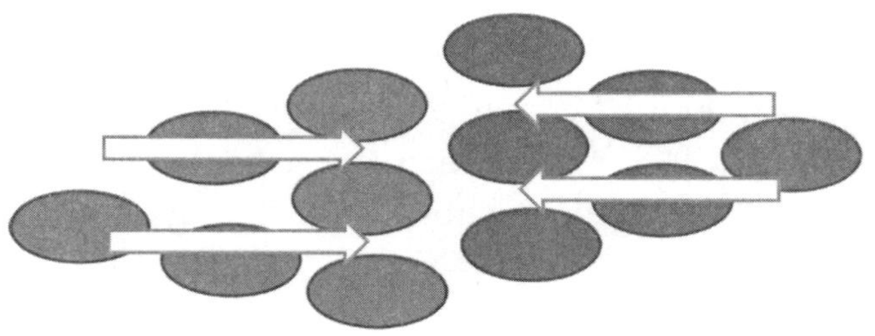

The rugby league 3-2-1 six man scrum formation.
The two rugby union flankers have been dropped from the second row.

the team awarded possession places the ball under his own players feet then runs around the back and picks it up to pass to his backs.

The team that puts the ball in always gets it back. The object of the scrum is, apparently, to give the teams time to reset and allow the backs to run for a minute without hindrance from the forwards.

In all honesty, the same result could be achieved if all the forwards stood in a circle and covered their eyes!

Probably the biggest change was in the rucks and mauls. Rule 18 stated;

> *In the event of any player holding or running with the ball being tackled and the ball fairly held, he must at once cry down, and there put it down.*

In union, this was interpreted as an all-in tussle by the forwards gathering over or around a tackled player to try and get the ball back onto their own side, and could result in protracted, seemingly deadlocked play. League got round this by introducing a formalised 'play-the-ball'. When the attacking player is stopped he is immediately released, allowed to get to his feet unhindered and ruck the ball back. Like the scrum, this change was intended to let both teams reset and led to a fast, open game, which was much better for spectators.

The problem was that limiting contests for the ball also limited the opportunities for it to change hands. To overcome this a maximum number of times a team could be tackled was introduced (initially four, increased to six in 1972), after which the ball is handed over to the opposition. To gain field position, the ball is normally kicked on the second to last tackle to make the opposition start their play as far down the field as possible. The result was a fast, open game, but one where only a limited number of players were involved at any one time.

The changes make league and union look very different, but most of the rules and skills involved remain the same, and since union became professional rugby players regularly alternate between codes.

League beyond Northern England

After the formation of the NRFU, the professional game was taken to Wales by returning workers in 1907. But in Wales union was a working man's game, not the elite sport that it was in England, and the Welsh workers were not so ready to give it up. Some changed, but most stayed with the amateur code.

It took a while to cross the channel, and then only to France. Rugby union was well established in France, especially in the south, and the French were playing in the Home Nations competition until 1932 when the British refused to play with them. That didn't go down at all well with the French, who decided that they'd play professional league instead. It was adopted in droves and became so successful that a 1939 French team beat the English on English soil, a first for any French team.

But the success was not to last. In France relations between the codes deteriorated to a level not seen anywhere else in the world and became political. In WWII the Vichy government saw league as a tool of the left wing socialists and the French Resistance, and banned it outright, seized its assets and actively encouraged players back into union. Even the name 'league' was banned and it became known as '*jeu à treize*' (game of thirteen).

After the war union managed to keep its dominance, but in the south-east, particularly Catalonia where there's a very long history of separatist agitation, rugby remained a political football and the region clung to league. The Rugby League International Federation (RLFI) was formed in Bordeaux in 1948 to fix the rules and regulate the game worldwide, and the French went from strength to strength until, by the 1950s, they could beat the best teams in the world.

But French league has remained largely in its south-eastern stronghold and, with a limited player base, has failed to maintain its former glories. In the mean-time French rugby union has gone on to become a major world force.

League failed to make an impact anywhere else in the northern hemisphere, although a few teams appeared in the middle to late 20th C in North America and Russia. It also failed to make an impact in the staunchly union South Africa. There was no serious attempt to introduce it there until the 1950s, when an entrepreneur organised French and English teams to stage exhibition matches. But the public thought they lacked the strong physicality of union and rejected the game. Further sporadic attempts were made to introduce it, but they mostly failed because the ruling Boers were heavily invested in union and it wasn't until the fall of apartheid in the 1990s that South African league began to be competitive.

It was in the Antipodes that league found truly fertile ground, first in Aotearoa-NZ and then Australia.

It all started when the All Blacks toured Britain in 1905 and saw first-hand the popularity of league in the north—and saw its potential. On their way home they stopped in Australia and one of the team, George Smith, began discussing with an Australian entrepreneur the possibilities of league in Australasia. At about the same time another Aotearoa-NZ player, Henry Baskerville, saw a newspaper report on the huge crowds that were being attracted to league games in England, recognised the financial potential and set about organising a professional team. He joined up with Smith and they took their team, known as the 'All Golds' off on a tour of Australia and England. They played three games in Australia (under union rules because they didn't know any of league's) where they persuaded Dally Messenger, one of Australia's top players at the time, to join them on tour. When they arrived in England the first thing they had to do was intensive training—not on the field, but in the classroom to learn the different rules they'd be playing under.

Altogether they played 46 games; ten in Australia, one in Sri Lanka and 35 in Britain, including a test against Wales—the first ever rugby league international test—and three against England. The All Golds won 26 of their 46 games, including two of the tests against England (the Welsh had a narrow victory), and scored a massive financial victory.

They stopped in Australia on the way home to discover that they had inspired Australian rugby players to turn professional in large numbers and in the time they'd been away the game had gone ahead to the extent that they were able to play three test matches. The first ever match between Australia and Aotearoa-NZ was played on the 9th of May, 1908, which Aotearoa-NZ won 11-10. They also won the second, and the third went to Australia.

But, while the All Golds were touring, Albert Asher, a player who couldn't tour due to injury, organised a Maori team to play in the 1908 season in NSW and Qld. Their win/loss was about even, but their style of play was entertaining and drew good crowds. They were hugely successful in promoting the game and today are credited with kick-starting league in Eastern Australia. It all ended in tears, however, when the NSWRL failed to pay them and the dispute ended in court. At the end of the tour they had to stage a rugby union match just to get the fare home, but despite that, they came back the following year—and didn't get paid for that one, either.

Great footballers, slow learners.

The All Golds' and the Maori successes inspired the eastern states of Australia to embrace league as nowhere else outside of the north of England. The Australian public was already disillusioned with union because it wasn't a great spectator sport. League was much faster and more open so the fans could see what was going on, and, although it was very physical with hard tackles, it had none of the close contact rucks and mauls where most of the violence happened. And, possibly most importantly, it was a game for the working man, not the elite. People were happy to pay to watch fellow working men play league.

And the players got paid. Not much, but they were happy.

At the time Australian Rules football was making a major push into Qld and NSW and was on the verge of gaining mass acceptance, but the sudden popularity of league, brought on by the All Golds and Maori, forestalled it. This possibly had as much to do with interstate rivalry between NSW and Victoria as anything else, but it wasn't for another hundred or so years that Australian rules again got a foothold in the east, or league in the west.

The New Zealanders had greatly enhanced league in Britain, and inspired the eastern states of Australia to embrace the game, but back home their success brought interest, but failed to make much of an impact. Union was far more entrenched with the general public who didn't see it as elitist, possibly because the class structure was much weaker than in either Britain or Australia. The social structures in Australia and the 'mother country' were different—in Australia it was born out of the convict system and land allocations rather than hereditary, but it was possibly stronger because of that.

Other reasons that league failed to make an impact in Aotearoa-NZ were because the style of union played there was more open and entertaining and the national team's successes had elevated the game to an almost religious level. The parallels with Wales are quiet marked.

All the Rugby Unions deregistered players who turned professional, which meant that returning New Zealanders couldn't go back to union at home and many of the All Golds went back to England to take up lucrative contracts.

But in Australia league went from strength to strength, the Australian National League (NRL) became the biggest and richest in the world and it was another half century, 1952, before Aotearoa-NZ won another game against Australia, and not till 1971 against Great Britain. It's fared better in recent years with an Auckland based team, the Warriors, competing in the NRL, but it still lags far behind union in public support. However, unlike Australia which is still far more partisan, most people who follow rugby in Aotearoa-NZ tend to support both.

Pacific Islands

Anybody that watches rugby league cannot help but notice the very large representation of Pacific Islanders on the field.

That's because they make up about 20% of players worldwide, and something like 50% of all league players in Australasia have Polynesian heritage. For such a tiny population base this is unprecedented, especially when you consider that Polynesians have really only been involved in league since the 1970s.

Actually that's not quite true. In 1923 a Sydney club imported a Maori player—the first person ever to be imported specifically to play rugby. But at that time Australia had a very strict 'Whites Only' immigration policy, so it would have been impossible for any other Pacific Islanders to come to Australia, but Maori were reluctantly exempted in 1905 after the NZ Government formally complained about its Maori citizens being banned.

But it wasn't exactly a flood of Maori players, the next (that I can find) was a cane-cutter in the 1940s. The White Australia policy was gradually abandoned in the 1960s and '70s and the doors cracked opened for Polynesian footballers. Uptake was slow to start but once word got around that they could actually get paid to play the game they loved (actually they played rugby union, but many were prepared to jump codes for the money), numbers increased exponentially.

Today league is often seen as a better option than union for two reasons. The first is simply because it pays more, which means a lot more money going home to families in the islands. Polynesians are very family oriented and being able to provide well for family is very important. The second is pride. Worldwide union is a much bigger game with a lot more countries and people participating, so no matter how good they are, the island nations size means that they will rarely reach the top (although they regularly get damned close!). But with the small number of nations competing in league, and with so many of their people playing in top level NRL, when those players choose to play for their home country the Islanders see their nations as leading the world. In union they see their players on top when they play for the All Blacks or Australian Wallabies or some other nation, but in league they see themselves on top.

But it's still far from a level playing field. The Islands are too poor to pay their players much and top international players that opt to represent their homelands lose money—occasionally they've even have had to pay for the privilege.

Having said that, times are changing. On the league side, the NRL is contributing financially to the sport in the Pacific. On the union side, Island teams, especially Fiji and Samoa, are making significant impressions on the world stage. The situation is fluid, which is perhaps reflected by the regular two-way flow of players between codes.

In all this I haven't mentioned the one Pacific nation, in fact the only nation in the world, that has adopted league as its national game—Papua New Guinea (PNG). League was introduced there after WWI when Australia was granted a mandate over former German New Guinea, making it essentially an Australian colony. The people of PNG are passionate about the game, but for various reasons they have not seen the successes of other Pacific nations.

Women in rugby league

Women's rugby league followed a very similar trajectory to their union-playing sisters, only in a far more restricted geographic area—mostly Australia, northern England and Aotearoa-NZ. In England they made little progress on the field, but female interest in the game was high and they made up a significant proportion of spectators. Some of that off-field interest was directed into administration rather than actual play, and women began to take on senior roles in the game, including refereeing, but it wasn't until the '70s and the sexual revolution that they began to appear on the field as players.

In the Antipodes it was a different matter. In Sydney in 1921 two female fans, Nellie Doherty and Molly Cane, asked the NSWRL for help in setting up a women's competition and, surprisingly, they agreed to form a women's league with at least five teams. It's not at all certain that the matter was being taken entirely seriously by the NSWL, because the secretary commented that the ambulance man at the games would have to include paint and powder in his kit, a suggestion that drew the frosty remark '*It won't be needed. We're going to play football as the men play*'.

As word got out about the proposal there was a groundswell of public opposition from those that thought the game too rough for women, including an invitation from the NSW Soccer Association for the ladies to play soccer because they thought it better suited to women. The response from the ladies was:

> *This is an age of changes and we must move with the times. I can't see how one girl's life can be ruined if she bumps into another girl. I think girls are as hard as men*.[1]

Training sessions were organised for every Friday. Men were banned from watching, except for the Secretary of the NSWRL and two policemen there to enforce the ban on men. But the good will and support didn't last. The ladies signed a deal with a sports gear company to finance the game and promote their products, the NSWRL didn't like it and threatened to ban anyone from the league who helped the ladies.

Unfazed, the first NSW ladies game went ahead on 17th Sept. 1921 in front of a crowd of between 20,000 and 30,000. The game proved a surprise because many had come expecting just a bit of fun, a novelty, similar to the crowd's expectations at the early English soccer games. Instead they were treated to a game of quality football—so good, in fact, that the Telegraph reported that

> *The football generally was so good that the suggestion was made that some of the players were boys, but that was not based on truth. Those who had come to laugh settled down to watch a machine-like display of correct football.*[2]

1 https://www.nrl.com/news/2018/12/23/how-a-courageous-duo-helped-womens-rugby-league-kick-off-in-1921/. Accessed 21/0723

2 Mary Konstantopoulos and Mike Meehall Wood. 17 Sep 2021

But two year later the women's league folded under constant pressure from the NSWRL, who saw their success as competition.

Further women's games were played sporadically in both Australia and Aotearoa-NZ throughout the next few decades, but it didn't gain momentum until the tentative beginnings of gender equality in 1960s and '70s. Then it paralleled union in development and rapidly became accepted, first in the UK, Australia and Aotearoa-NZ, and then as a world game.

And those 1921 pioneers were absolutely right—girls are as hard as men, when they choose to be.

Rugby's children

Modern rugby spin offs are mostly very similar, regardless of whether they were originated by league or union, so rather than tediously repeat myself, I'm unapologetically lumping them all in together.

There are four that are played regularly—touch, tag, sevens and nines. There are probably several other variations played locally, but these are the ones played officially.

Touch is essentially a non-contact version developed to introduce children to the game, and for when teams are ill-matched; for instance when they're mixed sexes or contain older people who are more prone to injury. They are also used by competition teams as training exercises to reduce the chances of accidental injury. The playing field is roughly 50 x 50 m, or about half a rugby field. Each team can be up to 14 members, but only 6 can be on the field at any one time. Play is over two 20 minute halves with a five minute break between, although that's not hard and fast and is often varied to suit local conditions or players. Most of the rules of rugby—league or union—remain, except that there's no tackling, rucks, scrums or kicking. A player in possession of the ball is considered 'tackled' if he or she is simply touched by an opposition player and must immediately dispose of the ball. It's fast and very good at teaching evasive skills.

Touch rugby is claimed to be an Australian invention, but as far back as the 1950s it was played in schools in northern England which had only asphalt play grounds, too small and too hard to play actual rugby.

Tag. There are two types of tag, one developed in Ireland and one in Australia. In the Irish version the actual ball must be tagged before the player is deemed 'tackled' and must play the ball, while in Australia players wear two tags attached with velcro to a belt. The ball carrier is deemed tackled when one of the tags is pulled free. Unlike touch, eight players per team are allowed on the field at any one time, and scoring varies depending on where it's being played.

The origins of tag are thought to have been in Gibraltar where there is very limited space for grass playing fields and was then picked up by the navy as a game that could be safely played on board ship. It was codified in England in 1990, taken to Australia in 1992 and then spread right around the world to become an international game in its own right. American football has its own version of tag called flag football, but I'll get to that.

Rugby league nines. This shortened form of league was introduced in 2014 in Auckland and spread across the Tasman a couple of years later. It's played under similar rules to the full game, except that each team has a playing squad of 15, of which only nine are allowed on the field at any one time but with unlimited substitutions. There are two halves of nine minute each with up to two minutes (depends where you are) break between.

It's a fast, full contact sport, usually played in a festival format where several games are played in the course of a couple of days, however so far it's failed to gain much traction with the public.

Rugby union sevens is the child that's gained the most attention. It's played between two teams of twelve players, of which seven are allowed on the field at any one time, over two seven minute halves with a maximum of two minutes at half time. Play is on a full sized rugby field and most of the rules that apply to the 15 man game apply to sevens, except that it allows for less substitutes and interchanges, has a modified three man scrum with a single front row, and the scoring team restarts the game with a kick-off. Because of the limited number of players and the size of the field, more open tactics are employed leading to a fast, open and entertaining 'running' style of play.

The origins of seven-a-side-rugby are surprisingly old. A short, open game was pioneered in a Scottish school sometime in the 1860s or '70s to improve the school rugby team's passing. The teacher responsible, Hely Almond, thought that if they would '*pass constantly and systematically to each other, they would baffle any side unaccustomed to such tactics*.'

This style of play was known as collectivism, but the English rugby playing fraternity were unimpressed, the game got caught up in the rift between league and union and the English RFU banned all games with less than 15 players.

In Scotland, however, it was a different matter. In 1883 a couple of butchers from the border town of Melrose reinvented seven-a -side as a fundraiser for their rugby club. It caught on and a couple of years later had spread throughout Scotland—presumably the Scottish Football Union had no issues with it—and by the early 20th C it was major sporting event. The Melrose Sevens tournament has remained a major fixture on the sevens calendar ever since.

The game gradually seeped through the border until the RFU was grudgingly forced to accept it, so long as it wasn't professional. Then it spread south through England and Wales and by the 1930s had become a popular spectator sport.

Scottish Emigrants took the game overseas, Aotearoa-NZ in 1889, Australia in 1891, Ireland and Argentina in 1921. The Argentine game had an interesting problem, the Buenos Aires cricket and Rugby Club have hosted a sevens tournament since the 1920s, but they have had great trouble recording a winner due to a tradition of friendly pitch invasions during finals. Adds to the atmosphere, I suppose. National teams and international tournaments began to emerge in the 1970s, the first was, of course, in Scotland. Then the Hong Kong Sevens tournament was inaugurated in 1976 and demonstrated that even very small nations could be highly competitive. After that the game spread rapidly around the world.

Today it's a thriving, very popular and lucrative professional travelling tournament where points are accumulated over the course of a season. Sevens has become so popular that it's been included in the Olympic Games—Fiji are the inaugural champions and as a result have adopted sevens as their national sport. They even issued a seven dollar banknote to commemorate their win.

A very good case could be made for counting sevens as a completely separate code. After all, it developed almost alongside union and it predates league by more than ten years. But it's never cut its ties with union and the two remain intricately linked, at least in the public's eyes, and players often move back and forth between the two forms of the game.

Chapter 6
NORTH AMERICAN FOOTBALL, GRIDIRON, TACKLE FOOTBALL

Organised chaos, total confusion, or just something that happens between commercials.
Again, it all depends how you look at it

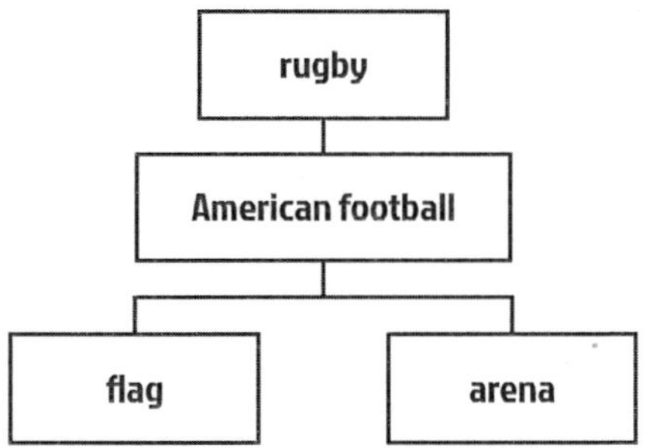

North American football is the third (or is it the fourth) of rugby's siblings. Otherwise known as gridiron because, from above, the field markings resemble a cooking griddle-iron North American football is played with slightly varying rules in both the US and Canada. It's difficult to get a handle on exactly how many people actually play it as the Americans seem to be more interested in how many people watch it on TV—about 40% of the population—than actually play, but as far as I can see there are about 5.3 million registered players in the US. The lack of solid data may be due to there being no single overarching American governing body for the various competing leagues in the country.

The National Football League (NFL) is the dominant American professional league, below that there are minor leagues, and below that is the university based amateur National Collegiate Athletic Association (NCAA) which, in turn, is fed by the high school system. In Canada there are about 600,000 registered players and officials, governed at the professional level by the Canadian Football League and at the amateur level by Football Canada. It's a major problem for the code that there is no organised play outside school, college or the professional league, which means that when most players leave high school or college they can't play any organised football unless they turn professional, they can only watch their kids or the professionals play. This lapse has benefitted both soccer and rugby across the continent.

North American football, or a game approximating modern North American football, was first played between Harvard University and Montreal's McGill University in 1874. The two teams played by quite different rules so they played twice, once under soccer-type rules for Harvard and once under rugby-like rules for McGill. After the games the Harvard men decided that they preferred McGill's rugby game and opted for it in their future games.

On the basis of that game the Canadians claim to have invented American football.

Over the next decade more and more teams adopted rugby rules and began modifying them; for instance 11-man teams were introduced and play was stopped when the ball carrier was tackled. The game moved out of universities and more into the public domain when athletic clubs, institutions that had sprung up after the American civil war and become very popular throughout the US, embraced football as part of their curriculums. But it was in Yale where a rugby player named Walter Camp truly developed it. He began introducing and refining rules in the 1880s which, over the next couple of decades, gradually turned a rugby style game into the gridiron of today.

Athletic clubs developed football as an integral part of their activities and competition was hot, with each club vying for the best players and all providing incentives to attract them, like well-paid sinecures or valuable trophies that could be readily converted into cash. At the time the game was officially amateur and the club's governing body, the Amateur Athletic Union tried unsuccessfully to keep a lid on professionalism, but in 1892 a player was paid $500 cash—a huge amount in the day—to play a game, and the floodgates opened.

Professional American football was born and within less than a century became the behemoth we know today as the NFL.

The Canadians claim that Canadian football developed separately to the American game, and certainly there are differences between the two, but those are completely overshadowed by the stark similarities. And I find it very unlikely that two such similar games could have evolved so close to each other without major cross-fertilisation.

Unlike the other codes, as far as I can see American football's development had absolutely nothing to do with pubs or alcohol, or at least none that are recorded. Nor is it possible to put a finger on exactly when it was born because there is no clear date that it was codified, it just seems to have evolved out of rugby over time. And, I suspect, most of its later rugby influence came from the northern English professional game, rugby league, because there are still very recognisable similarities between the two. This isn't surprising, given the American attitude to professionalism, it would have been natural for them to turn their eyes to professional rugby.

Or perhaps it was the other way round, the two games developed pretty much at the same time so it's impossible to tell what went which way.

The mechanics of the Game

Gridiron is a full contact sport played by two opposing teams of 45 players each, of these only 11 (12 in Canada) can be on the field at any one time. Teams are allowed unlimited substitutions, so they rotate their entire team on and off during a match. Games are played on a rectangular pitch measuring 100 yards (91.5 m) x 60 yards (55 m) wide, in Canada (110 x 65 yards, or 101 x 59 m). The field is marked off cross-ways at 5 yard (4.5 m) intervals—hence the resemblance to a griddle-iron—and there is a 20 yard (18 m) end-zone at each end.

At both ends of the field, centred on the line dividing the field of play and the end zone, is a 'tuning fork' shaped goal which has one central post in the ground, connected to the centre of an 18' (5.6 m) long cross-bar 10' (3 m) above the ground with approximately 30' (9 m) high uprights fixed at either end.

The game is played with a pointed oval ball measuring 11' – 12' (280–300 mm) long, a circumference of 23' – 24' (580–620 mm) and weighing between 14.5–16.2 ounces (410–460 g). The object of the game is to score a 'touch down' behind the opposing team's goal-line, either by carrying it over or throwing it to a player who has positioned himself behind the line. Despite it being called a 'touch down', there is no requirement to touch the ball to the ground to score.

Matches are played over four 15 minute periods with a two minute break between 1st and 2nd, and 3rd and 4th quarters, and a 15 minute half time break. Play is started by an official flipping a coin to decide who has first use of the ball (offence or defence) and which direction the teams will play, this is reversed at the start of the second half of play and the loser of the coin toss is given a choice of attacking or defending. The game is started by a 'kick off'—either a punt or a place kick—from within the defence's end of the field and the opposing team attempt to run it back against the team that kicked off.

The attacking, or offence, team is given four (three in Canada) attempts to move the ball ten yards toward the opponent's goal line. Each attempt is called a 'down', which is counted every time the ball's progress is halted either by the carrier being tackled or held up, or the ball touching the ground. The term 'down' is a hangover from the games origins in early rugby where, when a player was held he was required to acknowledge that he could not proceed and was told to '*put the ball down*'. In modern rugby union the referee calls 'tackle' when a ball carrier's knee touches the ground and they must release the ball into a ruck, and in rugby league when a player's progress is halted the referee calls 'held' and the player must immediately play the ball by rucking it back. The difference between rugby league and American football is that in rugby league only the ball carrier and a marker are involved and the game does not stop for more than the time it takes to play the ball. It's also interesting that in the original rugby league rules teams were only allowed four attempts to advance the ball before they had to relinquish it, the same as gridiron.

Each play is measured by a 'chain gang' on the side line who have a ten yard long chain with three poles. At one end of the chain the rear pole marks the spot where the set began, the pole at the other end marks the ten yard point that the attacking team must reach, and the middle pole is moved up and down the field parallel with the play to indicate each down.

After each down an imaginary line, called the 'line of scrimmage', is drawn across the field at the point where the ball was halted. Seven of the offensive team, the forwards, line up along this line with the quarterback immediately behind the centre. The defending team form up 11 inches (28 cm)—the length of the ball—in front of, and facing them, creating a narrow neutral zone. This formation is called the 'scrimmage'. The Canadian game has the same formation, except the neutral zone is one yard (91 cm) wide.

Plays are started when the quarterback calls 'hike' and the centre 'snaps' the ball back by passing it between his legs to the quarterback. Once the ball is snapped back play begins and the defence charge into the offensive forwards to try and interrupt the play. The quarterback either passes the ball to one of his three backs who runs it forward, throws it down field to a back who has managed to run past the defence, or back to a kicker. The forwards run interference to protect the ball carrier or kicker, but they're not actually permitted to handle the ball at the scrimmage, although they may occasionally pick it up if it's been fumbled in general play.

If you cast your mind back, you may remember that this was almost identical to early rugby play, only more organised. Come to that, it's not too far removed from a modern rugby scrum.

And, despite appearances, the only player that can be actually tackled is the ball carrier, everything else is merely blocking by forwards trying to protect their backs. Nor can catchers, be interfered with until they actually have the ball in hand—these rules are also in common with both rugby codes.

Plays, or downs, tend to be very short, usually a matter of only a few seconds, before a down is declared and the ball is taken out of play, at which point it all stops to reset the field.

If the offensive team make the required ten yards the count restarts for them to make another ten yards. If, on the other hand, they fail to move the ball forward 10 yards in three attempts and don't think they can make it on the last, they either kick it as far into the opposition territory as they can, throw or kick it to one of their own players who's managed to get down the field, or take the last down and surrender the ball to the other team. Again, this play is identical to rugby league, but that's where the similarities end.

After the last down the entire on-field teams are taken off. The offensive players, or the 'offensive platoon' as they're known, leave the field and are replaced by their team's 'defence platoon', similarly the opposition swaps its defence platoon for their attackers.

Multiple squads of players came about because of the unlimited substitution rule that allowed the development of specialised players—offence, defence and special teams.

The special team is mostly concerned with kicking. There are players brought on specifically to take place kicks, or occasionally drop kicks although those are rare today. Place kickers will usually have a specialist holder whose job it is to receive the ball and hold it in place for the kicker. In most cases the kicker will kick the ball off to start or restart play after points have been scored and then leave the field. Another player is brought on to take punts. When a holder or punter are to be used there is a specialist 'long snapper' who replaces the centre to throw the ball back to them instead of just handing it back to the quarterback.

There're also returners, employed to catch or receive the ball and run it back as far as possible, 'gunners' who specialise in running down the field to intercept the returner, and 'jammers' who try to intercept the gunners.

There may be more specialists, depending on the team's management style, but all of them come on for a single play, like one kick, then go off again.

Organisation between plays can be a very long and involved process and contributes in a big way to the marked 'stop-start' nature of the game. In fact there are far more stops than starts—it's been calculated by the Wall Street Journal that the average game lasts for three hours and 12 minutes, in which the average play lasts a mere four seconds on average, and out of the entire game the ball is actually in play only around 11 minutes. On average, television broadcasts spend 17 minutes on replays; 75 minutes watching players, coaches and officials wandering around on the field between plays; and about an hour on advertisements spread over 20 commercial breaks.

Scoring is by one of four ways:

- A touchdown is worth six points. This can be from either carrying over or catching the ball behind the opposition goal line.
- A conversion, worth one point. This is taken from a scrimmage five yards from the goal line after a touchdown. The ball is snapped back to a kicker who must put it over the cross-bar between the uprights
- Field goal, worth three points. This is taken by a place kick (or occasionally a drop kick) from anywhere on the field, usually on the last down. Like a conversion, the ball must go over the cross-bar and between the uprights.
- A safety, worth two points. This is awarded to the defending team when they trap the ball behind the attackers own goal.

After points are scored the game is restarted by the scoring team with a kick-off from their own 35 yard line. If the scores are tied at the end of the game an additional quarter is played.

The game is controlled by seven (or occasionally eight) on-field officials, by far the most of any football code. They are:

- **Referee** who heads of the official team and has overall responsibility for the game. They wear a different coloured cap to differentiate them from other officials on the field and are normally positioned behind the attacking team, where they watch for fouls from the offensive side and adjudicate on kicks. They also announce fouls and penalties, and the player number or position of the offending player to fans and media—a sort of name-and-shame. If a decision is in doubt the referee confers with an 'instant replay centre', which may be a long way from the game—there's a big one in New York City—before making a decision. They're also responsible for keeping track of the number of players on the offensive side.
- **Umpire.** Until recently the umpire stood behind the defending team to adjudicate on fouls and penalties in that part of the field. They were required to be pretty quick on their feet because their position on the field was exactly where most of the action takes place and they were in constant danger of being caught up in the play. Injuries were not uncommon and, after several umpires required hospitalisation in 2009, their position was moved to next to the referee. The umpire also keeps track of the number of players on the field and sees to the legality of player's equipment.
- **Down judge** patrols the sideline at the line of scrimmage to keep an eye out for rule infringements and determine when the ball goes out-of-bounds. They also keep an eye on the play's progress and direct the chain crew where to place the poles. The name 'linesman' was used until 2017, when the advent of female officials and gender neutral terms prompted a change to 'down judge'.
- **Line judge** works the sideline opposite the down judge to help them determine infringements and out-of-bounds on that side of the field.
- **Field judge**, or back judge, is stationed on the same sideline as the line judge, but further down the field, behind the defending team, to rule on infringements in that part of the

field and keep a check on the number of defence player on the field. Field judges sometimes also double as timekeepers and direct the crew that run the game clock.

- **Side judge** is stationed on the same sideline as the down judge but behind the defensive team, opposite the field judge, and does the same job for that side of the field. They may also be responsible for directing the timekeepers with the time clock.
- **Centre judges** are positioned beside the offensive team to assist the referee and the umpire with decisions. They also act as alternative referees if the main referee is injured or can't continue in their duties.

There is also a television network coordinator on the side-line who wears a long pair of orange gloves that they hold up to signal time-outs for commercials.

A major and very distinctive feature of American and Canadian football is the uniform. There are currently about nine pages of rules covering uniforms, and massive fines for violating them. Initially uniforms were made of plain wool to protect against the winter cold, then players began sewing patches of leather over the wool to give themselves protection. In 1901 the leather pads started to be worn under the jerseys and held in place with elastic, and over the years more and more padding was added and it all sort of grew from there. In the 1960s much of the leather was replaced with plastic and fibreglass, and knee pads, which started with players tying sponges to their knees, grew over time to be specialised padding warn inside the knickerbocker-style pants.

Rugby-style soft leather helmets were added in 1893. By the 1920s these had become hardened and cushioned leather, then in the 1940s plastic was introduced and helmets became mandatory. In the 1950s guards were added to protect against facial injuries.

Today gridiron uniforms give the players a robotic appearance—I expect the next step will be power assisted exoskeletons—but it's dubious just how much protection from injury they provide. Certainly there is protection from actual body, head or facial injury, but they have a minimal effect on concussion because that occurs when the head stops suddenly but the brain doesn't, which is what happens in heavy contact and whip-lash. Other codes, all of which use minimal padding and ban players from wearing any hard material, are attempting to minimise concussions by heavily penalising any direct head contact, something which gridiron seems reluctant to do.

Native Americans

Native Americans make up only a very small portion of the American population, but they've managed to have quite an influence on American football. Back in the game's formative years, First Nation's children were removed from their families and placed in 'Native Schools' where they were actively de-Indianised and have their culture beaten out of them. One of the tools employed was to have them play what was considered a white man's game—football—and the kids took to it with enthusiasm.

They developed their own style which emphasised speed and agility over bulk, and when the authorities realised they were good, games were organised against some of the top ranking university teams. Much to the embarrassment and chagrin of the likes of Yale, the First Nations kids won, and they quickly realised this was one of the few ways they could turn the tables and exact considerable violence on whites. And along the way the kids introduced new tactics and a high degree of athleticism that enhanced the game overall.

But one innovation was quickly outlawed—war-paint.

Some First Nations kids went on to become great athletes in their own right, but I can't find anything about their continued participation in football beyond the Indian Schools experiments.

I have, however, found evidence of considerable resentment over their culture being appropriated and disrespected by some of the NFL teams.

The Native American experience is reminiscent of the Polynesians, in that they were introduced to football through the white school system, but I suspect the schools were very different.

And while we're on the subject of Polynesians, when America acquired Western Samoa in 1889 they gained an unexpected bonus—footballers. It's estimated that a modern Western Samoan is 56 times more likely to play in the senior American football leagues than a non-Samoan. I can't find figures on other Polynesians, notably Hawaiians, but West Samoa, at least, has gained a very good income stream.

We can't leave this section without mentioning African American players. Today African Americans make up about 65% of professional players, but it wasn't always that way. The first to play was Fritz Pollard in 1920, but in 1926 clubs opted for segregation and he, along with a few others, was banned. It wasn't until 1946 that another African American played professionally.

At the time American society was racially segregated, very much like the later apartheid system in South Africa, and gridiron teams had an agreement that none would take on African Americans. That agreement was first breached in Los Angeles, and it happened under a certain amount of coercion. The Los Angeles Coliseum, home to the Los Angeles Rams, threatened them with eviction if they didn't sign African Americans onto their team. The Rams caved and signed two players. A few months later the Cleveland Browns followed suit with another two, and the floodgates slowly, almost imperceptibly, creaked open. The last club to hold out, the Washington Redskins (now the Washington Commanders), signed three African American players in 1962.

But when those first players arrived at their clubs they suffered a barrage of racial taunts, abuse and outright hatred that caused at least one to quit after just one season.

It took another 26 years, until 1988, for the first African American to officiated at a game.

Beyond North America

Gridiron is played throughout the world but, unlike rugby and soccer, has never really become popular and is played mostly where the American military are stationed, particularly in Japan, Germany and England. There is a reasonable worldwide audience for TV coverage of the big NFL games, like the Super Bowl, but that doesn't translate into interest in the actual game—perhaps many of the viewers are as much attracted by the very high-profile half-time entertainment as the football.

One of the primary reasons why gridiron has not achieved the success of other codes is the high cost of participating—the uniforms alone are out of reach of most would-be recruits. But the stop-start nature of the game is very strange to people used to continuous action.

Women in American football

Women's gridiron has had a very chequered history. Although, like every other code, women have undoubtedly been playing since it was invented, the first actual women's competition didn't happen until the Women's Professional League (WPL) was formed in 1965 with four teams—the Cleveland Daredevils, the Pittsburgh All-Stars, the Canadian Belles (Toronto), and the Detroit Petticoats. The WPL was formed expressly to play demonstration—or novelty—games, probably similar to women's soccer and rugby in the early 20th C. The WPL disbanded in 1973, reformed in 1999 as the Women's Professional Football League (WPFL), which merged in 2001 into the Independent Women's Football League (IWFL), established by women, for women. The IWFL lasted until 2018.

Canadian women have fared little better. The first league wasn't established until 2004 with only two teams. Canadian women's football has a few modified rules; there are 11 players per side, four downs are permitted instead of the normal Canadian three, and quarters are 12 minutes long (except in finals when they revert to 15 minutes). It struggled to gain traction, but it has grown to five teams, so unlike its southern cousin, it's hanging in there.

Most of the reasons advanced for the failure of the women's game to gain traction is put down to a failure to attract audiences and the financial challenges that this has brought.

Gridiron's children

Aside from Canadian football which, apparently evolved separately, American football has produced only two significant offspring—Flag football and Arena football.

Flag football was first officially played in the 1960s, although there are records of it being played by American troops during WWII as a safe keep-fit exercise. It's the American version of touch where tackling is not allowed, instead players wear a flag attached to their belts which the defence must pull off. When players are 'deflagged' it is deemed a down and the ball must be played. For the most part gridiron rules apply, except that it's usually played by teams ranging from four to ten players and, because violent contact has been all but eliminated, padding and helmets have been dispensed with. Although nominally a non-contact sport, some variations allow blocking where the forwards charge each other, but in flag contact is limited to chest to chest.

The game has been dubbed the 'future of American football' and has gained considerable support from both men and women at home and, unlike the tackle version of the game, made inroads overseas. Its growing popularity is probably due to players not needing expensive equipment or playing fields—it can be played pretty much any suitable surface, especially on sandy beaches. The NFL is currently campaigning to have it included as a demonstration sport in the 2028 Olympics in Los Angeles.

As the name suggests, **Arena** or **Indoor American football** is gridiron adapted to playing indoors, usually on ice hockey or basketball arenas. It dates back to pretty much the start of football in America—the first recorded game was in 1890—although the early matches were on almost full sized grounds and with the standard rules of the time. Over the next half century or so there was some tinkering with the rules to accommodate indoor conditions, but it wasn't until the 1980s that a serious attempt was made to get the sport going. Ice hockey arenas were formally adopted as the standard pitch size, with artificial turf overlays that could be rolled up to allow other sports to use it. A taut net was placed either side of each goal so that a kick or pass that missed the goal rebounded and remained in play and teams reduced to eight with only one platoon—meaning that, apart from specialised kickers, players had to be multi-skilled. Punts were outlawed and a number of restrictions on player positions and play were introduced.

In response to others trying to make money out of his game, the inventor, Jim Foster, patented the rules in 1990, particularly the name and the rebound nets. The patent's expiry in 2007 saw several new and competing leagues, lured by the big money to be made, rise and fall. There was even a version that had fans voting on plays. Inevitably, with absolutely no cohesion and bitter rivalries, the sport went through a range of bankruptcies, the most recent in 2019.

In 2023 there is another attempt to revive it with a promise to return in 2024.

I wouldn't hold my breath.

Women became involved in arena football in much the same way as they did in their early days of other codes, mostly as novelty entertainment. But the American ladies weren't always presented in a particularly constructive way—one franchise was known as the Lingerie Football League and featuring scantily clad women. I suspect that it's unlikely that it was the football that drew fans. None of the women's arena leagues, clothed or otherwise, seem to have caught on.

Chapter 7
AUSTRALIAN RULES FOOTBALL

Our game
or Aerial ping pong
All depends on your bias

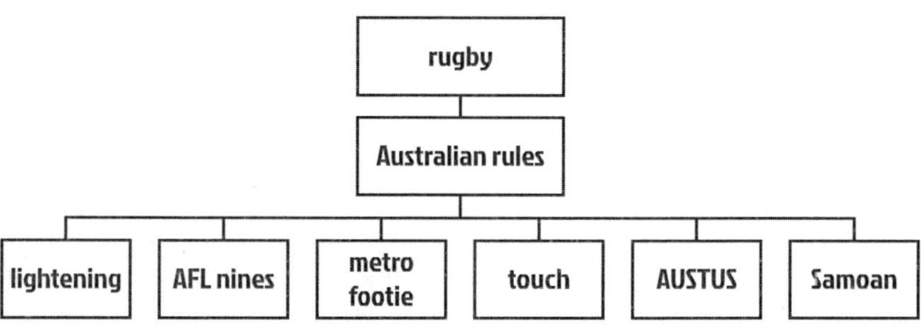

Australian Rules football (Aussie rules) is another of rugby's siblings, albeit the 'different' one, that was invented and codified in 1859 in Melbourne, Australia. It's the first of the modern codes to be codified (which doesn't necessarily mean it's the oldest), predating soccer by four years and rugby union by 12. Today it's governed by the Australian Football League (AFL—this is now normally used to refer to the game) and is the country's most popular sport, with leagues in every state and territory. In 2022 there were 1,190,671 AFL club members, including 75,568 members of Australian Football League Women (AFLW).

The mechanics of the Game

Games are played by two teams of 18 players on an oval grassy field, measuring between 135 and 185 m (443' – 607') long and 110 and 155 m (360' – 508') wide. The field is marked with a 50 x 50 m (164' x 164') centre square, in the middle of the centre square is one

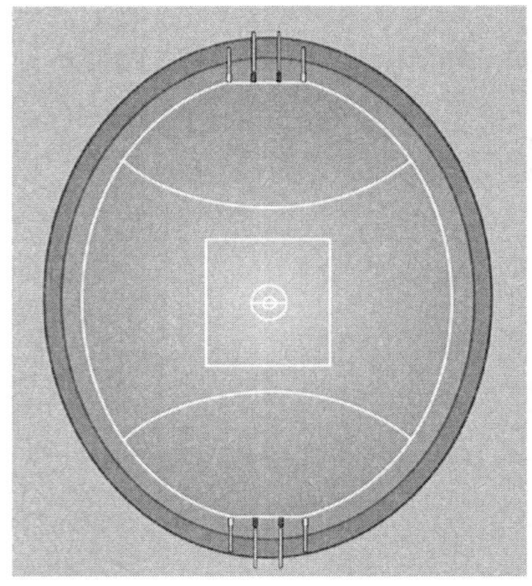
Australian rules playing field *(Wikipedia)*

circle 10 m (33') in diameter, and inside that another circle 3 m (10') in diameter, and at each end of the field a line describes an arc 50 m from the goal line.

The goals, located at each end of the field, are four posts set in a straight line 6.4 m (20') apart. A goal, worth six points, is scored by kicking the ball between the central goal posts without it touching either the posts or another player. Kicking it between a central goal post and one of the outer posts, or if the ball touches any post as it passes through, is called a 'behind' and earns one point.

Games are started by the Umpire bouncing the ball—throwing it hard onto the ground so that it bounces above the heads of the players—inside the central circle. They last for a nominal two hours, divided into four 20 minute quarters, but the clock is stopped for injuries or other stoppages, so a quarter can extend to half an hour or more. There is a six minute break between the first and second, and third and fourth quarters, and 20 minutes at half time. For lower level games there are two Field Umpires who control the game on the field, two Boundary Umpires who patrol the side line to adjudicate when the ball is out and throw it back in—this is done by standing with their back to the play and throwing it in over their head. They may also assist the Field Umpires in identifying rule infringements on the field, but they can't actually go onto the field. There are also two Goal Umpires whose task is to adjudicate on goals. Multiple umpires are needed because the field is too large (nearly twice the size of a rugby pitch) and the game too fast for one person to cover effectively—a single person would inevitably be caught too far away from the play to be able to fairly judge a situation. At the elite level, games need four Field and four Boundary Umpires to keep up.

Aussie rules uses an oval ball designed in 1880 by T.W. Sherrin specifically for the game and most balls used today still bear his name. They are similar to a rugby ball but vary in size, depending on the age and sex of the players, but commonly from 720–730 mm (28' – 29') circumference measured end to end, 545–555 mm (21' – 22') around the middle, and inflated to between 62 and 76 kPa, which makes them slightly longer, thinner and less pressurised than a rugby ball. Normally red balls are used for day matches and yellow at night.

The game is comparatively simple. There are no off-side rules and, while there are nominal defender, midfielder and attacking positions, they're comparatively loose. Each player is paired, or 'marked', by an opposition player—which means that the two remain close with a great deal of jostling for position throughout the match.

AFL's simplicity keeps play free-flowing and the ball moves rapidly about the field through long kicks between players. A player catching the ball on the full is awarded a 'mark' and permitted a kick free from interference, but otherwise pushing, tackling (grabbing between the knees and the shoulders) and general interference is permitted. If the play threatens to get too rugby-like the umpire calls a halt and bounces the ball to restart play. Bounces are somewhat unpredictable, which is, I suppose the object of them, but if the ball bounces out of the circle it has to be retaken. If two bounces are unsuccessful the umpire just throws the ball in the air so that the players can compete fairly for it.

At close quarter's players move the ball between each other either by short kicks or by 'hand-balling', where the ball is held loosely in one hand and punched out with the other. Passing, as in rugby or throwing like in American football is not permitted. When players are tackled with the ball they must either kick it or hand-ball it away, otherwise they are penalised for either holding the ball or dropping it. Carrying the ball is permitted but it must be either bounced or touched it to the ground every 15 m (50'). Provided this happens, players can carry it as far as they want, or until they're tackled.

History of AFL

Like soccer and rugby, Aussie rules had its origins in a letter published in a newspaper, the 1858 'Bell's Life in Victoria and Sporting Chronicle', in which Tom Wills, captain of the Victorian cricket team and pioneer of Australian football, asked for a meeting of interested men to form a football club and codify a new game.

Tom's specific purpose for his proposal was simply to keep cricketers fit in the off-season.

At that time random styles of football based more-or-less on rugby, soccer or Irish caid (we'll get to that), were played in the Australian colonies. When new migrants arrived in Australia they passed their games on to the locals, often via the Australian private school system where wealthier Australians sent their boys. Even wealthier Australians, like Tom Wills' parents, sent their sons off to England to complete their education as gentlemen, and learn to play proper football first hand.

Born rich in Sydney, Tom was raised on his father's extensive property in remote Victoria where his only companions were the local indigenous kids. There he is said (although not proven) to have played an Indigenous game called *marn grook*, which involved kicking and catching a ball made of stuffed possum skin. At the tender age of 14 he was sent off to Rugby School in England to have his rough edges knocked off and there, as a natural athlete, he played rugby and cricket so successfully that he captained both school teams. It's unusual that anyone fresh from the bush and with no experience of team sports, could just walk in and immediately become successful, so it's probable that his prowess on the field was the result of skills he'd learned with his childhood Indigenous play-mates.

When he returned home he brought his experience and enthusiasm with him and set out to create a uniquely Australian game,which coincidently, involved a lot of kicking and catching.

In the same year as his letter was published, Wills refereed a game that pitted 40 students from Melbourne Grammar against 40 from

Scotch College. It was played over two consecutive Saturdays with a round ball and very much in the early rugby style, with both teams spending much of their time in a huddle kicking the crap out of the ball and each other (that game became an annual fixture which has endured to the present day, albeit in a modernised format).

That style of play was pretty much the norm then, but Wills found it unsatisfying, so he and a couple of friends set out to devise a game that was both gentler and more suited to Australian condition. The Melbourne Football Club was established in May, 1859, and three days later Wills and others gathered in the Parade Hotel (the first association between alcohol and football, a tradition later continued by soccer and rugby) to draw up a set of 10 rules for a new game.

They were known as the 'Laws of the Melbourne Football Club' and published in the Victorian Cricketers Guide:

1. *The distance between the Goals and the Goal Posts shall be decided upon by the Captains of the sides playing.*

2. *The Captains on each side shall toss for choice of Goal; the side losing the toss has the kick off from the centre point between the Goals*

3. *A Goal must be kicked fairly between the posts, without touching either of them, or a portion of the person of any player on either side.*

4. *The game shall be played within a space of not more than 200 yards [180 m] wide, the same to be measured equally on each side of a line drawn through the centres of the two Goals; and two posts to be called the "kick off posts" shall be erected at a distance of 20 yards [18 m] on each side of the Goal posts at both ends, and in a straight line with them.*

5. *In case the ball is kicked "behind" Goal, any one of the side behind whose goal it is kicked may bring it 20 yards [18 m]*

in front of any portion of the space between the "kick off" posts, and shall kick it as nearly as possible in line with the opposite Goal.

6. *Any player catching the ball "directly" from the foot may call "mark". He then has a free kick; no player from the opposite side being allowed to come "inside" the spot marked.*

7. *Tripping and pushing are both allowed (but no hacking) when any player is in rapid motion or in possession of the ball, except in the case provided for in Rule 6.*

8. *The ball may be taken in hand "only" when caught from the foot, or on the hop. In "no case" shall it be "lifted" from the ground.*

9. *When a ball goes out of bounds (the same being indicated by a row of posts) it shall be brought back to the point where it crossed the boundary-line, and thrown in at right angles with that line.*

10. *The ball, while in play, may under no circumstances be thrown.*

Teams were to be 20 aside and winners decided by the first team to kick two goals. And the captains were the umpires.

Several other clubs were formed soon after Melbourne Football Club and in 1860 they held a meeting at the Argus Hotel to thrash out a common set of rules, resulting in the publishing of the Victorian Football Rules. These were further refined at a meeting in the Freemason's Hotel in 1866 where the field size was set at maximums of 200 yards (183 m) long and 150 yards (137 m) wide, with four goal posts at each end of the field set seven yards (6.4 m) apart. Game length was 100 minutes and had to have two proper umpires instead of the team captains.

They also introduced the rule that says players must bounce the ball while running with it.

Initially neither the shape, size, nor weight of the ball were specified, but most favoured the old style round ball. Wills, however, preferred the oval rugby ball, saying that it was more aerodynamic and easier to handle, but it's possible that his bias had more to do with nostalgia for his triumphant time at Rugby than any real concern for the characteristics of the ball. He didn't get his way immediately, but he persisted and eventually the oval ball was accepted. Despite adopting the rugby ball, the game was rapidly diverging from the rugby style that it had started out with. That was probably a deliberate move to curry favour with the public because many Victorians, like those in NSW, regarded rugby as too boring and too violent and were turning away from it in droves.

After the 1866 rules were set, development of the game was rapid and in 1877 the Victoria Football Association (VFA) was established, but infighting over funding dogged the sport and, in 1896, the stronger teams in the competition broke away and formed the Victorian Football League (VFL). The new league introduced the modern scoring system—six points for a goal kicked between the centre two posts and one for a behind kicked between a centre and a side post—and a 'finals' series of games at the end of the season to determine the year's champion instead of just the team that had accumulated the most wins.

Rivalry continued to be bitter between the two bodies for most of the 20th C—they couldn't even agree on how many players teams could field at one time. In 1911 the VFL allowed their clubs to pay players, as opposed to merely reimbursing expenses, and the age of professionalism began, but it wasn't until the late 20th C that most players could earn enough not to need a proper job.

The rival associations continued to bicker right up until 1990s when they both became professional under the newly formed Australian Football League (AFL). Under the AFL the game officially became truly Australian with 18 teams drawn from every state except Tasmania competing in a national competition.

The Australian spread

Like Victoria, the other Australian colonies had played football of one sort or another pretty much from their founding. For example, in South Australia (SA) which borders Victoria to the west, the first recorded game was old Irish caid, played in 1843 between Irish migrants to celebrate St Patrick's Day. Ten years later a letter appeared in a SA newspaper calling for Irishmen to gather to play football—probably also caid.

About the same time a businessman imported five round balls and paid to have goal posts erected at St Peter's College for games to be played under 'Harrow rules', which encouraged kicking the ball but not running with it. SA schools began to include football in their curriculums, and it featured in the 1857 celebrations of the state's 21st birthday.

The game was obviously gaining general acceptance in SA, but exactly what style was continually under debate. Everyone had a different idea of the rules and, as a result, games tended to be chaotic and occasionally farcical. We do know that in 1866 a football club was formed in Kapunda, then one of the larger settlements in SA, which used a round ball, rugby style goal posts, few rules and as many players as turned up. Ten years later another club was set up in the same town that used four goal posts, a rugby style ball, and possibly the first ever use in Australia of goal umpires. SA football was evolving along Victorian lines—despite the occasional vehement opposition. Like that from the local a newspaper, the Herald, whose editor regarded it as barbaric. Although he did make the constructive criticism that games shouldn't be played on gravel, he used the Herald to keep up his attacks for two decades. As an example, in 1892 he wrote:

The projected visit of the Adelaide Boys' Field Club has been abandoned because an agreement cannot be reached with the Railways Commissioner for reduced fares. If the club were a football team with the mainstrength brutality and stupidity as

> *the chief feature, and could command a following of brainless yahoos, there is not the slightest doubt that the required concession would have been granted but, because the field club is a body of smart intelligent youths—they must pay full fare or stay home.*[1]

The divide between pro- and anti- football has always been wide and, at least on one side, occasionally bitter.

Eventually, in April 1877 after a plea for a set of rules to be drawn up that may, possibly, enable a future inter-colonial game, a meeting was called at Adelaide's Prince Alfred Hotel—a pub, where else?—to thrash out a uniform code. At that meeting SA adopted Victorian rules (more-or-less), the oval ball and established the South Australian Football Association, predating the Victorian Association by one week and making it the oldest in the country.

It was a very similar story in Tasmania to the south. Football games, played under various English rules, were recorded from the 1850s, but with improved communications a problem became apparent. In 1879 a Victorian club challenged the Tasmanian clubs to an inter-colonial 'test' match, but the Tasmanians had to decline because of their lack of uniform rules. The challenge eventually went ahead on 1881 under Victorian rules, and after that Tasmanian clubs adopted the Victorian code so that inter-colonial games could become a fixture.

Western Australia (WA) is the other stronghold of AFL, but they started somewhat later than their eastern compatriots. The first recorded football match in WA was, in all probability, an early form of rugby played in 1868 between locals and a visiting British army unit. British expatriates in WA heavily favoured rugby, so rugby clubs were formed and it was introduced to schools in the 1870s. It wasn't until the WA gold rush in the 1880s that Aussie rules began to make headway.

Back in 1851 huge deposits of gold were discovered in Victoria, sparking a gold rush that, at its peak, brought around

1 Charlton, R. The History of Kapunda. Hawthorn Press. 1971

6000 hopefuls a week to the colony. With that many men in one place it was inevitable that football games of one sort or another were organised, and by the time the gold fizzled out, the football they played was Victorian rules. When gold was found in WA many of those miners rushed west and took their AFL with them, ultimately swinging the balance of the football codes in WA and the West Australian Football Association (WAFA) was formed in 1885. Further gold discoveries in the 1890s combined with a massive international depression to increase the flow of the hopeful and the desperate westward and boost Aussie rules still further.

It was a very similar story in Aotearoa-NZ. Gold was discovered in several places across the country in the 1850s and '60s and miners flooded across the Tasman from the overcrowded Victorian fields and, of course, brought the Victorian game with them. The first organised match was played in 1868 and Australian football enjoyed a brief flowering in Aotearoa-NZ through the 1870s and 80s. The New Zealand Football Association (NZFA) was established in 1880, but it struggled with its image, mostly because of a hostile NZ press, and in the 1880s rugby reasserted its dominance and the Australian game had all but died out by 1884.

The early 20th C saw a wave of migration across the Tasman and a second coming for Aussie rules. Several new clubs and leagues were formed, inter-colonial matches were set up and in 1905 the Australian Football League was renamed the Australasian Football League. The league blossomed and the New Zealand Australasian Football League (NZAFL) was formed at the Naval & Family Hotel in 1907.

For a while it looked like Aotearoa-NZ would be a hub for Australasian football, but for some reason the Australians were quick to pour cold water on it, declaring that the game's focus must remain Australian. Perhaps that had something to do with an Aotearoa-NZ Aussie rules team defeating both Qld and NSW in 1908 at a carnival to celebrate the games 50th year. After the tournament the New Zealanders got only 20% of the proceeds, with 50% going to NSW despite them losing. That was the same year that the NSW rugby league reneged on a visiting Maori team—perhaps there was something in the water that year.

After that the NZAFL went into steep decline and by the 1910s the Australian members of the council began withdrawing funding and support. Rugby rapidly reasserted itself (again) as the premier game and AFL declined and died, the last NZ club folding in 1912. Trans-Tasman relations went from bad to worse, until the Aotearoa-NZ delegates were expelled and 'Australasian' reverted to 'Australian' in 1914.

Ironically, in NSW and Qld, where the AFL had concentrated most of its energy and funds to attract adherents, Aotearoa-NZ-inspired rugby league relegated it to a very minor role at about that same time.

With TV coverage of AFLs becoming available in Aotearoa-NZ in the 1970s, AFL began to make a comeback, but it remains a minor sport, well behind both rugby codes and soccer.

In Australia's remote far north Aussie rules began to make an appearance in the early 20th C and the first recorded match was played in Darwin in 1916. Since then it has developed a fanatical following, particularly among the Indigenous population, and especially on the remote communities. Today more than 7% of the Northern Territory's (NT) population play the game and, per capita, the NT contributes more players to the AFL than any other state or territory. Most of those are Indigenous and their success generates immense pride in their communities.

Overall Indigenous players are over-represented on the national level, with somewhere between 10% and 13% of players identifying as Indigenous, whereas they make up a mere 3% of the overall Australian population.

Further afield, Australians travelling overseas and expats returning home from Australia in the late 19th and early 20th C took AFL with them, but, while it enjoyed a brief flowering in some places—like the US, which temporarily replaced Aotearoa-NZ with the most players outside Australia—it failed to make a lasting impression. One reason that's been put forward for its failure to make inroads is that it requires a large ground, something that is often not readily available in more populous places.

As an interesting aside, one of the strangest AFL stories I've heard is that of L/Sgt Peter Chitty, 1943 winner of the game's most prestigious award, the Brownlow Medal. Peter's Brownlow was unique—it was the only Changi Brownlow ever awarded.

During WWII Peter was among thousands of Allied troops taken prisoner by Japanese forces and held at Changi POW camp in Singapore. While there the Australians realised that they had enough AFL players to form a six-team league, complete with the administration needed to oversee it. The Japanese approved and they played for nine months, culminating with a match between Victoria and the rest of Australia. Peter captained Australia and was awarded the medal after the match. Oddly enough, it wasn't the Japanese, but the Australian officers who ended the matches because of concerns that competition was becoming too fierce.

AFL wasn't the only game played in Changi and other Japanese POW camps. There were rugby games, soccer, tennis and organised boxing tournaments where the camp commandant presented prizes. The Japanese were probably quite entertained, after all, they were trapped in the same boring routine. There are even reports of them playing sports like baseball with the prisoners, and of after-game socialising.[2]

Which is curious because it's contrary to all we've been taught, and just goes to show that histories should all be taken with a very big grain of salt.

The Changi Brownlow Medal is now in the Australian War Memorial in Canberra (www.awm.gov.au). No one seems quite sure what it's made of, guesses range from part of an aircraft to some sort of kitchen utensil.

2 Grant, Lachlan. Enduring myth of Changi as "POW hell' overshadows stories of survival. Sydney Morning Herald. September 201

Women in AFL

Just like in all other codes of football, women had been playing AFL since its very beginning—they just weren't acknowledged as doing so. They were probably discouraged from playing by incidents like the Bendigo woman, who was charged with public nuisance for kicking a ball in the street in 1892. That probably wouldn't have happened if she'd been a man. That changed in WWI when women organised games to fund-raise for a range of causes, like the war effort, the Red Cross, a victory arch to celebrate the end of the war, and for soldier's rehabilitation.

The first recorded women's game was played in WA in 1915 and matches were well attended, not just because of the novelty value of women playing a men's game, but also because the public would have been well aware that they were raising money for good causes. Attendance was probably helped by the limited number of men's games being played because so many were away at the war. By 1918 women's teams were springing up across the country and attracted huge crowds—one game in Ballarat attracted 7,000, the largest ever seen there.

Between the wars women kept playing, mostly as fund raisers, and in 1921 they made the daring move of ditching long skirts for male football attire—shorts! That probably brought in more men to watch them play, which is a little sad. The press didn't help the ladies, with most reports adopting a patronising tone with comments about 'the softer sex', and coverage tended to be local and not considered worthy of the larger publications. Then there was a backlash in the 30s with protests about all-female tournaments and at least one club captain (a woman) stating that the game was too rough for girls. It got so bad that, like in the early days of women's soccer, some lady players felt the need for anonymity and took to wearing masks to conceal their identity.

The game was given a boost in WWII and in 1947 there were calls for the leading clubs to field women's teams, an initiative that continued through the 1950s. But it wasn't until the 1980s that women's competition began to be taken seriously and it grew steadily until the turn of the 21st C, when it took off with the number of registered teams growing by 450%. In 2015 there were 284,501 female players registered in Australia and 530,166 worldwide.

The modern AFL Women's (AFLW) was launched in 2017 with eight teams, all affiliated to one or other of the major clubs. Within two years that expanded to ten teams, then 14 in 2020, and 18 in 2022.

AFL's children

AFL has a limited geographic range, but within that range it commands a dedicated, often fanatical following. Perhaps because of that, an attitude of 'we love our game just the way it is, thank you', AFL doesn't seem to have spawned robust offspring.

Like soccer and both codes of rugby, there is a format that has fewer players on the field. The AFL version features nine players a-side (AFL 9s), and is generally played on a half size, rectangular field, often a rugby or soccer pitch, but the size of the field doesn't seem to be fixed and games are occasionally played on full sized grounds. The rules mostly remain the same as in the full game, the main differences seem to be that players can't run as far with the ball and if it goes out an opposition player throws it back in. AFL 9s is often played to introduce the game outside Australia.

There are variations on the limited-player-number theme, like touch AFL, AFLX (a version that only has seven players a side), Metro Footy which is primarily played in the US to introduce Americans to AFL, and Samoan rules—a 15 a side game played on a rugby field which sounds like a mish-mash of rugby and AFL.

Historically there were other variations that were briefly popular and then died, like a shortened version of the game called Lightening Football that was introduced in South Australia in 1940, and became common throughout the country, until the covid pandemic in the 21st C severely limited it. It's still played in some places, but so far has failed to recover.

The 1914 battle for hearts and minds in Australia's eastern states led to the creation of a hybrid game called Universal Football (UF) which blended AFL and rugby league rules. The blend seems to have strongly favoured league and there was some progress towards amalgamation, but the war intervened and by the time things returned to normal the momentum had been lost. This particular game may have been inspired by the old Victorian Football Association (VFA) rule that allowed the ball to be passed with both hands from below the shoulders—similar to a rugby pass. If that was the case, rivalry between the VFL and VFA may help explain why it didn't progress.

An attempt was made in America in 1915 to establish a hybrid between AFL and American Football called National Football. This was to be played on an American football ground with throwing the ball, as in the American game, allowed. America's entry into WWI stymied the game before it could get established, however during WWII when there were many Americans station in Australia, the idea of a hybrid game was revisited. A game called '*Austus*' was created, but this time it heavily favoured Australian rules. The main issue with the cross-over was that Australians were used to kicking the ball while the Americans threw it, so the rule was altered to allow either; and an American ball was used because it could be both thrown and kicked more easily.

Other than that, it seems that it was all Australian rules. Both armed forces endorsed the game as a suitable sport for their men, but it didn't live long after the Americans went home after the war, possibly because both the AFL and the American National Football league (NFL) had far too much invested to encourage a potential competitor.

But it's just possible that Australian Football had one robust child, although it's never been properly acknowledged. That's Gaelic Football, but because there is no firm link between it and Aussie Rules I'm looking at it as a completely separate code.

Chapter 8
GAELIC FOOTBALL

Caid, GAA

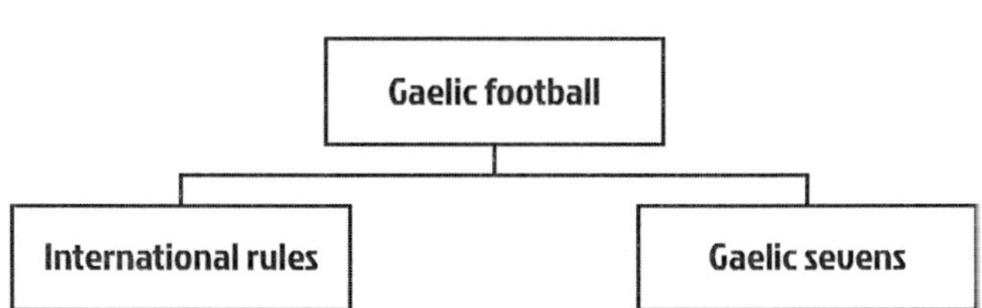

Gaelic Football was codified by the Gaelic Athletic Association (GAA) in the Hayes's Commercial Hotel in County Tipperary, Ireland, in 1884. It was a deliberate attempt by a group of fervent Nationalists to oppose the spread of soccer and rugby, English games they believed damaged the Republican movement. The first match under the new rules was played in 1885, and by 1887 the game were widely known throughout Ireland.

The mechanics of the Game

Gaelic football (GAA) is played with a round ball, similar to a soccer ball but slightly smaller and heavier, by two teams, each with 15 players on the field at any one time. Minor matches are played over two 30 minute halves and more important inter-county games are two 35 minute periods. The pitch is a rectangular grass area roughly 137 m (450') long by 82 m (270') wide with an 'H' shaped goal at each end (similar to a rugby goal) 6.5 m (21') wide with a cross-bar 2.5 m (8') above the ground. The goal area beneath the cross-bar is netted, as in a soccer goal.

The object of the game is to get the ball between the posts. Getting it into the net is worth three points and above the cross-bar one point. Each game is controlled by eight officials, a referee, four umpires, two linesmen and a sideline official. The referee controls the game by interpreting and applying the rules. One linesman patrols each side-line, changing sides at half time, and adjudicating on when and where the ball crosses the line, who put it out and who puts it in. They also keep an eye on play, advise the referee on any infractions or other matters that may have been missed, and one of the linesmen can act as stand-in for the referee if needed. Umpires are paired and each pair remains behind a goal-line throughout the game to indicate when the ball crosses the line, awarding either a free kick when it's crossed outside the goal, one point if it goes over the cross-bar or a goal if it hits the net. If a single point is scored the umpire waves a white flag and a green flag signifies three points for a goal. As with the linesmen, umpires also help the referee by keeping an eye out for infringements that may have been missed.

The sideline official keeps track of player substitutions and general interactions between on and off field.

Players move the ball up and down the field by kicking, running while bouncing it every four paces, hand-balling (punching it out of one hand with the other hand) and 'soloing'—running while dropping the ball onto the toe of the boot and kicking it back up into their hands every four steps. They may bounce or solo only twice in a run before they have to dispose of the ball.

There are fixed positions, including a goal keeper, but no off-side rules. It is a non-contact sport in-so-far as it's illegal to hold, drag, pull or rugby-style tackle an opposing player, but jostling or shoulder charging is allowed if there's a clear attempt to compete for the ball.

Despite its popularity, Gaelic football is one of the very few football codes in the world that has remained steadfastly amateur, which may be a part of its popularity but it also has the detrimental effect of a continuous stream of top players seeking their fortunes in professional codes.

History

The 1885 rules proved too vague to be effective, so they were revised in 1888 to make them clearer and add new facets to the game—like extra goal posts 6.5 m (21') either side of the goals with a point scored if the ball goes between the goal and the post (sound familiar?), and when the ball is thrown in players must stand in parallel ranks in the middle of the field and hold hands.

Yes, holding hands on a football field!

The extra posts were removed in 1910 and the holding hands rule was revoked in 1914 after a player revolt.

Today more than 20% of Ireland's population play GAA, making it the country's favourite participation (as opposed to spectator) sport, ahead of both soccer and rugby. The history of Gaelic football is contentious with an ongoing debate over how much influence the original Irish football, or *caid,* had on modern Gaelic football. Caid dates back to early mediaeval times, but it's seen as a bit of a catch-all for a variety of games whose only resemblance to each other was that they all featured teams chasing a ball. Some researchers have pointed to one of those games played in 1670 which featured catching and kicking a ball as a precursor to the Gaelic football, but others tend to dismiss this and insist that the modern game has little or nothing to do with early Irish games.

Then there's the obvious similarities to Australian Rules football.

Relationship to Australian Rules.

This is contentious! We know that the great 19th C Irish diaspora took caid around the world and there's documented evidence of it being played in South Australia in 1843. We've no idea what form that SA game took, but ten years later, in the same town, football was being played with a round ball and rugby style goal posts, which sounds very much like early GAA—or early rugby. Another ten years, more-or-less, and still in the same town, it had evolved into using a rugby ball, four goal posts, and umpires with flags.

We also know that there were games of caid being played by the many Irishmen on the Victorian goldfields in the mid-19th C, and as the game evolved the style they played probably morphed into Victorian rules. Many of those Irishmen went back to Ireland after the gold rush, around the same time as Victorian football was being codified and becoming popular in Australia, and, like the other miners who dispersed across Australia and around the world, they took their new sport with them.

In Ireland, soccer and, particularly, rugby were becoming popular in the 1860s and '70s. Then, in the mid-'70s, another game began to be played that was virtually indistinguishable from Australian football. Now, there's no documented evidence, but it seems to me a no-brainer that if a mob of men were playing and enjoying a particular style of football on one side of the world, they're going to continue to want to play it when they reach the other side. Especially if there's a group of them. Returning miners would form a cliché with a bond born out of shared experience—and probably money because if they hadn't been successful they were unlikely to have gone home. And if there was enough of them, and they had the money, they'd be able to organise and pursue their leisure interests—like their favourite game of football. And, because they had money and were the 'local-boys-made-good', they would influence others to play.

But the Australian game would have been, to most Irishmen, as foreign as soccer and rugby. So the 1884, Haye's Hotel and subsequent meetings set out to create a new Irish game by mashing them all together and adding a few novel rules of their own—like holding hands. Much of what they adopted was a direct take-off from the Australian game, which wasn't surprising because most of those at the meetings had either been to, or had close family links to Australia or Aotearoa-NZ. But it took them another 20 odd years to come up with a game truly of their own.

But there was a twist.

Ireland has another, far more ancient game, *hurling*, that's played with a very hard ball that they belt around the field with sticks like hockey sticks. It's hard, fast and very ancient—the first written record of hurling was in the 5th C, but it's thought to be much older and predate Christianity by a long way. We'll have a bit more on hurling later, but for now it's sufficient to say that it employs goal posts and playing fields that are identical to Gaelic football, the same number of players and officials, the same scoring system and scores are also indicated by the umpires waving white or green flags. If a player wants to pass the ball without using his stick he must kick it or slap (hand-ball) it on, and if he carries it, he must bounce it every four paces. Shoulder-charging is permitted when two players are competing for the ball.

It's likely that hurling has developed these rules over time and the ancient game was probably quite different, but never-the-less it predates all the modern football codes.

I suspect that:

- At least one version of caid was, essentially, hurling played by kicking a large round ball instead of hitting a small one with sticks. This may have come about with the introduction of the soccer ball, but it may have been much older. A version of caid was played in Ireland since at least medieval times that used a more-or less fixed size field and goals made from bushes or poles at each end. A similar game was played in Wales, called hurling to goals, and there's a strong suspicion that it may have originated with the Vikings (I'll get to them, they're really interesting), and that was the version of caid being played in Australia in the early to mid-19th C.

- It was played by some of the men present at the Parade Hotel in Melbourne when the rules for Victorian football were drawn up—there is no other logical way that some of the rules, like bouncing the ball, could have come into Victorian rules.

In short, I think it probable that Gaelic football went to Australia in the form of a version of caid, was picked up by Australians who altered it to suit their conditions, then re-exported it back to Ireland where it was modified and codified into modern Gaelic football.

Women in Gaelic football (Peil Ghaelach na mBan)

The women's version of the sport is governed, under the umbrella of the GAA, by a nominally independent body called the Ladies› Gaelic Football Association (LGFA). The rules are generally the same as the men's version, except that it is strictly a no-contact sport and deliberate physical contact is illegal, the ball is slightly smaller and all games last for 60 minutes.

Like all the other codes, women's Gaelic football had very humble beginnings followed by exponential growth in the late 20th C growth. The first women's league was organised in 1926 in County Claire, but it doesn't seem to have developed until the 1960s when it became a novel drawcard for charity events. After that growth was spectacular—in 2001 there were about 80,000 players, and by 2020 that number had risen to more than 190,000 in about 650 clubs. Like the men's game, ladies Gaelic football remains strictly amateur.

GAA's children

Like the other codes, Gaelic football has produced a shorter, faster form of the game in Gaelic 7s. These are matches played with seven-a-side over two seven and a half minute halves. For semi-finals and finals matches, games are extended to nine minutes per half. There are male and female 7s tournaments, played under the auspices of the GAA and the LGFA respectively.

There is also International Rules Football that was devised especially so that international games could be played between Gaelic and Australian players; these rules are used around the world wherever one or the other code played. International rules are a hybrid, although they seem to heavily favour the Irish—games are played on a Gaelic rectangular pitch, there are 15 players in a team and it uses a round ball. The primary differences is the scoring system and extra goal posts placed outside the Gaelic goal. One point is awarded for putting the ball between the goal and the side posts, three for putting it over the cross-bar, and six for under the bar.

International Rules began in the late 1960s and the first series between Australia and Ireland was played in 1984, but competition has been somewhat sporadic. It was suspended in 2020 because of the covid pandemic and, at the time of writing this, had not restarted. It's come under criticism as being not serious and just an excuse for the players to have a good holiday—both probably true—but it has also exposed players on both sides to the other code, with the result that several Irish players have been enticed to take up lucrative contracts in the professional Australian League.

This is probably good for the Irish game as it gives players a viable career path that may be enough to keep them in the game, rather than prioritising other careers options.

Part 2
THE ANCESTORS

He seized the ball and passed it to a team-mate while dodging another and laughing. He pushed it out of the way of another. Another fellow player he raised to his feet. All the while the crowd resounded with shouts of 'Out of bounds,' 'Too far,' 'Right beside him,' 'Over his head,' 'On the ground,' 'Up in the air,' 'Too short,' 'Pass it back in the scrum.'

Antiphanes, 408 – 334 BCE,

Chapter 9
THE PARENTS

None of the modern games materialized out of nothing, they all have ancestors—it's just a case of trying to work out who they were. The last couple of generations are quite easy, at least on the mother's side, because they all have the same mother—the English Public School system.

Mother

The evolution of Public Schools and the Gentrification of Football

The English call their private schools 'Public Schools', but to the rest of the world they're definitely private. Like many other traditions, the reason for the contradictory naming lies far back in history.

Before the 14th C the norm was to educate your children at home with a tutor. Or with the church, which ran 'Grammar' schools with the sole purpose of educating local boys in Latin grammar in preparation for clerical work in the church. All education was, by definition, private, and therefore for the children of the local rich.

But in the mid-14th C society was changed irrevocably. The plague, AKA the 'Black Death', swept England killing so many people—about one in three—that there were serious labour shortages across the board, from farm labourers to clergy.

The rich and the nobility were doubly hit. Firstly, riches were no guarantee against the disease, and they died, although probably not in the same numbers as the rest of the population. But they suffered a secondary affect that was, for them, possibly worse. Their workers died and left a severe gap in the labour force, which meant not only shortages of almost everything, but those workers that were left suddenly found themselves able to demand, and get, whatever they asked for. Previously comparatively static populations became mobile, no longer tied to any particular town, job or estate and able to follow the money. And, as wages went up, so did the living standards of the peasants. It was one of the very few times in history that the rich didn't get richer and the poor didn't get poorer.

The rich could no longer find staff, including tutors, easily. If they could find one, he was probably horrendously expensive and liable to jump ship for a better offer. Similarly grammar schools must have suffered because the clergy were not spared by the plague, and many would have been forced to close for lack of teachers.

Education was in crisis.

So, after the initial impact of the plague settled down, some far sighted people began to look for a solution to the teacher shortage, and they realised that, if reliable education couldn't be brought to the boy, then the boy must be sent to the education. The answer was to open a school where boys could be sent, from both within and outside the district, for a proper education. Many would have to board at the school and the fees charged ensured a reliable staff of tutors.

The first 'Public School' was opened by the Bishop of Winchester at Winchester in 1382, followed in 1440 by Eton, founded by Henry VI. These new schools were well funded with powerful patrons and had a wider curriculum than the old grammar schools, although still very heavily religion based. The concept harked back to Roman and Greek times, but was radical by medieval standards, and neither the Romans nor the Greeks boarded students.

But boarding came with a problem. Young boys are boisterous and, in groups, quite often disgusting. Healthy boys (and girls, but they didn't count) had an excess of energy that had to be released. Left to themselves they're usually manageable, but in a group they bounce off each other, create stupid ideas and act on them. That's mostly pretty normal and amounts to simply testing their bounds, finding out what society would let them get away with and what their limits were. Just finding their place in the world. But occasionally it was to the detriment of their own and society's health.

Diversions that provided an outlet for all that energy were needed.

Existing institutions that gathered boys together in groups had their own methods of dealing with and harnessing that energy. Chief among those would have been the Church, which gathered young novice monks in great numbers. But in the monasteries the boy's energy was kept in check and the normal urges of puberty were stamped on by vows of celibacy, a harsh regime and rigid discipline that saw them sleep deprived through long night vigils and rituals, and long days of work. Novice monks undoubtedly got up to all sorts of things, but, for most, monastery life was forever and the closed societies that harboured them reflected the age structure of the outside world. It included monks of all ages, so novices were in a distinct minority and were subject to the restraints and predations of their elders.

Trade guilds were another institution that gathered large numbers of young boys. Apprentices, which formed a major part of medieval society, were integrated into the guilds and formed what were, essentially, gangs that occasionally got out of hand and went to war with each other. But on the whole they were kept in check by the tradesmen who employed them and enforced a fairly rigid set of rules. That, along with long hours of work and some vigorous and violent games, (including football) saw off their excess energy. And, of course, unlike the poor novice monks, they had more or less free access to the town's wenches to see them through puberty.

The armed forces, such as they were, is the other institution that employed large numbers of young men and threw them together. But they did not employ children. Warfare required strength, and by the time a boy had developed enough of that, he was beyond the excesses of childhood—but not beyond the sense of immortality so common in youth and so necessary in war. Anyway, when a young soldier or sailor played up he normally did it in the company of his seniors, who taught him how to do it properly.

But Public schools were different. They were bringing boys together at exactly the time when they were beginning to test boundaries, when their energy was at its greatest and when the confusing hormones of puberty were raging at their highest. Added to that, the schools were mostly religious in nature and the moralistic authorities had a particular horror of masturbation and sodomy, which had to be prevented at all costs. In monasteries hard work and long prayer kept youthful aberrations more-or-less in check, but in schools the boys were there to learn, for which they needed to be alert, so they couldn't be kept up most of the night to make them somnolent and pliable like novice monks. Harsh discipline could be employed, but the pupils were almost all from rich and powerful families, probably mostly spoiled, and there was always the risk of protective parents coming down hard in defence of their little darlings.

There was also the problem of staff. They were tutors, not baby sitters. They were employed on the basis of their expert knowledge of one subject or another and not trained to deal with young boys en mass. When they'd taught in private homes the family took care of discipline outside the classroom—and any major issues that arose within it—so the tutor's responsibility was minimal.

But in the public school system their expert knowledge wasn't enough, they had to develop into a whole new profession—teachers. And teachers had to develop new ways of dealing with boys. And over time it was realised that hard, even brutal, physical exercise was the answer.

This idea was summed up as:

> *A daily proper portion of bodily fatigue is the antidote to all wandering of the thoughts and dwelling on improper objects.*

The Victorians embraced this as the ethos of '*mens sana in corpore sano*' (a healthy mind in a healthy body), sort of the same as the modern concept of the body being the temple of the soul.

But back in the first schools such ideas were far in the future. To begin with the boys would naturally have formed themselves into groups, cliques that competed for dominance. These would have been uneven, at one end of the spectrum the strong and sporty would band together, at the other the nerds, and in between boys that shared similar interests would have found each other. Over time staff discovered that with the judicious allocation of new students to one group or another, balanced groups were created that were capable of competing on a more-or-less even footing across a range of intellectual and sporting fields.

From this came the modern concept of school houses, and with it fixed teams of players and supporters. But players at what? At home some of the boys would have hunted, rode, perhaps jousted and trained at arms, but in the confines of the school all but training at arms was impractical, and not everyone was suited to, or even eligible for that. The school needed a sport they could all be involved in, one that didn't require particularly wide open spaces and one that the boys were familiar with.

They discovered that football was ideal. A boisterous mob affair, by that time football was being played vigorously, in one form or the other, throughout the country. And although it was generally played by the lower classes, the children of the gentry probably all joined in at one time or another. Boys brought the game to their schools, where it was soon realised that it was exactly what was needed to let off steam—hard, brutal without being deadly (usually, although there was an incident in the 14th C when a boy was found dead and Irish students were suspected of having killed him during a game), and hugely enjoyable for most.

It was, however, a bit of a balancing act for the schools. The boys needed to be tired, but not so exhausted as to make them unable to study. In 1519 William Horman, headmaster at Eton, wrote,

> *There muste be a measure in gyuynge of remedies or sportynge to chyldren, leste they be wery of goynge to theyr boke if they haue none, or waxe slacke if they haue to many.*[1]

1 Living Sports History: Football at Winchester, Eton and Harrow

Which roughly translates to 'sport for children must be balanced, too little and they'll be too full of energy to study and too much and they'll be too exhausted.' Horman also gave us our first reference to football, or something like it, being played in public schools when he wrote:

We wyll playe with a ball full of wynde.

The right balance would see the boys return to their dormitories exhilarated, battered, bruised and too exhausted to do anything but sleep. At least that was the idea, personally I doubt if exhaustion stopped any boys masturbating—or sodomising each other if they were that way inclined.[2] The 'house' system with its organisation, competitive teams, loyalties, leaders, heroes, followers and fitness regimes, provided a framework for functional teams.

But public school authorities did not all embrace the game. In Winchester in the mid-17th C it was described as '*innocent and lawful*', whereas other academics, like Samuel Butler, headmaster at Shrewsbury, described it as '*more fit for farm boys and labourers than young gentlemen*'. For the most part, however, the benefits of football were recognised and it was generally welcomed in most schools. In fact Butler's successor made it compulsory.

Initially playing in fixed teams, albeit probably loosely organised, football was found to be good for fostering cooperation. It was later described as key to developing character through teamwork, sportsmanship and self-sacrifice. Teams became more coherent and positions on the field began to evolve—in fact Hely Almond, a late 19th C headmaster, sai:;

Games in which success depends on the united efforts of many, and which also foster courage and endurance are the very lifeblood of the public school system.

2 Clearly it didn't stop them because I've often heard footballers of all codes being referred to as ardent practitioners of both practices—almost always by followers of rival codes.

This ethos still maintains in the 21st C when many of the more prominent schools pride themselves on their sporting prowess and, provide a disproportionate number of top flight players, especially in rugby union.

But all that was far in the future when the good Bishop opened his school at Winchester in 1382. Then, as I said, football was an unruly (in the true sense of the word) and barely organised affair. Although broadly the same, each region, even each village, had its own way of playing and each boy brought his own style of play from his home. There would have been endless conflict over minor details.

So each school began to amalgamate the various interpretations into some sort of coherent code that evolved over the years and centuries into unique games, peculiar to each school and reflecting the broad region from which their students were drawn. But they were all organised around one new constraint imposed by the schools—a limited playing field. Back home games ranged far and wide, usually without boundaries, however schools had limited grounds available.

It obviously took time and generations of students to hone the game in each school and they took pride in their uniqueness, until each school played a game that was unintelligible to any other.

Although all were violent and 'hacking'—kicking an opponent's shins—was particularly prevalent, levels of violence varied considerably. Some schools only allowed the ball to be caught and kicked while some let it be carried. By the 18th – 19th Cs a bewildering range of terms for plays had been invented, for instance at Eton they played (still play) two forms of the game. The first is the 'wall game' where two packs battled along a wall to get a ball into a zone at each end, called a calx. The rules of this game, which included such things as sneaking, picking up, throwing and rolling in straight, were described as being 'as intelligible as Hebrew'.

The second Eton game sounds similar to rugby in some respects but quite alien in others. It was played with a round ball, had goals like soccer goals behind which the ball had to be touched down to score a 'rouge'. Anyone familiar with modern rugby will recognise things like heeling the ball back in the ruck (furking in the bully), off side rules (sneaking) and allowing a free kick to anyone who caught the ball on the full. But many of the other rules were similar to the wall game and equally incomprehensible.

Other schools had their own peculiarities. Harrow played on particularly muddy fields with a heavy 'pork pie' shaped ball, and included goals with no crossbars called 'bases'. The ball could not be passed forward, a free kick was awarded for catching the ball on the full and players were free to run interference.

Winchester had a game called 'Winkies' which was even stranger to the outsider. It involved scoring by kicking a ball into an end zone (worms), but the teams took turns to kick the ball, play was restarted with a scrum (a hot) and there was an allowance for bonus scores (behinds). There were no side lines, but instead there was a net on either side to keep the ball in play.

The rules of all these games changed constantly, and rarely to simplify them. Running with the ball would be brought in, then banned, then allowed again. Tripping, hacking and shoulder charging would be legal at one year, then not allowed, then legal again. Actual murder was never made legal, but anything short of it seems to have been legitimate at one time or another.

All these games could exist because they were only played 'in house', there was no such thing as inter-school games, so different rules did not matter. That changed with the introduction of railways in the early 1800s. Before that it was an horrendously expensive major mission to get teams from one school to another, so the idea of inter-school meets was not an issue, but with railways …

However, once the idea did arise it was predicted that so much enmity existed between schools that to set boys from rival schools against each other in a violent sport would be a recipe for disaster. This prediction was borne out by a match between Marlborough and Clifton in 1864, which was such a blood-bath that most schools were convinced that inter-school football matches were a very bad idea, and they would be far better off limiting inter-school rivalry to non-contact sports, like cricket. An Old Etonian put it quite succinctly in 1863 when he said:

The feud between Eton and Harrow is sufficiently well known to make an increase of hostile feeling very undesirable.

A major part of the problem was the lack of any comprehensive over-arching rules, and such was the independence—some would say pig-headed snobbery—between the schools that few were willing to sit down together and draw up anything workable, because it would inevitably mean that some, or all, would have to compromise.

That's not to say that more-or-less sensible rules weren't being made. The first seems to have been at Eton in 1815, but all they were doing was laying out a few rules to cover the more contentious, often localised, issues. Like what happens if the ball ends up in the trees or the pond. The games were only played within their schools and everyone knew the central rules, so there was no need to write them down.

In the mid-19th C more and more public school boys were going on to university, and they expected to carry on playing football while there, and beyond. The problem, of course, was that they all played the form of football developed at their school, and when ex-students from various schools ended up at the same university they all thought that their game was the proper one. It was like the public schools' problem all over again. In 1846 two Shrewsbury old boys attempted to organise a game at Cambridge, but, as one of them complained:

When an attempt was made to introduce a common game, and form a really respectable club at Cambridge, the Rugby game was found to be the great obstacle to the combination of Eton, Winchester, and Shrewsbury men in forming a football club.[3]

3 Football, Simple and Universal. The Field. Dec.1861

And thus started the great disagreements that ultimately resulted in the births of all the modern codes.

In 1845 the first tentative rules for rugby were written down at Rugby Public School, then, in 1848, an attempt at a unified code was tried at Cambridge. The result was complete confusion, with the Eton men getting very aggravated at the Rugby men for handling the ball. After that debacle, it was agreed that two men from each public school, plus two who were not public school graduates, should meet to try and work out a uniform set of rules. Each brought a copy of their school's rules, such as they were, and argued about them far into the night, until, just before mid-night, the Cambridge Rules were agreed on.

Unfortunately no copies of these rules has survived (that I know of), but some of them are known. Goals were scored by kicking a ball between uprights and under a crossbar, players were permitted to catch the ball from a kick and kick it on immediately, but forbidden to run with it, and only the goal-keeper could hold onto the ball, and he was allowed to punch it on from anywhere in his own half. They also decided on the most logical of things—players of each team should be identifiable by the colour of their caps.

In 1862 Cambridge further refined their rules to specify eleven men a side, an umpire plus linesmen, a standardised goal and field size, a ban on handling the ball except to stop it, a new offside rule and a fixed period for each game. The Cambridge rules went on to eventually become the basis for the Football Association's (soccer's) code.

The rules gradually got out into the public domain when students occasionally played against local town boys. The games weren't pretty and often ended in a brawl, but the idea of football with rules gained traction in the wider community. And graduation from university didn't mean that men couldn't go on playing. They formed clubs, often only open to graduates of one school or university, but non-school based clubs were also formed that had a broader base, and it was from these that many of today's clubs grew.

One of those was Barnes FC, formed by a London solicitor called Ebenezer Morley in 1862, the same year as the people at

Cambridge were formulating their rules. Ebenezer managed to get several public school men to join his club, but this inevitably led to disputes about play and Ebenezer, who hadn't attended any public school, became so frustrated that he wrote to a newspaper suggesting that football should follow cricket's lead and fix a cohesive set of overarching rules. That letter led to a meeting of about a dozen clubs at the Freemasons' Tavern in London on 26th October 1863, which resulted in the formation of the Football Association with Ebenezer as its first chairman.

Eleven clubs joined the FA that night, but it took a further six meetings to agree on a comprehensive set of rules and a blueprint for the game, based on an amalgamation of public school and university games.

But all was not sweetness and light.

Those first rules allowed for both dribbling and handling the ball, a fair catch marked with a heel resulted in a free kick, and, after much discussion, hacking or kicking an opponent's shins, was outlawed. These all raised serious divisions between those advocating for a Cambridge style game and supporters of the Rugby one.

The two rules in contention were:

- Rule No 9: A player shall be entitled to run with the ball towards his adversaries' goal if he makes a fair catch, or catches the ball on the first bound; but in case of a fair catch, if he makes his mark to take a free kick, he shall not run.
- Rule No 10: If any player shall run with the ball towards his adversaries' goal, any player on the opposite side shall be at liberty to charge, hold, trip or hack him, or to wrest the ball from him, but no player shall be held and hacked at the same time.

Arguments for and against these rules became heated, with one side suggesting that they were uncivilised while the other said that they embodied the true, masculine spirit of the game. One hacking and handling advocate, Francis Campbell, representative of the

Blackheath Football Club which was formed in 1858 by old boys from Blackheath Propriety School and an ardent player of the Rugby game, even went so far as to say:

> *you will do away with the courage and pluck of the game, and it will be bound to bring over a lot of Frenchmen who would beat you with a week's practice.*

At that time in history, to suggest that a Frenchman could defeat an Englishman was undoubtedly serious talk (although it was to prove prophetic on many occasions on the football field) and that comment can only have deepened the divisions. As Campbell was the FA's first Treasurer his opinion carried weight, and the 'Hackers' managed to maintain a slim majority throughout these discussions, right up to a meeting in November when Morley again advocated for the non-hacking and carrying rules, invoking the Cambridge style rules supported by six of the most influential public schools. At the end of that meeting supporters of the Rugby style game were still in the majority, but when another meeting was called just a week later many of the Rugby supporters failed to show and the non-hackers carried the day.

It's not recorded, or at least that I can find, why they didn't show. Perhaps they were just fed up with the whole thing and decided to go their own way, perhaps they weren't informed of the meeting, or maybe there was some other reason, but that meeting on December 1st 1863 sealed the rift between association football and rugby.

Francis Campbell resigned from the Football Association after the vote and went on to be instrumental in the formation of the Rugby Football Union seven years later.

Curiously, by then hacking, the issue at the centre of the rift with the FA, had disappeared from rugby everywhere except its place of origin—Rugby School—where it was considered an integral part of the game. Ironically, because the new rules forbade hacking, Rugby School did not join the Rugby Union until 1890, nearly twenty years after its formation.

As we've seen, association football went on to be the most popular game in the world, played with various degrees of intensity almost everywhere. Apart from some tinkering with the rules—like banning all handling and the introduction of a free kick and half a dozen minor variants, it has remained more or less static for the last one hundred and fifty years.

The first game played under the FA rules was between Barnes and Richmond on the 19th December 1863. It was a nil-all draw.

Meanwhile students at Rugby Public School made a first tentative attempt to codify their game in 1845, but it wasn't until 1871 that ex-Rugby students managed a comprehensive set of rules and rugby went on to become the world's second most popular football code.

Their mother should be proud of them both.

The Fathers: acknowledged and not

Soccer

It will come as no surprise that paternity can be very difficult to prove. The modern football codes all have the same mother, but they have different fathers. In fact some of them have more than one, which is a bit weird. The most straight-forward is soccer which, at first glance, would seem to be simply the offspring of the Public Schools and the northern Sheffield Football Association. Pure English, unsullied by foreign genes.

But it's just possible that a foreigner snuck in. Totally unprovable, of course, but…

First the indisputable father:

Northern Football and the Sheffield Football Association

The 18th and 19th C were traumatic times for the British working people. Land enclosures—property owners fencing off land to exclude others from using it—had been a feature of the English country-side for centuries, but it accelerated in the 18th C with Parliament, made up entirely of property owners, passing act after act allowing themselves and their mates to appropriate common land. In most cases the 'common' land was the property of the land owner, but it included tracts where tenants and the landless were legally entitled to graze a few animals and raise small crops, usually in return for supplying labour or other service to the lord of the manor. Many of the rural poor relied on common land not only for food and income, but also for fuel, hay, collecting berries and running pigs.

Until the 19th C each enclosure required an Act of Parliament, but in 1801 a General Enclosure Act enabled landowners to 'enclose' their property and exclude all others without referring to Parliament. This resulted in many of the villagers suddenly finding themselves without income or access to any means of subsistence and being forced to look for work in the rapidly expanding industrial cities. In some cases the enclosures were actually to make land available for the rapidly expanding cities and factories.

I'm pretty cynical, and in most cases I don't believe in coincidence, and I definitely smell a rat here. The Industrial Revolution was in full swing and needed a labour force that wouldn't have been there if not for the enclosures and the forced migration of the rural poor. And the factories that needed the labour were owned by the same land owners that were forcing people off the land.

The vast majority of the people that moved to the towns found work. Too much work. It was, for the most part, hard, exhausting, long hours six days a week and poorly paid. Even the children were included in the work force and suffered the same conditions and the same exhaustion. And along with work came poverty, appalling living conditions and rampant disease. The filthy streets and houses and, especially, the lack of sanitation and clean drinking water sparked epidemics that killed thousands too weak from exhaustion and poor diet to resist. So more enclosures were needed to replace them.

But the factories flourished, England and the Empire grew rich and the ground was laid for football's worldwide expansion.

The theory goes that the removal of the people who played mob football (the father of them all, we'll get to that) to the close confines of the urban environments and the general exhaustion of the working men saw the death of working class football. As a result it was left to the leisure classes who attended public schools, mostly in the not-heavily-industrialised south, to develop and civilise the game and claim it as their own. According to that theory, working class football was dead and it was up to the southern gentry to send 'missionaries' into the industrial bad-lands to introduce their new game.

But that theory doesn't stand up too well to scrutiny. In fact it is an excellent example of those who can pay, write history.

Reports of the demise of working class football were premature. Football is an incredibly good way to let off steam and vent frustration, and very few people needed to let off steam and vent frustration more than the 19th C British working man. Especially if he happened to be working in one of the big, ever expanding northern industrial cities. The men, children, and probably women used any vacant space or piece of wasteland that they could find in their desolate environments to kick something around on a Sunday, as borne out by a witness in an 1842 Parliamentary inquiry into the conditions of working-class children in the mining areas of Northern England:

> *Although Christmas Day and Good Friday were the only fixed holidays in the mining region of Yorkshire, children had at least one day off a week and a fair portion of time in the evening. This they could use to play sport on the considerable areas of wasteland in the neighbourhood. Their games included cricket, nur and spell* [a bat and ball game] *and football.*[4]

4 Social Class and the Invention of Modern Football. John Storey, Culture Matters Saturday. 23 January 2016

The old games of the wide open spaces, or at least the more open villages, were not possible, so they had to improvise—and quickly. New, tighter versions were invented, and new rivalries and loyalties developed.

It wasn't possible to play village against village, so factories and other work places banded together to form teams, then clubs. As they increased in size and popularity they attracted sponsors when bosses realised that there was a certain amount to be gained from the collegiate influence of a football team on their workforce. Very much like the public school students, it gave the workers a degree of loyalty to their workplace, whether as players or spectators, and with the bosses on board areas of more suitable land were acquired for inter-club matches. And to play inter-club new rules needed to be written and agreed upon. This happened quite early, as can be seen in an 1838 article in 'Bell's Life in London':

> *A match at football will be played at the cricket ground, Leicester, on Good Friday next, between eleven (principally printers) from Derby and the same number of Leicester. The winners to challenge an equal number from any town in England, for a purse not exceeding £25*[5]

It's probable that the rules they wrote and the game they ended up playing was heavily influenced by the 1848 Cambridge rules and, in 1857, five years before Ebenezer Morley called his London meeting to form the Football Association in 1862, Nathaniel Creswick and William Prest formed the Sheffield Football Club and instigated Sheffield Rules. In 1860 neighbouring Hallam Football Club was established and by 1862 fifteen clubs had been formed in the Sheffield area, all playing to Sheffield rules. They joined the London based Football Association in 1863, but continued to play under their own rules, which presented a bit of

5 Social Class and the Invention of Modern Football. John Storey, Culture Matters Saturday. 23 January 2016

a problem for north vs south games. For a time both sets of rules existed side by side, influencing each other as cross-code games were played, but ultimately it was Sheffield that capitulated in 1877 by adopting the FA rules—with, as I mentioned earlier, the odd compromise.

After that, organised football developed rapidly in the working classes of the industrialised cities, clubs were no longer all work place based—some developed from church affiliation and others were organised by teachers and pupils in schools. And fan bases grew. If you couldn't play you could still participate by attending and giving full and very partisan support to your team. It all became very tribal.

In 1882 Blackburn Rovers from Lancashire challenged Old Etonians for the FA Cup—they lost 1-0, but came back the next year as Blackburn Olympic, and won. Their team of workers, weavers, foundry workers, plumbers, clerks, a dental assistant and a gilder, defeated the pride of the English upper class public schools, and the upper classes never recovered. No Public School based team ever won the FA Cup again.

Undoubtedly, the British working classes fathered soccer, but, as I alluded to earlier, I suspect that they weren't the only ones to get their genes in there. As I said, I am, by nature, a cynic and don't, as a rule, believe in coincidences. And there's a couple of glaring ones in soccer's story. The main one is the 'no physical contact and no ball handling', aspects of the game that just beg investigation.

Every other football game in Europe up until 1848 involved ball handling and a high degree of physical contact. All the public school games and everything that came before was violent.

Soccer was like a ballet dancer born into a family of bricklayers, and its paternity was just as questionable.

One theory on the origin of the radical 'no hands, no contact' ethos is that Ebenezer Morley got badly frightened in a rugby-like game and decided to write physical contact out. But that doesn't explain the 'no handling part'. I suspect the truth is a little more exotic.

Oriental Football[6] and the Chinese connection

The only other styles of football in the world (that I can find) that outright banned the use of hands was Chinese *tsu' chu* (which translates to 'kick ball') and Japanese *kemari*, both of which were very ancient and immensely popular. After Huang di's troops played with their enemy's stomach 5,000 years ago, football must have been quietly spreading across Asia because the next vague reference to it is from Japan around 3,000 years ago, where there was a game that involved several people trying to kick a stuffed ball into a hole in the middle of a large field. That's the first reference anywhere to a goal and a definite purpose to kicking a ball.

About two and a half thousand years ago tsu' chu was written into a Chinese military manual called the zhan guo ce as a training exercise. The manual was written during an extremely violent period in Chinese history that involved huge armies of hundreds of thousands of men. As the wars progressed the victors absorbed defeated armies and, by the time peace returned, millions of soldiers had been taught to play football. When all those men returned home they took the game with them and football boomed throughout China and beyond.

It's claimed that a football match was played between China and Japan as far back as 50 BCE. That's unproven, but probably true because Japanese mercenaries were fighting alongside Chinese troops and, being associated with the Chinese army, they would have played tsu' chu.

When they returned home those mercenaries began the Japanese Kofun Period, a time of huge cultural development involving the adoption of both Chinese and Central Asian practices, even importing whole Chinese clans to kick start industries such as silk production. By the 5th C the Samurai class had become established with a hierarchical organisation with the Imperial family at its head, similar to that employed by Central Asian warlords.

6 For a more complete history of Chinese football go to www.graemedobson.com.au

Back in China in the 7th C the Tang dynasty ushered in a Chinese golden age of culture and innovation, and tsu' chu evolved into a highly organised institution. Under the new regime it also acquired a new style of ball. The old one, which was just two hemispheres of leather sewn together and stuffed with straw, hemp or feathers, was replaced by a more spherical one made of eight shaped pieces of leather sewn around an inflated pig's bladder. The new design made the ball lighter, more responsive and much more manoeuvrable, enabling top players to develop skills that would have been impossible with the old ball.

The Chinese use of animal bladders came about when the Tang expanded to pacify border tribes and establish 'protectorates' from Afghanistan to the frozen north, where they encountered the practice of using the inflated bladders of slaughtering animals as footballs. All it would have taken for the Chinese to make a durable, standardised ball was to encase the bladders in leather.

The new ball would have been expensive and not easily obtainable by the rabble, who probably still had to use the old style, but those rich enough to get the new ball became obsessed with it. Its lightness and predictability spawned innovations that changed the game and spurred fundamental changes that ultimately led to the professionalization of the sport, which came to be known as *bai da*.

Meanwhile, a more refined game called *zhu qui*[7] began to be played among the elite. It had different rules, employed different skills and was played for a different audience to bai da.

It was as if tsu' chu had produced two sons, one a professional wrestler, the other a ballet dancer—very much like public schools would produce soccer and rugby. And somewhere, somehow,

7 A word of caution is needed here. I have browsed several references to zhu qiu and Bai Da and they seem to be split as to which name refers to which code of tsu' chu. I have taken what seems to be the majority decision and called zhu qiu the refined one and bai da the populist, but it could well be the other way round. In the long run it makes no difference, they're only names.

A 14th C game of zhu qui. *(Painting by Qian Xuan, Yuan era. Wikipedia. Public Domain.)*

zhu qiu was introduced to Japan and became the Japanese game of *kemari*. Or perhaps it was the other way round, but it's a moot point and it doesn't really make any difference.

Zhu qiu and kemari were gentile games with none of bai da's physicality. They were played at court for the entertainment of Emperors and aristocrats, often during feasts and on important occasions, such as the Emperor's birthday, where the emphasis was on form rather than substance. I'm not sure about zhu qiu, but it was similar to kemari which was played by six to eight players on a square field about seven metres on each side. The object was to keep the ball in the air using the feet and legs, or any part of the body except arms and hands (think modern day hacky sack). Players from each team passed the ball to each other in the air, but if it touched a hand or the ground possession went to the opponents. Points were scored for style and difficult moves. There may also have been a central pole that players were awarded points for bouncing the ball off and retaining control.

The strong similarities between kemari and zhu qiu enabled an international match between China and Japan in 611.

Meanwhile bai da went from strength to strength among the great unwashed of China. It retained the rough structure of original tsu' chu and drew huge crowds, along with commercialism and gambling. Players were lionised, idolised and demonised just as footballers are today. The lighter ball encouraged women to play and female teams were introduced—there was even a story of a teenage girl showing up a squad of soldiers with her skill, which probably went down really well.

Bai da clubs employing professional players were founded in the major cities and towns, each with distinctive uniforms and their own organised fan base. A league was formed and competitive games scheduled, very similar to the way football is organised today. The game took on a commercial aspect because the clubs had to pay their players. One stream of income was from 'apprentice' players—amateurs who wished to play for a club had to pay a professional to train them before being allowed to play.

Ming dynasty ladies playing bai da. *(Painting by Du jin, Ming Dynasty. Wikipedia. Public Domain.)*

The Tang dynasty came to its inevitable end and was replaced by Song emperors around a thousand years ago, and under them both codes rose to new and glorious heights. The ball was again improved and the norm became twelve pieces of hexangular shaped leather sewn together around an inflated pig's bladder, with a standardised weight of 600 gm (21 ounces)—don't forget, all this was over 700 years ago! The rounder standardised ball allowed better control and players could reach even greater skill levels, and the crowds went wild. Both male and female teams competed professionally under an over-arching body known as the 'Clouds High League', and crowds in the tens of thousands turned up to watch high profile games.

The sport became a national obsession.

Sound familiar?

The Mongols ousted the Song in 1279, and they, in turn, were overthrown by the Ming in 1368, and bai da began to lose its lustre. The new Ming emperor doesn't appear to have had any great love for the game and didn't encourage it, but it wasn't him that ended its glory days.

In 1331, just 60 years into the Mongol reign, bubonic plague struck northern China and killed around 90% of the population, not leaving enough people to work the land. Famine added to the misery of disease and football must have suffered a severe loss of both players and administrators, not to mention fans. This wasn't like earlier times when hardships were caused by war and oppression and a good, hard game could let off steam.

This time gathering in crowds could be fatal.

Banning bai da, may have been a public health measure, because games were one of very few, if not the only occasion when people congregated in huge, tightly packed crowds and they became, in modern parlance, super-spreader events. But it might also have had something to do with the corruption that had entered the game. Bai da became associated with the under-belly of society, and officials and workers were neglecting their work and wasting huge sums on gambling. It was even said that brothels sponsored teams of prostitutes to attract customers, although how much of that one was true and how much was invented by palace eunuchs and misogynistic imperial advisors, is questionable.

Across the sea the Japanese escaped the plague completely. The Mongols tried and failed to invade in 1274, and afterwards Japan was effectively cut off from the mainland and kemari went its own way. It lost its elite tag and spread to the general population, who played it enthusiastically throughout the country. Clubs and schools formed, players wore uniforms specific to them and the colour and pattern of their socks denoted their social status and skill level. During Japan's push for industrialisation in the 19th C its popularity began to fade as Japan adopted Western ideas, technology and sports. It remained popular with some of the elite and the nobles pushed the Emperor to establish the Kemari Hôzô Kai (Kemari Preservation Society) so the game would not be lost. Today it's only played ritualistically on special festival days.[8]

In China organised bai da officially ceased to exist publicly and, after two thousand years of almost continuous growth, popularity and imperial approval, bai da went into very rapid decline and, by modern times, was supposedly virtually extinct in China.

But I think it unlikely that something as universally popular with millions of people would simply disappear overnight. After all, it had survived more hardships and regime changes than it could poke a stick at. The extreme rigours imposed on late 19th and early 20th C China, followed by the introduction of new western sports, may have administered the last rites, but it's very likely that it was still being played at a grass roots level in China in the 19th C when Europeans, especially the English, infested the country.

I suspect, although it's impossible to prove, that the no-contact and no-hands rules were introduced at Cambridge by one of those Englishmen, or someone who had close association with one.

A prime candidate was Henry Charles Malden who attended Trinity College at Cambridge from 1847 until 1851. He was

8 US President George H W Bush caused great insult when, on an official visit, he intruded on a demonstration game of Kemari and began kicking and heading the ball. When ushered off the court he was heard to mutter 'we won'.

one of the movers at the 1848 meeting that set the Cambridge rules and, according to his daughter, always considered himself 'the father of soccer'. Henry never, as far as I'm aware, actually travelled himself, but his father, Charles Malden, was a navy man who'd travelled in the Pacific and could certainly have had contact with China and/or Japan, perhaps even encountering kemari among the Japanese migrants to Hawaii where he spent some time.

And Henry was close to his father, after his time at Trinity he went to work as a tutor at Windlesham House School where his father was headmaster. If Charles encountered and liked Oriental football, he would undoubtedly have passed it on to his son—most fathers play football with their sons.

Tsu' chu had survived and thrived in its homeland for millennia, but like many old families, it fell on hard times at home, so migrated to greener pastures where it thrived. Perhaps with the assistance of an English sailor named Charles Malden and his son Henry, it sailed to England and became great again.

And perhaps that same gentleman also imported the idea of a multi-panelled, standardised ball. At the start of this section I said that there were a couple of glaring inconsistencies in the development of soccer, coincidences that I find hard to swallow. The first is the no-hands rule, the second is the ball. What are the chances of a game and ball being invented, both of which bear remarkable similarities to an ancient game and ball on the other side of the world?

It's not as if Europeans never 'appropriated' anything.

Just saying…because I don't believe in coincidences.

Rugby

Initially there was just rugby as played at the Rugby Public School. It was a strange, violent—some might say barbaric—game, but one much loved by its adherents who, sometimes, hailed from remarkably far away. Rugby, it seems, was the school of choice for many colonials (and Americans) to send their sons for an education. The game spread rapidly throughout the British Empire and around the world, but in its original form it met with a mixed reception because of its violent nature, and it was clear that, if it was to gain universal acceptance, it needed to be modified.

There were several ideas on how this should be done and it rapidly divided into four—rugby union, rugby league, American football and Australian rules—all with a probable input of foreign genes (although most will deny it, it's like finding a convict in the family).

Rugby union was established and codified by Rugby School Old Boys in the Pall Mall Restaurant in London in 1871, but once out there it wasn't long before games that were more skilled at ball handling began to have an input to it. The first of these was very close to home—the Celtic games of Wales and Cornwall.

The Celtic Connection: Welsh Cnapan

The Welsh had a traditional ball game called *cnapan*. It was fast with an emphasis on ball handling, although the ball in this case was small, wooden, very hard and soaked or boiled in oil, fat, or some other slippery substance to make it difficult to handle[9]. Although it couldn't really be called football because the ball was probably never kicked, the skills involved were very close to those required for open, running rugby.

The playing field was vast and not defined, there was no out-of-bounds and 'goals' could be several kilometres apart. The object of the game was to try to get the ball so deep into your own shire, perhaps even into the foyer or porch of your own church, that the opposing team lost hope of retrieving it.

9 Collins, Tony; Martin, John; Vamplew, Wray (2005). Encyclopedia of traditional British rural sports. Sports reference. Abingdon, Oxfordshire: Routledge. pp. 66–67. ISBN 0-415-35224-X.

Despite their size—each team could be upward of a thousand men—teams seem to have been organised in a similar way to modern day rugby, or at least as organised as a mob that big could be. Each team had big, burly men who matched each other in rucks and smaller fast men that could move the ball swiftly once the big men secured it.

The majority of cnapan players were peasants and poor workers who played on foot, but the wealthy played on horseback. This would seem to negate the fairness of big man on big man and small man on small man, but there was a mechanism of control. Each team had groups waiting at hedgerows, bridges, streams, or some other narrow places they knew a rider must pass, and when he did they ambushed and unseated him. Mostly the horsemen just moved the focus of play to a new location and probably to a new set of players.

Cnapan seems to have had few discernible rules, short of outlawing outright murder, but one feature that stands out was a mechanism to stop the game becoming bogged down. If a ruck became too chaotic it was stopped with a cry of 'Heddwch!' (peace—the same as modern day calls of 'held' or 'down') and the ball was thrown in the air to restart the game. The same word could be used to temporarily halt the game if someone was seriously injured and had to be removed from the field.

The game is described as originating as a form of war training for the Ancient Britons. Given that there must have been tactics, leadership and organisation involved, this is entirely possible. But probably not Ancient Britons, but Romans. We'll get to them.

Late 20th C attempts to stage cnapan games between the Welsh parishes of Newport and Nevern were unsuccessful because, even with much smaller teams, rules and a referee, the organisers couldn't get insurance. But the ball handling skills it engendered were very transferable to rugby. Which explains why the Welsh workers and miners took to it so readily, were so successful and were able to inject those skills into the wider game and helped make it faster and more open.

Cornish hurling (hurlian)

There were two Cornish games, both called hurling (*hurlian* in Cornish) but very different to each other, as John Norden, a visitor to Cornwall, wrote in about 1584:

> *The Cornishmen they are stronge, hardye and nymble, so are their exercises violent, two especially, Wrastling and Hurling, sharpe and severe activities; and in neither of theis doh any Countrye exceede or equall them. The firste is violent, but the seconde is daungerous: The firste is acted in two sortes, by Holdster (as they called it) and by the C is very littleoller; the seconde likewise two ways, as Hurling to goales, and Hurling to the countrye.*

Hurling-to-country, was a game very similar to cnapan. The main differences that I can see are the games objective—hurlers tried to get the ball into a goal behind the opposition rather than keep it themselves—and the unique ball, traditionally hand-made from apple wood sheathed in silver. The size was not fixed, but it generally weighed in at about 600 grams with a circumference of about 23 cm. It was small, heavy, hard, and, as John Norden said, dangerous.

Games were started in the late afternoon by the ball being thrown into the crowd of players. Play began slowly as the ball was passed sedately around so that everyone could touch it, it was even given to spectators because handling the ball was considered lucky and promoted health and fertility. It was a breach of the game's etiquette to try and carry the ball away too early, before all the spectators who wished to hold it had done so. Even during play, if a player held the ball above his head it meant that he intended to give it to a spectator to hold and it was considered very bad manners to tackle him.

But once everyone had had an opportunity to hold the ball, the game exploded with violent skirmishes and scrummages as the teams tried for their respective goals, both located somewhere outside the town. The game was won when one team managed to put the ball into their respective goal, or, alternatively, carried it across any part of their Parish or Shire boundary. Once the ball reached a goal or boundary the game was over. The man who actually goaled was carried back to the Market Square on the shoulders of his team mates amid much cheering and the singing.

Then, of course, everyone retreated to the pub, where the ball was dropped into a jug of ale and all players got to drink their fill of 'Silver Ale'. The man who'd actually goaled got to keep the ball—provided he could afford the considerable cost of a new one for the next season.

The second Cornish game, **hurling-to-goals**, was markedly different from almost any other form of football around at the time—except for an Irish game called 'field caid'—but information on both is scant. Pretty much all of what we do know comes from 17th C Richard Carew. I'll quote his description here because it's important to rugby's history, but I've used modern spelling and a bit of interpretation because reading the original 1602 document is difficult.

> *Hurling takes its denomination from throwing of the ball, and is of two sorts, in the East parts of Cornwall, to goals, and in the West, to the country. For hurling to goals there are 15, 20 or 30 players, more or less, chosen out on each side, who strip into their slightest apparel, and then join hands in rank one against another. Out of these ranks they match themselves by pairs, one embracing another and every of which couple are specially to watch one another during the play.*
>
> *After this, they pitch two bushes in the ground, some eight or ten foot asunder, and directly against them, ten or twelve score off, other two in like distance, which they term their Goals. One of these is appointed by lots, to the one side, and the other to his adverse party. There is assigned for their guard, a couple of their best stopping Hurlers, the residue draw into the midst between both goals, where some indifferent person throws up a ball, the*

which whosoever can catch and carry through his adversaries goal, hath won the game. But therein consisted one of Hercules labours, for he that is once possessed of the ball, has his contrary mate waiting at inches, and assaying to lay hold upon him. The other thrusts him in the breast with his closed fist to keep him off; which they call 'Butting' and place no small point of manhood in doing it well.

If he escape the first, another taketh him in hand, and so a third, neither is he left until having met (as the Frenchman says) 'Chausseur a son pied' [this literally means 'hunter at his foot' I think it meant tackler, but your guess is as good as mine], *he either touches the ground with some part of his body and begins wrestling, or cries 'Hold', which is the word of yielding. Then he casts the ball (Deals it) to one of his fellows, who catching the same in his hand, makes away with it as before, and if his agility be good enough to shake off or outrun his counter-weighters, at the goal he finds one or two fresh men ready to receive and keep him off. It is therefore a very disadaantageable* [indecipherable, but probably means unequal] *match, or extraordinary accident, that sees many goals; however that side which gives most falls in the hurling, keeps the ball longest, and presses his contrary nearest to their own goal carries away the best reputation. Some-times one chosen person on each party deals the ball.*

The Hurlers are bound to the observation of many laws, as, that they must hurle man to man, and not two set upon one man at once; that the Hurler against the ball, must not but, nor hand-fast under girdle: that he who hath the ball, must but only in the others breast: that he must deal no Fore-ball, viz. he may not throw it to any of his mates standing nearer the goal, than himself. Lastly, in dealing the ball, if any of the other part can catch it flying between, or before the other have it fast, he thereby wins the same to his side, which straightway of defendant becomes assailant, as the other, of assailant falls to be defendant. The least breach of these laws, the Hurlers take for a just cause of going together by pairs, but with their fists only.

Neither does any among them seek revenge for such wrongs or hurts, but at the like play again. Therefore hurling matches are mostly used at weddings, where commonly the guests undertake to encounter all comers.[10]

The similarities to modern rugby are obvious. It was played by two equally matched but comparatively small teams on a defined field with a goal at each end, each team's goal being *appointed by lots* (by the 'flip of a coin'). Players had set positions and were matched against each other; big man against big man, fast against fast, and specifically a couple of good *'stopping hurlers'* (full backs? goal keepers?).

The *'and then join hands in rank one against another'* bit is interesting. If that also applied to the Irish game it would explain the very odd early 20th C Gaelic football rule that said that when the ball is thrown in, players must stand in parallel ranks in the middle of the field and hold hands. This has echoes in the modern rugby lineout where players don't actually hold hands, but they do space themselves to arms-length.

There must have been some sort of umpiring system because players were *'bound to the observation of many laws'*. The aim was to get a ball across a line between goal posts (bushes) behind the opposition, and in getting it there the attacker was permitted to 'but' or punch in the chest (fend), but the defender was prohibited from 'butting', or from *'hand-fast under girdle',* which probably meant he couldn't hit or grab his opponent below the belt (now known as 'squirreling'—going for the 'nuts'—in some codes). Violation of the rules gave the opposition the right to punch the offender. Brawls must have abounded!

The prohibition on forward passing is particularly significant. *'That the hurler must deal no foreball, or throw it to any partner standing nearer the goal than himself'*

10 Richard Carew of Antonie Esq. The Survey of Cornwall and An Epistle concerning the excellence of the English tongue. Printed for B. Law» in Ave-Mary-Lane ; and J. Hawatt, at Pensnce, London,1602. Pp.75

This rule did not apply to any other game of its day (that I know of), but somehow it's come down to be a major aspect of modern day rugby.

Interestingly, unlike all the other forms of medieval football, hurling-to-goals seems to have completely disappeared in the latter half of the 17th C. But for it to have influenced modern rugby, it must have persisted in some form. Either that, or the 'no forward pass' rule, along with a number of other aspects of the game, were reinvented quite independently in the 19th C.

Or perhaps some scholar with an interest in football discovered Carew's work and thought 'this looks good, let's revive it.'

But I think the most likely explanation is that the game continued to be played locally in Cornwall and Ireland in a very quiet way, perhaps only in one or two villages or towns, until a player found himself at some school, perhaps Rugby, introduced it to his fellows and it caught on.

That's just a theory, I doubt we'll ever know for sure.

Cornish hurling achieved some national attention in 1654 when Oliver Cromwell, Lord Protector and winner of the English civil war, and his Privy Council watched a game between fifty Cornishmen and fifty others in Hyde Park, London. It seems odd that it was being played in London, but perhaps it was, what we would now call, a 'demonstration match' put on for Cromwell's benefit. It's not recorded whether it was hurling-to-country or hurling-to-goals, but by Cromwell's time hurling-to-country was, apart from the silver ball, essentially the same as other forms of mob football common in England, so it would have lacked the novelty value necessary for a demonstration match worthy of the Lord Protector.

Also, hurling-to-country does not lend itself to spectators because it's a moving feast. To follow it a spectator would need to be continuously on the move, and even then would likely miss most of the action. But hurling-to-goals was played on a defined field where a spectator could watch the entire game without needing to move.

On balance, I think it was more likely to have been a game of hurling-to-goals, or perhaps a hybrid of hurling-to-goals played by the Cornishmen and the mob football played by the 'others'.

It is recorded that Cromwell and his attendants thoroughly enjoyed it, which runs somewhat contrary to all we've been taught because, as a Puritan, Cromwell was not supposed to enjoy anything, especially sports. Then again, at university he was reputed to have been very good at football.

So why, if the game achieved recognition at the highest echelons of power, did it seem to disappear? Was it simply overwhelmed by the English forms of mob football which were more dominant at the time, or was there another explanation?

Sadly, I suspect that the answer lay in the politics of the time.

Mid-17th C England was in the grip of civil war. Oliver Cromwell and Parliament had revolted against the autocratic rule of King Charles I and, like in civil wars everywhere, regions, villages, and even families were divided. In Cornwall the bulk of the county declared for the King, only in the NE, along the border with Devon and in the border cities of Plymouth and Stratton did they fight for Cromwell's Parliamentarians. Plymouth, in particular, resisted repeated sieges by Royalist forces throughout the wars.

Carew tells us that hurling-to-goals was played in the east part of Cornwall, the very part that was loyal to Cromwell, so I think it likely that after the war men from that part of the county were permitted—as a favour and reward for their loyalty, or as part of the victory celebrations—to put on a display of their unique game for the great man.

In other parts of Cornwall, those places that supported the King, hurling-to-country seems to have been the dominant sport. When Parliamentary forces passed through the southern Cornish town of Penryn after putting down a Royalist uprising, they displayed three silver hurling balls stuck on the ends of swords. This was done no doubt to taunt the locals and it probably meant that hurling-to-country was officially frowned upon.

It seems that a Cornishman's political allegiance could be inferred by the code of football he played.

As an aside from this—I have found no mention of the style of ball used in hurling-to-goals, but if Cromwell's troops used the silver balls to taunt the Western Cornish it would make sense that silver balls were not used in hurling-to-goals. And the style of play would have lent itself more to a larger, more pliable ball, possibly one made from leather stuffed with either some soft substance or an inflated pig's bladder.

But going back to the question; why did hurling-to goals-disappear?

Cromwell died in 1658 and was succeeded by his son Richard, who was not a success and was forced to resign in 1659. The Monarchy was restored under Charles II a year later and in January 1661 Cromwell's body, along with those of his chief aides, was taken out of Westminster Abbey, put on trial for high treason, hung in chains from Tyburn gallows before being beheaded, their heads put on high stakes at Westminster Hall and their bodies thrown into a common grave. The heads remained displayed on stakes for 24 years, until a storm dislodged them.

Now, that is what I call vindictive!

By contrast, after Cromwell had Charles 1st's head cut off, he allowed it to be sewn back on, just so his family could grieve properly and… actually I'll talk about the British executioner and his place (or not) in football's evolution later.

Given that the two forms of Hurling seemed to have become politicised, it is quite probable that the one that had been played by Cromwell's supporters fell into serious disfavour and was suppressed by the Royalists, never to be heard of again, while other versions of the game gained Charles II's royal approval and playing them was officially approved. Especially on Sunday afternoons after church. Which was probably a snub to Cromwell's Puritanical disapproval of such levity on the Sabbath.

As in Wales, when modern rugby was introduced to Cornwall in the late 19th C it was taken up with enthusiasm by the working classes, especially the miners, and never became an elite sport as it was in England and Scotland. It went on to become the County's most popular, and most successful, sport. Cornwall even represented Great Britain at the 1908 Olympics, and they can probably put their success down to the traditions and skills they gained from hurling.

The Welsh and Cornish had an early and significant influence on rugby, but it was the Maori of Aotearoa-NZ that really opened up the game.

The South Seas

As far as I can tell only one pre-European ball sport evolved in the vastness of the great Pacific Ocean, the game of *kí-o-rahi*, and the Maori in Aotearoa-NZ were the only people in the Pacific who played it, which, if true, would place kí-o-rahi's origins precisely in time and place—after the first Maori migration to Aotearoa-NZ eight or nine hundred years ago.

But it's quite possible that they brought the sport with them from Tahiti and the Cook Islands and it subsequently died out and was forgotten there. Missionaries were very quick to intercept traditions and erase anything that they saw as sinful, which were most things non-European, or fun, including ball games.

They were very good at it. South America is a prime example where a major sport, one with organised leagues, fan clubs and royal patronage (of course we'll get to that later), was supressed to the point that it all but disappeared. In the Pacific their job was probably much easier in comparatively small islands where almost everyone was within reach, but Aotearoa-NZ was an exception. It's much larger than any of the other Polynesian islands and, in many parts, very rugged and inaccessible. A sport could survive hidden among its bush-clad hills and valleys.

If the origins and evolution of kí-o-rahi are shrouded, its later development is not. After years of anonymity it emerged from the remote '*marae*' (the Maori equivalent of the village green) in the mid-20th C and, after a slow start, is rising rapidly in popularity. Unlike the Celtic games, there are no records of how it used to be played, so we don't know how true the modern version is to the original, but it clearly incorporated all the ball handling, running and evasion skills present in modern rugby—even though, like Welsh cnapane and Cornish hurling, it's not football in the true sense of the word.

In the modern version teams of seven players compete against each other on a circular field to touch a small round ball to posts set at intervals around the perimeter, or hit the ball against a larger central post. Each player wears two ribbons, one on either side of their hip, and must relinquish the ball if one of the ribbons is pulled off. The size of the field and specific rules vary and are agreed on between the teams before the game starts.

It's fast, non-contact (although one version, *nonoke,* permits tackling) and in many respects resembles touch football. The sport is being promoted internationally and in 2010 men's and women's teams went on a demonstration tour of Europe. It was nominated as one of fifteen ethnic sports to be part of a 'Passport to Play' program aimed at getting America's school children more physically active. Oddly, that program is run by a fast food chain noted for fattening children.

There are claims that 19th C English colonists saw the game, took particular notice of ball handling skills that were notably lacking in their own game, and took them back to England to be included in the emerging game of rugby. I think a more likely scenario was that warriors fighting alongside the English in the Aotearoa-NZ land wars saw their allies playing rugby and used their ki-o-rahi skills to thrash them at their own game.

Then the Maori took those skills on an 1888 tour to England and, with the help of the unique Polynesian build, thrashed the English (tellingly, not the Welsh) at their own game, on their own soil. Non-Maori New Zealanders were quick to adopt the skills, and the game was changed forever.

Rugby League

Rugby league inherited all the genetic makeup of union, but added a healthy input from the working men from the north of England, pretty much the same people who had such an important input into soccer. It was them, with their new interpretations of old rules and the introductions of new ones, that made league the unique game that it is today. But we went into all that back in part one, so we'll just leave it at that.

North American Football

At first glance North American football looks so different from rugby that you'd think it had completely different parents, but on closer inspection they're not too far removed. The American game's paternity is, however, very murky. Originally the Americans played a variety of games in their schools and universities, then, in 1874 a match was played between Canadian McGill University's rugby style and America's Harvard University's soccer. The rugby style won general acclaim and became the dominant code, but its violence was not particularly to the liking of the wider American public.

Enter Walter Camp, the undisputed father of American football. Just like soccer's Ebenezer Morley, Walter had been on the wrong end of some fairly rough play on the rugby field, and he didn't like it so he set out to formulate a less violent code. He, and then others after him, tinkered with rugby over the next several decades until they had something not necessarily less violent, but uniquely American. Canadian football developed in parallel to the point where, to the casual observer, there is little difference between the two.

But, once again we've been there, it's the other possible fathers I'm interested in. The first (or the last, depending how you look at it) was an Italian game called *calcio.*

Italian Calcio

Between about 1880 and 1924, exactly coinciding with gridiron's formative years, more than four million Italians migrated to the US, a significant input to a population of around 75 million. And it would be surprising if they didn't bring their sport, calcio with them.

Originally named *giuoco del calcio fiorentino*, or Florentine kick game after the place where it was supposedly invented, it came to be called simply *calcio,* or 'football'. The first recorded match was played on the frozen Arno River in Florence in 1490, but just because it was first recorded then doesn't mean that that's when it began, it was probably played in the slums for centuries before it emerged onto the river during an exceptionally cold winter and came to the attention of the more affluent.

Initially there was an unlimited number of players allowed on the field and the only rules seem to have been that weapons could not be brought onto the field, and the ball could only be passed or kicked, not thrown. It was played on a field about the same size and shape as a modern football ground, and the object was to get the ball across a line, called the *caccia*, behind the opponents. Any and every means was permitted to achieve this, even punching below the belt and all in brawls.

The game began by the ball being placed in the middle of the field and kicked off by the team that won the toss, after which the forwards surged together and began an all-in brawl to soften up the opposition. Over time, to minimise the damage, it was made illegal for more than one man to attack another. When enough of the opposition forward pack was out of action the backs got involved and could use any part of their body to propel the ball through or around the opposition. A goal net was later introduced on the *caccia* and a point was scored when the ball hit the net, but if it went over the net the opposition was awarded half a point. Teams changed ends after every point was scored.

Serious injuries and deaths were common. And, just to liven it up a little, sometimes a bull was introduced onto the field, or at least that's what some sources say. Can't say I'm convinced.

In the 16th C the powerful Medici family became interested in the sport and began sponsoring it. As a result it became the preserve of the upper classes and was played by students and other young members of the nobility. Undoubtedly the unwashed masses continued playing in the back-streets, but, as usual, they went unrecorded as the rich enjoyed themselves by inventing versions to suit themselves. One example of their inventiveness was a version called *calcio storico*, which was played between epiphany (January 6th) and lent (mid-February) each year. Players would take to the field in the Piazza della Novere or the Piazza Santa Croce dressed in their finest and richest clothes and groomed to the max, ready to put on a show of upper-class physicality.

The game spread beyond Florence and there are records of the rich and famous, including future Popes, playing it in the Vatican. In 1544, a game was played in the French court at Fontainebleau, just south of Paris, between 30 French aristocrats led by no less than the Dauphin (heir to the French throne) against 30 Italians led by the Duke of Orleans. At the time there were a large number of Italians, mostly Florentines, at the French court and they were obviously keen to show off their game. And this was a special match indeed, attended by some of the richest and most influential people in Europe.

As it progressed, rules were introduced to limit injuries, although official control remained minimal and violence was a common factor. Player (*calcianti*) numbers were limited to 27 aside and games to 50 minutes. Teams were organised into fixed positions; four goalkeepers (*datori indietro*), three fullbacks (*datori innanzi*), five halfbacks (*sconciatori*) and fifteen forwards (*corridori*). Team captains took no active part in the game, but instead organised and controlled their teams from the sidelines. Although some sources say there was a referee and linesmen a code of honour seems to have been the controlling factor, but just in case pikemen were stationed around the ground ready to intervene.

Calcio became entrenched in Florentine culture in 1530 when the city was under siege by Spanish troops of the Holy Roman Emperor after Florentine republicans rebelled against the Medici family. The Pope at that time (Clement VII) was a Medici and he was able to turn to the Emperor for help. Although the Florentines were outnumbered, outgunned, starving and staring at certain defeat, they remained defiant and to demonstrate their defiance they organised a game of Calcio—just to taunt their enemies. The game was played in plain view of enemy troops stationed on the hills surrounding the city, who were so incensed by the demonstration of defiance they lobbed a cannon ball into the middle of it. No one was hurt.

Apart from a brief psychological victory, the game didn't do the Florentines any good and they were forced to surrender soon after, but the gesture left such a mark on the city's tradition that it was replayed every year for some time after.

The Republic didn't last, but calcio was a winner.

Twenty five years later the city of Sienna used the same tactic, this time against a besieging Florentine army. Like their enemies a quarter of a century earlier, the good people of Sienna were starved and facing certain defeat, so they organised a game of football. They played in the town's main square, in full view of the besieging troops.

It didn't do them any good either, they surrendered soon after.

By 1606 it had become such a strong institution in Florence that a law was passed to the effect that any bystander who interrupted an official game would be flogged—this at a time when lawmakers in the rest of Europe were doing their utmost to wipe out similar games. The passing of such a law demonstrates the sport's links to the powerful ruling class, but that was to be its downfall. It was so closely tied to the Medici family that when the last Grand Duke of the Medici died in 1737 the aristocratic version of the game pretty much died with him. The last official match was played just two years later, in 1739.

That a game could die so quickly strongly suggests that it was not, at least in the end, a game of the people. If it had been, the death of one aristocrat would not have had such an impact, or, probably, none at all. But it's likely that it was only the official game that died and the general mob kept playing their own version. And it wasn't only played in Florence, as the good people of Sienna showed.

The game was officially revived in 1930 to celebrate the 400th anniversary of the siege of Florence and, after a spluttering rebeginning, it's still played in a somewhat sanitised form, mostly for tourists.

Some of the Italians who migrated to America would certainly have brought calcio with them, but just how much it influenced American football is an unknowable, but certain similarities

A 1688 game of Calcio Florentino. *(Artist unknown. Wikipedia. Public Domain.)*

between the two suggest that it did slip a few genes into the new-world game.

The other game that I think had an influence on American football's development, one that was always in the background, was Native American Pasuckuakohowog.

Pasuckuakohowog

In pre-colonial North America, north of about Arizona and south of the arctic tree-line, tribes were playing a game called *pasuckuakohowog*, which roughly translates to 'they gather to play ball with the foot'. It was a chaotic game with up to a thousand players at a time on an open, rectangular field about 1.5 x 1.25 km (roughly 1 x ¾ mile).

The object of the game was to kick, carry or throw a ball made of leather stuffed with grass or straw across a goal line drawn behind the opposition. Almost nothing seems to be known about the rules for getting it over that line, perhaps because there weren't any to speak of. If there were the early colonists had adequate opportunity to record them because they often observed the game being played and, by all accounts, were fascinated by it. Sometimes they even joined in.

Actually, it probably wasn't too far removed from the mob football they'd experienced at home.

Just thirteen years after the English colony at Jamestown, Virginia, was established in 1620, the colonists played pasuckuakohowog on a beach with, apparently, one thousand members of the local Powhatan tribe. There weren't that many colonists at the time so that game was either mixed teams or very one sided.

Most illustrations show players holding a stick or club, so it seems that sticks or weapons were permitted, and there is general agreement that pasuckuakohowog-related injuries were common. In fact it was so violent that players disguised themselves with heavy paint to avoid accountability and later reprisals. Games went on for an indeterminate time—all day or over more than one day, depending on the occasion, and generally it was played as part of a festival. Or maybe it was the game that was the occasion for the festival, and it was a case of play hard all day and party hard all night.

Whichever way it was—a part of a larger festival or just a festival of football—it had a serious side. It was alternatively known as 'The Little War' and was used as a means of settling intertribal disputes without resorting to costly wars. A few injuries on the football field, even a couple of deaths, were nothing compared to the dozens or hundreds that would die in a war, not to mention all the accompanying misery, damage and loss of resources. And if a game was accompanied by a good party and a fair amount of genetic exchange, all the better.

The fact that the colonists were able to so readily join in what should have been a foreign game raises the question—could the English have brought the game with them?

Probably not. By the time of colonisation pasuckuakohowog had a firm place in Native American culture and its use as a substitute for war is very unlikely to have developed so quickly.

But there is another possibility, entirely hypothetical and which can never be proven one way or the other, which would explain why the English and American games were so similar.

It may have been introduced by earlier European colonists—Vikings.

That the Vikings, colonised North America in the 10th C is now undisputed and a Norse settlement is now a UNESCO world heritage site at L'Anse aux Meadows in Newfoundland, Canada. But the Norse name for America was 'Vinland', or 'vine land', and Newfoundland is way too far north for vines to grow. So the latest thinking is that they must have at least sailed far enough south to encounter enough vines for them to name the place for them. This would have put them in the general vicinity of where the English encountered pasuckuakohowog between 4–500 years later, more than enough time for the game to become entrenched, but not long enough for it to have diverged too much from its roots.

And the Vikings were pretty ardent football players—we'll get to them later, too.

I can find no reference to any traditional football games on the west coast of America, which may lend weight to pasuckuakohowog being introduced into the west, but whatever its origins native American football must have got some of its genes into the mainstream American game when the colonists began playing it way back. Just how much remained by the time Walter Camp got his hands on it is debatable, but what isn't in doubt are the skills that the native kids from the Indian Schools injected during their short association with the game. They were also, probably, responsible for the short-lived use of war paint in gridiron.

South of about Arizona there was an entirely different ball game being played, one with proven roots in Central and South America many thousands of years ago. Although it was definitely not football as we know it, it's often mistaken for one of football's ancestors. It did, however, make one significant contribution to the modern game that can't be ignored—rubber. It's also a prime example of the power of the missionaries to destroy cultures and games.

Southern ōllamaliztli

Ōllamaliztli fits into football's family tree like the weird old uncle that everyone seems to have, no one's quite sure if he's really related, but you were warned to stay away from him anyway. Ōllamaliztli was different, and almost as ancient as Emperor Huang di and tsu' chu.

Highly organised and formalised, ōllamaliztli (or *tlachtli,* or *pitz*—depending where you came from, or, if you were a 16th C Spanish Conquistador, it was *juego de prlota Maya* — 'the Mayan ball game') was a game for the Mayans, Aztecs, Incas, and all the other civilisations that lived in Central and Southern America.

We know about the game mostly from the Spanish, who seemed to have been both fascinated and appalled in equal measure. They left written descriptions of play, but, so far, no one's found any actual rules. Lots of images and even some ceramic dolls of players have survived which give the impression that the

Image of a ōllamaliztli player from the Tepantitla murals.
(Photo by Da Quella Mantera Futbol, cropped and enhanced by Daniel Lobo, Sept 2006, Wikipedia.)

ancient game was very like the modern Mexican game of *ulama,* where the players try to hit a heavy ball backwards and forwards between teams, using only their hips or, in some versions, their forearms or legs. Broadly, the rules of ulama are that there's two opposing teams of two to four people who hit a 4–5 kg (about 9–11 lb) rubber ball to each other across a centre line, without it hitting the ground. Points are gained when the opposition either fails to return it, hits it out, or for hitting the opposition's end wall.

There may not be any ancient records of the game, but there is a lot of archaeology associated with it, especially the elaborate enclosed stone courts where it was played. These have survived in their hundreds across the region—at the last count there are about 1,500 of them, the oldest at Paso de la Amada on the Pacific coast is about 3,500 years old. The courts vary considerably in size, from 96.5 x 30 m. down to 16 x 5 m. (316' x 98' down to 52' x 16'), but they maintain the same basic proportions. The older ones are open ended with vertical or sloping walls on either side, newer ones have one end enclosed by an extended wall to form a 'T' shape and in some cases both ends are enclosed to form an 'I' shape.

Ōllamaliztli court in El Salvador. *(Wikipedia)*

By the time the Spanish arrived stone rings had been added to the sides of the courts for players to put the ball through. That must have been immensely difficult to do, because successfully threading a ring won the game outright, but points were deducted for a failed attempt. Successfully ringing the ball was probably rare because the rings were set high, so attempting to put the ball through them was reserved for teams hopelessly behind and trying to snatch an unlikely victory.

Players used hard, solid rubber balls (rubber is an early Meso-American invention), some of which have been found preserved in bogs and dated to nearly 4,000 years old. But rubber was not the only thing the balls were made of, early Spanish records say that on occasion the game was played with a stone ball or a sack of stones.

It was a hard game.

It was also fast and, according to the 16th C Spanish, brutal—and if the Spanish Conquistadors thought something was brutal, it must have been truly harsh! Leather, wicker or wooden girdles were worn, sometimes together with a chest protector to give some protection to the players from the worst of the impacts but, as one Spaniard wrote, bruises could still be so bad that they had to be lanced and sometimes men died from being hit in the head or stomach.

Mind you, players, especially team captains, sometimes died from winning, too.

Quite late in the game's development it appears to have become associated with human sacrifice. When games were played as a part of special festivals it seems that it was the actual players, probably the losing side but sometimes the winning one, and possibly just the winning captain, who was sacrificed at the conclusion of the match. It doesn't sound like much of an incentive to win, but different times, different values. Perhaps it was a direct line to a seat with the gods.

Whatever the truth of the 'player sacrifice' scenario, human heads feature fairly strongly in pictures of games, enough for some historians to suggest that on some occasions the game was actually played with them. On the positive side, like pasuckuakohowog, the game was used as a substitute for war and as a method of ritually settling disputes without resorting to bloody and expensive battles. Perhaps the sacrifices were token bloodshed to keep the war gods on side.

In its day it was as popular as any modern sport, so much so that teams had sponsors and an organised competition was played in front of vast crowds who were kept fed on venison snacks and lubricated with corn beer.

Football, pies (or hotdogs) and beer—sound familiar?

The Spanish observed that there was universal and heavy gambling on games. Everyone, from peasants to kings, laid bets that could cost them anything from a bit of property to their wives and children, themselves as slaves, or even their lives. And it wasn't inconceivable that affairs of state were decided on a ball game.

The arrival of the Spanish signalled the beginning of the end for ōllamaliztli. They brought new weapons, armaments and ways of waging war that were totally unfamiliar to the old civilisations, and new diseases so reduced the populations that they were unable to fight back effectively. But it wasn't the violence or disease that rang the death knell for ōllamaliztli, it was religion. The Spanish priests saw the game as pagan and tried to have it outlawed. After initially being fascinated with it, and even taking players to the Spanish court to show off their skills, the Conquistadors eventually agreed to the churches demands, the priests had their way and the game all but died out, leaving only a shadow in the form of ulama.

And, perhaps, modern volley ball.

But it did leave a great contribution to modern football—rubber—without which the modern football could not have been made and none of the current codes could have evolved to the point they have.

Australian Rules Football

Australian rules is the game that's moved furthest away from its rugby roots. Despite their grounding in rugby, its originators made every effort to make it as different as possible and denigrated rugby at every opportunity. As far as Tom Wills was concerned, was odd because he had excelled at rugby.

I think it's generally accepted that Tom Wills was the midwife for Australian football, but as far as its genetics are concerned it's pretty obvious that Irish caid, of one sort or another, had a major input. But that wasn't all one way, Gaelic football also has a large pool of Australian genes, so I guess you could say there was a lot of cross fertilisation going on.

But there was another father, one that's become the elephant-in-the-room when the origins of Australian rules is discussed.

The Australian Indigenous game, *marn grook*.

Marn grook

In the mid-19th C explorers and settlers in the Australian colony of Victoria witnessed Australian Aboriginals playing a ball game called *marn grook*, and about the same time (1855) William Anderson Cawthorne made images of an indigenous ball, referred to in Kaurna language as Pando. I'm sure it was neither realised nor appreciated by the Europeans at the time, but they were witnessing what may have been the world's oldest unadulterated form of football (stone-aged balls excepted, of course).

The game was traditionally played on a field of indeterminate size by two teams of varying numbers using a ball made of possum skin (or in one account, a big kangaroo's scrotum) stuffed with scraps of old skins or flexible bulrush roots. There were no goals, nor any identifiable points system, nor, apparently, any rules. The object of the game was to keep the ball in the air and away from the other team by passing or kicking it to other members of your own team. Players competed to see who could kick it higher and who could leap the highest above his (or her) compatriots to catch it.

Great care was taken in selecting teams, which were normally divided according to moieties—an ancient and very complex social division designed primarily to prevent incestuous marriage—and skin groups, which are sub-divisions of moieties. Once players were selected, teams were further refined to ensure they were balanced in number and gender, and that each was as diverse in body shape and ability as possible. Then play began in earnest. One description said that the game was begun by a woman kicking the ball high in the air followed by a general free-for-all to catch it and kick it again. Games could go on all day, or perhaps for days on end, and were the occasion for great merriment, showing off and boasting, then the night time was given over to feasting. At the end the winner was decided by general consensus between the teams, but it seems that winning or losing was of limited importance—it was the game that counted.

In 1878 William Thomas, Protector of Aborigines (a government official charged with controlling, rather than protecting) describes a game of marn grook he witnessed while performing his duties.

> *The men and boys joyfully assemble when this game is to be played. One makes a ball of possum skin, somewhat elastic, but firm and strong. ...The players of this game do not throw the ball as a white man might do, but drops it and at the same time kicks it with his foot, using the instep for that purpose. ...The tallest men have the best chances in this game. ...Some of them will leap as high as five feet from the ground to catch the ball. The person who secures the ball kicks it. ...This continues for hours and the natives never seem to tire of the exercise.*[11]

Sounds very much like a prototype for Australian rules.

This was the game that a young Tom Wills grew up playing with the indigenous kids at his father's property in Western Victoria. And he didn't just play football with them, he learned their language and became so familiar with their dances that the locals complimented him on it. He became immersed in the local indigenous culture; if he didn't he would have had a very lonely and deprived childhood because there were no other kids around. If he hadn't learned his social skills with the tribe, he probably wouldn't have been able to function anywhere near as well when he was sent off to an English boarding school.

It's quite possible that Tom adopted more than marn grook's style of play, he may have included a couple of its terms in his new game. For example 'mumarkee' awarded when the ball is caught from a kick (a mark), and 'barek' or 'barak' for cheering for a particular player or team (barracking). Tom never acknowledged

11 Robert Brough-Smyth, *The Aborigines of Victoria*. 1887, p176

the games Indigenous roots, probably because to do so in the late 19th C would have killed the new sport stone dead.

Even today the Australian Football League (AFL) remain reluctant to discuss their game's indigenous roots. And it could get even more interesting, because the origins of marn grook itself may not be as ancient as thought.

It's impossible to trace marn grook's history through the ages because Aboriginal society was one without writing and where time can be a slippery concept. Knowledge was passed orally from generation to generation and skills, including football, were passed down physically. Different styles were played across the vastness of the Australian continent as clans as tribes adapted it to suit their own circumstances. But the substance, the basics, remained the same over distance and time.

Conventional wisdom tells us that Australians had been isolated from the rest of the world since the seas rose about 10,000 years ago, therefore we can say with a reasonable degree of confidence that marn grook developed wholly in Australia as an indigenous game.

Conventional wisdom can, however, be a fickle thing, and in this case it's wrong. Northern Australia has been in almost constant contact with the outside world for at least the last 1,000 years, probably much longer. That contact was particularly intensive over the last few hundred years when fishermen (and others) came to the coasts of the Northern Territory and Western Australia in their thousands, and the coastal people took ship with them and travelled far and wide.[12]

Quite early on Chinese zhu qiu moved into SE Asia, where it adopted a hard ball made of woven rattan 15–20 cm in diameter, and changed its name to **sepak takraw**.

Modern sepak takraw is a fascinating, very energetic and very highly skilled sport that's played fanatically from Vietnam in the north to Indonesia in the south, from the Philippines in the east to Myanmar in the west. The game resembles volley ball where two teams of two or four players compete to get a rattan ball across a

12 Dobson, G. Under the Banyan Tree. Boolarong Press; 2021

high net, usually by kicking but any part of the body except hands can be used. The object is to volley the ball back and forth within the court without allowing it to touch the ground.

In its original form, sepak takraw did not have a scoring system, the object was simply to pass the ball backward and forward while keeping it in the air. The winner, if there was one, was decided on style, technique and adherence to etiquette—just like zhu qiu and kemari.

The earliest positive reference to sepak takraw is from the 15th C city of Malacca, on the Malay Peninsula, when it was recorded that someone was executed for accidentally hitting the Sultan's son with a sepak takraw ball and knocking his hat off. The sport's official website, however, says that it was played in the Philippines, Brunei, Myanmar, Indonesia and Laos as early as the 11th C. There's no actual proof of this that I can find, but it's quite probable because at that time a huge and very powerful Sumatran maritime kingdom, called Srivijaya, dominated the region. The Srivijayans had very close ties with first Tang, then Song China and was frequented by Chinese merchants, diplomats and adventurers at the very time when zhu qiu was at its most popular. It was inevitable that the game came with them.

From there it went to the kingdom of Bone on the island of Sulawesi in Eastern Indonesia, where the Buginese, the pre-eminent sailing and trading people of the region, adopted it enthusiastically, called it *sepak raja* (or *pa'raga, ma'raga or a'raga*), and took it to the remotest parts of the Indonesian and Philippine Archipelagos.

And, probably, to Northern Australia. It would be surprising if they didn't because Arnhem Land and NW Australia were a big part of the Buginese trade network. The 'Makassan' fishermen who were active in Northern Australia in their hundreds, if not thousands, during the 18th and 19th Cs, were mostly Buginese. They got called 'Makassan' because Makassar City was the only port where their Dutch overlords would allow them to trade with their customers, the Chinese, so they based their fleets there and became known by their port, not their ethnicity.

The Makassans had close relationships with the Australian coastal tribes and the Australians travelled extensively with them to SE Asian cities and beyond. They also adopted many of their customs, vocabulary and games, but sepak takraw appears to have left no trace in Australia.

Or did it?

There's not such a big step between non-competitive keeping a rattan ball in the air by kicking to non-competitive keeping a possum-skin ball in the air by kicking, and it would be a very natural progression for a decorous game to become a boisterous high-kicking affair in the hands of a comparatively unconstrained and exuberant people. Something that much fun would have travelled across the continent like wildfire via intertribal trade and corrobboree.

And if the settlers or missionaries saw it being played, most would have thought (if they thought anything of it at all) 'look at the Blackfellas, trying to copy our football'. They may even have thought that they'd picked it up by watching games of rugby in Sydney.

There's no way of proving this one way or the other, but it's entirely possible that Australian Rules football has strong roots in China or Japan.

Chapter 10
THE GRANDPARENTS

Medieval Mob Football

If the mother of modern football was the English public school system, then its grandfather had to be Medieval Mob Football.

Starting way back in the centuries after the Romans left Britain, the Scots, Irish, English, Welsh, Cornish and Southern French all began to develop their very own versions of football, collectively known as Medieval Mob Football.

Only a couple of snippets that even vaguely mention these games at their very beginnings have survived. One is by a 9th C Welsh monk called Nennius who wrote in his '*Historia Brittonum*':

> *'the field of Ælecti, in the district of Glevesing, where a party of boys were playing at ball'*

This quote was, apparently, borrowed from a 5th C source, but what exactly is meant by '*playing at ball*' is not clear. After Nennius there is no mention (that I can find) of football for several centuries. This is probably due to two major factors. Firstly; very few people could write, and those that could were fully occupied with higher things. Secondly; it was a time of major social upheaval. Everywhere whole peoples were on the move in the wake of Rome's collapse. In England the land was first invaded and settled by waves of Anglo-Saxons, then raided by Norse Vikings and settled by Norwegians and Danes, and finally by French Normans.

Medieval Europe was not a gentle place, not a nice place to live, and those that lived there seldom did so for very long because life for the average person was generally short, harsh and brutal. But as long as they occupied their mortal coils, people played football—unruly affairs that reflected the brutality of the times and societies. It was nowhere near the organised, almost genteel games of the future, nor was it always, strictly speaking, football because in many cases no ball was ever kicked.

The balls in question varied in size from about the size of a human head or bigger—sometimes it may have actually been a human head—down to that of a large apple. Almost universally amongst the many versions that sprang up—the aim of the game was to get a ball of some description across a line or into a goal which was, as often as not, a neighbouring village's church.

And that was pretty much all there was—a simple, violent game of mass participation. Virtually no rules, except that murder or manslaughter were officially frowned upon, no limit to team size and no control. Just carrying, kicking, passing, throwing and running. And fighting. There was a lot of fighting.

Each region, sometimes each town or village, had their own version. Often a few kilometres travel would be enough to find a whole new game, which won't come as much of a surprise to anyone who has travelled the byways of the English country-side and been baffled by the shift in accents, sometimes almost what seems like a shift in language, over very short distances.

In the early years there seems to have been a distinct division in football styles between Celtic and the Anglo Saxon regions that suggests different origins, although we don't really know enough about them to be sure. On the Celtic side we've already looked quite closely at the Irish, Welsh and Cornish, but what about the Celts in Brittany (France) and Scotland?

Breton la soule

The Bretons had a game called *la soule*, a simple, violent and unruly sport that involved two teams of indeterminate numbers trying to get a ball made of fabric, cork, wood or (most commonly) an inflated pig's bladder encased in leather—depended on what was available at the time and place—to the front door of the opposition village's church. Or perhaps into their own church, or any other place agreed on by the competing teams, there doesn't seem to have been any standard goal and it was probably determined by the players at the time of the game, or varied according to the game's location.

Like most football at the time, the playing field was the land between villages and could involve fields, forests, streams and ponds. Player numbers could be anything from a couple of men to hundreds. Teams were organised according to village allegiance, one village against another, or according to some other distinction—for example married men against single. 'Village versus village' was probably the long version of the game, which started on the boundary between parishes and could go on all day, or sometimes for days if time allowed, while 'married v singles' was the equivalent of randomly selected teams for an afternoon kick around.

There were no rules apart from the standard prohibition on murder or manslaughter. Broken bones were common and accidental (or deliberate) death was not unknown. The ball was moved forward by throwing, kicking, carrying or hitting it with a stick. Tackling and scrummaging were a major part of the game—and probably weren't restricted to activity around the ball, it was the perfect opportunity to settle old scores under the guise of playing.

La soule was mainly played on Christian festivals and feast days that fell between Christmas and Easter, a down-time in the agricultural calendar when there was time to play. All other seasons were mostly taken up with ploughing, planting, tending to crops, harvesting and preparing the land for winter.

It was also a season when pig's bladders and pig's skins were plentiful. In the harsh northern climate it was difficult to keep more than a few selected breeders alive during winter, so it was the practice to slaughter stock in the late autumn and preserve their meat before the worst of winter set in. Pigs were popular farm animals because they bred prolifically, grew rapidly over the warmer months and piglets born in spring were near full grown, fat and ready for slaughter by the time winter rolled around. Their meat was salted, smoked or eaten in great quantities to fatten people up ready for the hard times ahead (the Christmas ham did not happen accidentally), and the intestines and blood made into sausages. Skins were turned into leather and made into boots, clothes and an array of equipment, and stretched and dried in ball-shapes ready for bladders to be inserted and blown up.

In a nod to ancient tradition, the modern rugby ball is often referred to as 'the pig skin'.

The first mention of la soule appeared in a charter in 1147, where a reference is made to the payment of '*seven balloons of greatest dimension*' ('balloon' was a common term for a pig's bladder, which equalled a football) along with a sum of money. It's a pretty vague reference, but it does show that la soule was being played in Brittany at least 900 years ago.

It was a hard game and great entertainment for bored villagers and nobles alike—even the clergy got involved. The games popularity spread across France, and it was still being played in some areas as late as the mid-20th C. It was revived when France hosted the 1998 World Cup, which resulted in a modernised (and undoubtedly sanitised) 21st C version being played between villages at Vendôme in the Loire Valley. French players have extended invitations to players of Shrovetide Football (we'll get to that), a similar game played in England, and players from the Bulldogs Rugby Club in Twickenham, England, have been playing in Vendôme since 2008.

Scotland, Orkney and the ba' game.

In ancient Scotland one football game stands out—the ancient *ba' game* of Orkney.

The ba game ('ba' just means 'ball') is still played in the Orkneys and a few other places in Scotland, but in mediaeval times it was played across Scotland, primarily as a part of Hogmanay (Xmas and New Year) celebrations.

The Orkneys, along with the other Scottish islands, were once very closely associated through trade and kinship links with the Norse from Iceland and western Norway and, as a result, they were included in the ancient Icelandic sagas. These sagas tell us of the (supposed) origins of 'ba'. Technically, despite being written down, this is probably classified as mythology, but it has a substantial ring of truth about it.

The story is included in the Orkneyinga Saga and tells us that the first Earl of Orkney, Sigurd Eysteinsson, defeated a Scottish Earl called Maelbrigte Tusk—presumably the 'Tusk' refers to his odd shaped teeth. After the battle Sigurd strapped Maelbrigte's head to his saddle to take home and display on a spike for everyone to admire. But as he spurred his horse forward the head swung back against his leg and Maelbrigte's tooth scratched Sigurd's leg. The scratch became infected and Sigurd died of blood poisoning, and the good people of Orkney became so enraged at the death of their Earl that they kicked Maelbrigte's head through the streets of Kirkwall as a sort of 'payback'. This was probably just a good, disorganized kicking, but it was said to be the origin of ba.

You have to wonder, though, if Maelbrigte's teeth were so bad that a scratch from them could kill a strong, healthy man, how many people died of blood poisoning from scratches—or worse—that they got from kicking his head?

Today the Ba' Game involves competition between Uppies (Up the Gates) and Doonies (Doon the Gates). In this case 'Gates' is an Orkney word taken from old Norse meaning road or path, so whether a player was born 'up the road' or 'down the road' determined which team he played for. Modern social mobility has made this method of team selection impractical and today players choose a side mostly based on personal preference, but the names remain. Teams seem to be of indeterminate numbers and games can involve several hundred, or even thousands of players (although I don't think there were ever enough people living in the Orkneys to make up thousands).

The modern game is played with a leather ball stuffed with cork, weighing about 1.3 kg and with a circumference of roughly

70 cm. The cork historically used to stuff the ball was probably not the bark of an Iberian tree, but more likely the bracket fungus historically used to make balls in Northern Europe. This was often referred to as 'cork' and used to make everything from floats to bottle stoppers.

After the Maelbrigte's head kicking there are no records to tell us when, or how, the game was originally played, so all I can do is describe the modern game and draw conclusions from that.

The object of the game is not quite the same as the other Celtic games of the period, because it doesn't appear to involve either parish boundaries or churches, or cover a playing area anywhere near as big. The aim for the Doonies is to get the ball into the sea at Kirkwall Bay in the north, and for the Uppies to touch it against a wall at the south end of town.

The game began by the ball being 'thrown up' (tossed into a waiting scrum) at Mercat Cross on the Kirk (church) Green by either an older stalwart of the game or a local dignitary. The resulting melee surges back and forth, up the road, down the road, into side streets and even private yards as teams struggle for possession of the ball. Occasionally someone gets enough control to make a dash out of the scrum and into the crowd of spectators, but they don't appear to necessarily result in a gain for either side, those occur when there is a 'smuggle and run'.

Given that in the close packed mob few players actually know where the ball is, one tactic is for a player to make a break pretending that he has the ball, in the hope that the pack will be tricked into following him and allowing the player who actually has the ball a comparatively free run. Once free of the pack the ball carrier makes a run for his goal—straight up or down the street, or through alleys, through the crowds of spectators, even over roof tops—by whichever route he thinks best to evade pursuit. Once the scrum catches him the whole thing starts again. Games can go for several hours, five is the average but eight hours is not unknown, and there are few rules.

When one or the other goal is reached an individual winner (player of the match) is decided by a popular vote among the winning side and he is awarded the ball to proudly display in his home and a new one is handmade by a local craftsman.

Actually, it all sounds very much like Cornish hurling.

Despite the obvious roughness of the game, serious injuries are rare. Those that do occur are usually to unwary spectators who can't get out of the way in time, so children and the elderly are advised to stay clear. The game itself is held in check by some sort of unspoken code of conduct, similar to the Welsh and Cornish etiquette that does not tolerate 'inappropriate behavior', and if someone is hurt badly the game stops to allow them to be pulled out. Property in the confined spaces of the town is obviously at risk so houses and shops are boarded up and mobile property, such as cars, kept well clear.

The ba' game is, for the most part, a men's game, but in the winter of 1945-6 women's games were held, something to do with the new found equality springing up after women took on male roles during the war. But chauvinism quickly reasserted itself and after that one experiment the ladies were quickly sequestered safely away from such rough activity—very similar to what occurred across the post war world. Today, as far as I can make out, women and girls are taking an increasing role again, although not necessarily in the middle of the scrum.

Anglo Saxon England and Shrovetide Football

Shrovetide football was a name given to mob football when it was played during the three Christian festival days known as Shrovetide, which precede the Christian holy days of Lent. Shrovetide—Sunday, Monday and Tuesday—is a period of feasting, festivities and games. Particularly Tuesday, which is traditionally known as Pancake Day, when the people played hard and gorged themselves in readiness for Lent, which is forty days of abstinence, deprivation, fasting and penitence leading up to Easter itself.

It's a pagan pre-Christian festival dating back at least to the Egyptians, but practised throughout Europe from Spain to the far reaches of the North. Originally it was an 'end-of-winter' celebration when the dark spirits of winter were driven out to make way for the joyous ones of spring. In the southern European Catholic regions it became known as 'Carnival' and in the far north it was 'Fastelayn'.

Like most traditions. Shrovetide has its origins in practicality. As we said earlier, just before Christmas most livestock were slaughtered and the meat preserved for the winter, along with some fruit and vegetables. But preservation was not perfect and by March food was starting to go off, and the warmer spring weather only accelerated the rotting. So Shrovetide (or carnival or fastelayn) was a case of 'eat it all while it's still edible' and fatten up for the lean month or two ahead before more food could be produced.

Shrovetide football was first mentioned in 1180 by William Fitzstephen in his *Descriptio Nobilissimi Civitatis Londoniae*. In it he describes all the youth of London going out into the fields on Shrove Tuesday to play 'ball'. Each school and each craft guild had its own ball and all the older citizens came out to watch. He even talks about how wrapped up in the games the spectators became and how the older men reliving their youth as they watched the young men playing—as old men always have, and always will. Of course they'd always played it better, and always will have.

From about the 12th or 13th C references to football in Britain increased and we can get a reasonably accurate picture of some of the games, which were originally all essentially the same, with just a few variations from one town or shire to the next. They all lacked rules and were all played by indeterminate numbers of people over indeterminate areas. And all were extremely violent, but that had a very practical social side. Shrovetide came at the end of winter when people had endured comparative inactivity and living cheek-by-jowl with family and neighbours. It was a time when frustrations build up and offence could be easily taken and magnified, but venting those frustrations in such close conditions could lead to serious consequences so, wherever possible, a lid was kept on tempers for the greater good.

When the weather warmed and it was time to start life again, it made sense to have a sanctioned activity where steam could be let off, several months' worth of pent up frustrations could be vented and offences, real and imagined, avenged. Get it all out of the way in the guise of chasing an innocent ball in a game without rules and without fear of recrimination. Stories abound of extreme violence and serious injuries being joked about in the pub after the game, so it seemed that grudges were settled on the field and not carried off it.

Then everyone started over with a clean slate.

Well, almost everyone, there were exceptions. In 1321 Pope John XXII granted a special dispensation to Canon William de Spalding of Shouldham in Norfolk, absolving him of all blame for 'accidentally' killing a man during a game. Apparently, in the heat of play, a 'friend' had run into the Canon's 'sheathed' knife and died a few days later. Despite his position—or perhaps because of it—William was fearful enough of repercussions to seek the protection of a higher authority.

There's a short poem that seems to sum up the day pretty well:

> *When the pancakes are sated, Come to the ring and you'll be mated, There this ball will be upcast, May this game be better than the last*[1]

I assume the '*Come to the ring and you'll be mated*' means that you'll be paired with a team to play football, not that you'll be … Then again, Shrovetide was definitely a time of excess in all things.

Like most other codes of the day, Shrovetide football was played over a huge, but generally undefined, field with goals—usually houses, churches or town squares, often set kilometers apart. There were no rules to speak of, at least none that I can find, short of outright murder being frowned upon. There didn't even appear to have been the etiquette that was a feature of the Celtic versions.

1 Ditchfield, P.A. Old English Sports, Pastimes and Customs Paperback. January 31, 2006

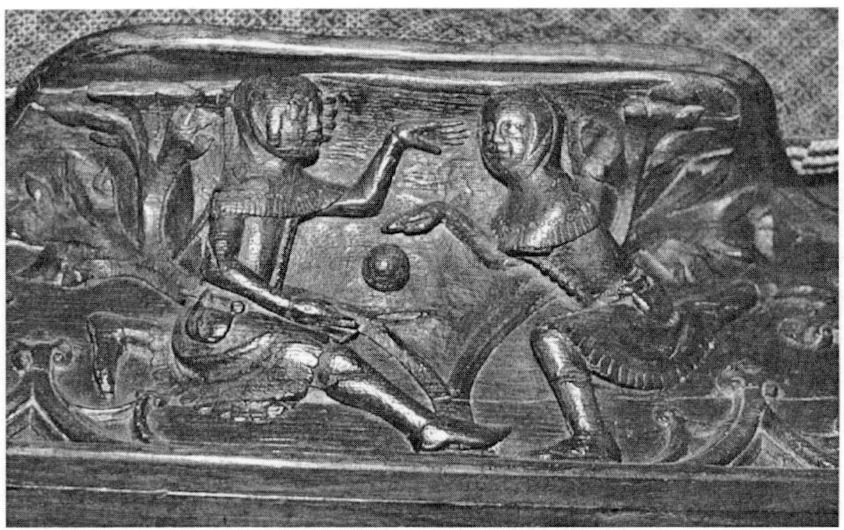

A 14th C depiction of ball play on a medieval misericord (a kind of folding church seat) in Gloucester Cathedral. *(Photo by Dominic Strange. www.misericords.co.uk)*

Because they were simple and without rules, games were pretty much interchangeable between districts. A group of men from the extreme south of England could play against a team from the Scottish border with no appreciable problems. Mostly, the only regional variations in the game seemed to be in the ball, or rather the stuffing that was used for it. Some were leather stuffed with cork (as in the ba game), some used a pig's bladder inside a leather casing, and some stuffed their ball with some other soft materials. Some balls were light and lent themselves to kicking, others too heavy to kick and more appropriate to carrying.

As time went by more and more people began moving from the country into the cities and took football with them. But it became no less boisterous and, while there was little chance of damage to property when the ball was fought over across fields and streams, the buildings that lined the streets in cities like London suffered considerably and disgruntled residents had to resort to putting barriers in front of their properties for protection.

And, of course, playing didn't remain confined to Shrovetide and people began playing whenever they could, and therein lay a problem. People became obsessed with football and neglected their work, and their civic and religious duties, which was a big headache for the authorities.

In England one of the public's most important civic duties was archery practice. The longbow was a super-weapon of its time, the medieval equivalent of the machine gun. It could shoot nearly 400 m (1300') and easily penetrate armour at a range of 230 m (750'), it was accurate, deadly and in the right hands was capable of a rapid rate of fire.

It was England's weapon of choice in its never ending conflicts and it won them some stunning victories—for example, at the battle of Agincourt in 1415, England's Henry V fielded an army of 6,000 against a French army of 36,000. The French lost an estimated 10,000 men, mostly to English archers, while the English lost just a couple of hundred. And in the battle of Crecy in 1346 English archers accounted for around 2,000 Frenchmen while the English lost only 50.

But such success did not just happen, men had to practise long, hard and regularly. In 1252 it became compulsory for all Englishmen between 15 and 60 to practice archery at least once a week to maintain a substantial pool of trained archers ready to be conscripted at a moment's notice. The law fell into abeyance when bows were replaced by guns in the 16th C, but remained on the books until 1960.

Anything that interfered with archery practice was a threat to the realm and had to be stamped on, and mass obsession with football certainly interfered with archery practice. Between Edward II in 1314 and the English civil wars in the 1660s, football was officially banned in England more than 30 times, but such was the strength of the game that not one of them stuck.

Over that time various administrators and clerics described football as:

- a useless and idle sport
- a devilish pastime
- involving beastly fury and extreme violence
- a pointless sport; meeter for laming than making able

- a bloody and murthering practice, rather than a fellowly sport or pastime
- football causeth fighting, brawling, contention, quarrel-picking, murder, homicide, and a great effusion of blood
- more a friendly kind of fight than a play or recreation.

Even the clergy put the boot in. In the 16th C a Puritan cleric named Philip Stubbs [2] railed against the game, saying:

> *Lord, remove these exercises from the Sabbath. Any exercise which withdraweth from godliness either upon the Sabbath or any other day, is wicked and to be forbidden.*

And it wasn't just football in the firing line. James II of Scotland passed an Act of Parliament in 1457 that banned all 'pointless games', including golf. Those caught playing games should be punished with a 40 shilling fine—a lot of money at the time.

None of it stopped people playing. In fact, it seems that football was becoming more organised. Between 1421 and 1423 the Worshipful Company of Brewers twice hired their hall out to *'footeballeplayers'* which implies that players were organised into a group or club and established the first known link between beer and football—a bond that has continued to this day.

And it wasn't just in Britain and Scotland that football was being condemned, slandered and banned. Across the water in France, where they didn't use the long-bow so didn't even have archery practice as an excuse, King Charles V decreed in 1365 that *the game of la soule could not appear among the games that serve to exercise the body*. And even in independent Brittany the game was stopped in 1440 when the powerful Bishop of Tréguier threatened players with excommunication or other severe punishment, as well as a fine of 100 grounds (I have no idea how much a ground was, but it was probably a lot).

2 https://archive.org/stream/phillipstubbessa00stubuoft/phillipstubbessa00stubuoft_djvu.txt

That didn't stop the French and Bretons playing, either.

So why were there such widespread bans?

As the early mediaeval world developed and the feudal system got more organised, the lands became more peaceful (relatively speaking) and there were less opportunities for lords to increase, or simply sustain their wealth by looting their neighbours. The ruling classes became more and more dependent on taxing their workers—merchants, artisans, peasants, serfs.

As administrations grew bigger and layers were added to government, and as armies grew bigger to defend ever expanding states and egos, so more and more was needed from workers. And as the feudal states' needs grew, anything that distracted the workers, the wealth generators, became an inconvenience, and ultimately a threat.

Play, initially shared across the social spectrum, was to become the preserve of the rich in their public schools, universities and courts—at least that was the theory.

There was also the small problem of the plague. The period of the first European bans roughly coincided with the time when plague was sweeping Europe and a 1363 ban coincided exactly with the height of an outbreak that killed 20% of Londoners. That order, which banned pretty much every sport where people gathered in groups, is very reminiscent of the 21st C response to the Covid-19 pandemic.

There probably wasn't any one thing behind the bans. Certainly interference with civic duties was a major factor, as was public heath, but the major reasons were simply efforts to keep the economy functioning by removing distractions from productive work.

But the plague also set in train mass reforms in land management and work practices, and the invention of labour-saving machines that changed the face of society forever and ultimately drove the free-flowing and lawless mob game of the wide open spaces into the cities, factories and public schools. Football was forced to clean up its act and, in the process, breed the parents of modern football.

Mob football continued to be played in the country, but as the population shifted both physically and socially, so the old football declined. Then the newly urbanised rising middle-class revolted against the violence of the game, and when nine men were killed or died of their injuries in a 19th C game the public outcry was the death knell for old style football.

But who were the medieval game's ancestors? Where did they come from, who were its forebears?

For that we have to look a lot further back in history—to the Vikings, Romans, Greeks, Chinese and Inuit.

Chapter 11
THE GREAT GRANDPARENTS, AND BEYOND

Mob football grew out of games played by Britain's invaders, Romans, Anglo-Saxons and Vikings—who were divided into Norse (Norwegians), Danes and Icelanders—and Normans. The Anglo-Saxons may have played football, but they didn't leave enough records to be sure, and it was all well established by the time the Normans appeared.

That leaves Romans and assorted Vikings as the ancestors.

The Romans and Harpastum

When the Romans invaded and settled in Britain they brought their customs and sports with them, including their ball game, *harpastum*. Primarily a sport for the army, harpastum was a rough, violent game played and loved by the legions across the empire. But it was also a mob game played in the streets of Rome and provincial towns, so it's likely that Romanised provincial natives happily participated and continued to play it after the Romans left.

Frustratingly, the Romans recorded minute details of their lives and they told stories about playing harpastum, but very little about the rules. This was probably because everyone who cared knew the rules, such as they were, so why write about them? But we do know that harpastum was a participation sport, not a spectator one. If the Romans wanted to watch games they went to the arena and watched gladiators, wild beasts and lavish shows. But, unless you were particularly unlucky, those weren't participation sports.

A Roman fresco of harpastum players.
(Author unknown. Wikipedia. Public Domain.)

Ordinary people enjoying themselves has never made the news, except when it had a consequence, like that described in court by 1st C BCE lawyer, Cicero. He told the court how a wayward ball from a street game of harpastum flew through a barber's open window and hit the barber on the hand, just as he was shaving a customer. The unfortunate customer died on the spot.

Makes breaking a neighbour's window seem pretty inoffensive.

Despite the high injury rate, harpastum was considered beneficial to health and fitness. About three hundred years after its introduction into the Legions, a Roman doctor named Galen described it as:

> *Better than wrestling or running because it exercises every part of the body, takes up little time, and costs nothing. It is profitable training in strategy and could be played with varying degrees of strenuousness.....When, for example, people face each other, vigorously attempting to prevent each other from taking the space between, this exercise is a very heavy, vigorous one, involving much use of the hold by the neck, and many wrestling holds.*[1]

A couple of hundred years later a 5th C Roman Bishop from Gaul named Sidonius Apollinaris described a game as it was then:

> *And now the illustrious Filimatius sturdily flung himself into the squadrons of the players, like Virgil's hero, 'daring to set*

1 P.N.Singer, «Galen: Selected Works» (1997), pages 299-304

> *his hand to the task of youth'; he had been a splendid player himself in his youth. But over and over again, he was forced from his position among the stationary players by the shock of some runner from the middle, and driven into the midfield, where the ball flew past him, or was thrown over his head; and he failed to intercept or parry it. More than once he fell prone, and had to pick himself up from such collapses as best he could; naturally he was the first to withdraw from the stress of the game.*[2]

From what we can make out of the play, each team tried to hang onto a small, hard ball and the other team tried, by whatever means, to get it off them. But how the scoring system worked and what constituted a score is unknown. I don't see how a team could score points—if, indeed, the object was to score points—perhaps it was just the team that held onto the ball longest won. It's difficult for us to conceive of a competitive ball game without scoring, but in other cultures games were simply ongoing melees until a victor was decided by consensus, or decided on style and etiquette, or just who held onto the ball the longest. One thing that is clear about harpastum is that feet were, at best, used incidentally. The early Europeans either never thought of kicking or didn't see the point.

From the description of play, it seems pretty obvious that harpastum was the immediate ancestor of Welsh cnapan and Cornish hurling-to-country. Cnapan even retained the Roman direction of play—keeping the ball on their own side. In its homeland, Italy, it's been suggested that harpastum is ancestor to calcio, but the whole style, the ball and the direction of play in calcio make this dubious at best.

The Romans invented many things, but harpastum wasn't one of them. Like a great many other things, they adopted it from one of the cultures they encountered across the empire—in this case, from the Greeks.

2 Sidonius Apollinaris, Letters. 5.17.7 (translated by O.M. Dalton)

Greek Episyros and Phaininda

The earliest definitely recorded European football was a game called *episyros* ('On the Lime' or 'Common ball') played in the Greek city of Sparta sometime around three thousand years ago. It was extremely popular among the Spartans, who used it to toughen up their youth, teach them cooperative attack and defence and prepare them for war, which was basically a Spartan's only job.

Episyros was played by two teams, each of between twelve and fourteen players who faced each other across a central line marked with lime (the skyros). The object of the game was to get a ball over a line behind the opposing team, usually by throwing it over the heads of the opposition. The ball was made of linen stuffed with some soft material that could be grasped with one hand while warding off opposition players with the other. It was light, loose and difficult to throw, so that a team couldn't put it over the opponent's line on the first attempt. Field sizes seemed to have varied, but I can't find any solid reference to sidelines or rules, possibly because there was no 'out of bounds' and rules were minimal. The only thing that was sure is that it was a hard game, tackling was hard, gang-tackles were allowed and injuries common. It didn't matter how the ball got over the line—carried, thrown or kicked—so long as it went over, a point was scored. Even if a player who had possession of the ball near his own line was forced back across it, pushed or physically carried, a point was scored for the opposition. This obviously encouraged cooperation in both the attacking team and the defenders as they rallied to help their team mates. Cooperation and tactics such as feints and throwing dummies were important and strategy played a major role.

It was perfect training for war and an ideally boisterous game for youth to let off steam harmlessly (more or less).

The sport was so popular in its heyday that a Spartan league was formed, made up of five teams drawn from the five tribes that made up the Kingdom of Lacedemonia, of which Sparta was the capital. The league's main fixtures were part of an annual festival held to celebrate the year's age group reaching adulthood.

Actually the name 'On the Lime' may have originated with this festival. Male children were taken from their families very young, six or seven, and sent to live in military barracks outside the city where they were seriously 'hardened up'. They were forbidden to re-enter the city until they had graduated to adulthood, which meant that they could not cross a border defined with limestone (Sparta thought the fighting prowess of its men a better defence than walls).

Of course the name may have simply referred to the lines marked on the field with lime, but the wall story sounds better, and it was so long ago no one can be sure.

Images of episyros being played, or at least athletes playing with a football sized ball, have been found that date to Sparta's heyday in about 400 BCE and claimed to be proof that Greeks invented football. One of those images has even been replicated on the European Cup trophy, although there are suspicions that that particular image, a man bouncing a ball on his knee, may actually be from an ancient 'keep fit' manual that detailed various gymnastic ball exercises. There's so little known about it that it's impossible to be sure, but the episyros ball was so loose that it would have been very difficult to bounce on a knee.

Neither is it possible, at this distance in time, to know for sure episyros's origins, nor if it retained its popularity after Alexander the Great's father relegated Sparta to an unimportant backwater in 338 BCE, but a look at Greek history might give the odd clue.

The ancient Greece that we know was a blend of four cultures, but mainly Ionian and Dorian. DNA analysis tells us the Dorians were nomads from the steppes of Central Asia and Siberia who reached the Balkans via the Caucasus and the Black Sea about 3 - 5,000 years ago, expanded across most of Greece, killed a large part of the population and destroyed the classical Greeks (the ones that fought Troy). They established Sparta, which became the Dorian focal point.

Football originated somewhere on the Central Asian steppes of Western China, about the same time and place where the Dorians set out, and if they brought it with them you'd expect to find vestiges of it along their path—and that's exactly what there is.

At the Eastern end of the Black Sea, in the Caucasus Mountains where Europe meets Asia, on the direct Dorian line of migration, is the little country of Georgia. In Georgia there is a village called Guria where an ancient game, *lelo burti* (field ball), is played each year to celebrate the Orthodox Christian Easter. Some say the game is three hundred years old and commemorates a victory by a small Georgian force over a much larger Ottoman army, but the game appeared in a 12th C Georgian epic called 'The Knight's Panther', so it's clearly older than the Ottomans. Others claim that it is at least three thousand years old and was played throughout the Caucasus's and used to identify the toughest and most resourceful men to be put in charge of village defences, which means originally it shared the military connections of the Chinese and Spartan games.

It was played between the men of neighbouring villages, team numbers were indeterminate and playing fields varied considerably—they could be several kilometres long and cross hills, valleys, swamps and rivers. The ball was a sewn leather casing which, according to some accounts, was folded into a concave cup from which wine was drunk on the eve of the game. The following morning the ball was stuffed with dirt, sand, sawdust, grass, fur, wine (yes, wine, it's the only game I've ever heard of that puts alcohol in the ball instead of the players) and anything else at hand to bring it up to a massive 16 kilograms. The game was started by the priest throwing the ball into the centre of the field resulting in an all-in melee with dozens, perhaps hundreds, of men all trying to get their hands on it. There were very few rules apart from the players couldn't be drunk and if someone got injured they raised their hands and the game stopped long enough for them to get to safety.

Actually, apart from the very unique ball, it sounds a lot like mob football.

In modern Guria it's played by men from the upper town against the lower town and the field is an area between two streams, about five hundred metres apart, which act as goal lines. Anything between the streams—backyards, orchards, fields—is considered part of the playing field and a team wins by carrying the ball into or over the stream behind the opposition. After the game the winning team is awarded the ball and, by tradition, it's carried to the cemetery and placed on the grave of someone that the team decided to honour. Lelo burti balls are a common sight in Gurian cemeteries.

Officially it's no longer played between villages, but I wouldn't rule out inter-village competition somewhere in the wild Caucasus Mountains.

During the Soviet era the game was altered in an attempt to remove any religious connotations or affiliations—in that respect the Soviet cadres were very like the missionaries that'd infested European colonies for the past couple of hundred years. Fields were more-or-less standardised to between 90 and 135 m long and 60 to 90 m wide. The leather ball was made rounder lighter and stuffed with grass, horse-hair and wool, although it's still a hefty 2.5 kg. Team numbers were set at fifteen men per side and games at two thirty minute halves.

And rules were introduced. Players could kick the ball, pass it forward or back and run with it. But they could only hold on to it for five seconds before they had to pass, and only the player with the ball could be tackled. Goals were scored by a player carrying the ball over a central area of the goal line, after which play resumed from the centre of the field.

I'm not sure if the old rule about sobriety was upheld in the new code.

The new game sounds a lot like rugby, and it's credited with being responsible for rugby's popularity in modern Georgia

Back to Greece.

The Dorians were followed by the Ionians from somewhere around what is now modern Türkiye, who moved into the islands between Greece and Türkiye and the east of the Greek peninsular, where they set up Athens as their capital and waged an endless war with the Dorians.

In Athens they began playing a game called *phaininda* (deceiving game). It was played with a linen ball on a marked field by teams of between 12 – 15 players, but instead of trying to get the ball past the opposing team as in episyros, players attempted to keep it on their side of a centre line while the other team tried to get it off them—the same as the Romans.

Antiphanes, a play-write who lived from 408 – 334 BCE, wrote:

> *He seized the ball and passed it to a team-mate while dodging another and laughing. He pushed it out of the way of another. Another fellow player he raised to his feet. All the while the crowd resounded with shouts of 'Out of bounds,' 'Too far,' 'Right beside him,' 'Over his head,' 'On the ground,' 'Up in the air,' 'Too short,' 'Pass it back in the scrum.'*[3]

Clearly both the Greek games involved throwing with not a lot of kicking involved, because soft, non-bouncy linen balls would be pretty unresponsive and unrewarding to kick, and not likely to last too long if they were. The records, such as they are, also state that the ball was 'thrown over the heads of the opposition', not kicked between their legs.

Where did the Athenian game come from? It may have been an adaptation of the Spartan one, the ball certainly sounds similar, but the hatred between the two states makes that unlikely, especially when you consider that the two games had different objectives and therefore different styles of play.

The answer may lie with Greece's most famous son, Alexander the Great.

In 334 BCE Alexander invaded Persia with about 40,000 troops. He defeated every army that he came up against and established an empire that stretched from Greece in the west to the edge of India in the south and the Chinese borders in the north east. It

3 Athenaeus: The Deipnosophists book 1. Translated by C.D.Yonge (1854)

was the greatest Empire the world had yet seen, and also one of the shortest lived. About ten years after leaving Greece his troops mutinied. Exhausted, homesick, missing family and friends and increasingly frightened of the huge and well organised armies that lay ahead, they refused to cross the Indus River and Alexander was forced to retreat. Which was just as well because if the massive forces waiting for them on the farther bank of Indus didn't destroy them, then the battle hardened Chinese in the north would have.

War had been raging in China for one hundred and fifty years and the Qin, the first army the Greeks would have encountered, was large, well organised and well equipped. They also had a novel, and very effective, training tool—football.

When the fighting was eventually over Ying Zheng, erstwhile king of the victorious western state of Qin, restyled himself Qin Shi Huang di, First Emperor of China, and set about unifying China and making his mark on history. He was an absolute ruler, a brutal tyrant who organised society along military lines and pressed the population into massive public works where harsh conditions killed hundreds of thousands, probably millions. He built a network of roads that linked all of China and joined and strengthened disjointed sections of wall to make the first Great Wall. He also built himself an enormous tomb and guarded it with the famous Terracotta Warriors.

Because tsu' chu was recorded in military manuals, we know quite a lot about the first games. There were two teams of twelve to fourteen players, each trying to get a ball of some description across the other team's (or their own) goal line by throwing, passing or kicking. Rules were few and excessive violence the norm. But there's no way of knowing for certain exactly how it was played, or even whether the object was to keep the ball or put it over the opposition's line.

But back to Alexander.

If he'd attacked the Qin, Alexander the Great may have simply been Alexander the Vanished, a footnote in Chinese history, but he stopped in the Fergana valley in what is today Tajikistan in Central Asia, just a few hundred kilometres short of Qin territory.

There he established a Greek city called Alexandria Eschate (Alexander the Furthest) and populated it with his wounded, those too tired to march all the way home again, and those who opted to become colonists.

Friendly contact between the Greeks and Qin must have begun almost as soon as, or before, the city was founded. This is borne out by the Sampul tapestry, found in China's far west, which pictures a Greek soldier with blue eyes and carrying a spear, and a centaur. That the picture is of a soldier together with a creature from Greek mythology suggests familiarity and friendly relations. The Qin probably hired Greeks mercenaries, and there's speculation that the Terracotta Warriors were either inspired by Greek art, or even that Greek sculptors had an input into their creation.

As it turned out, the centaur was quite apt for Alexandria Eschate, because in addition to wounded and weary soldiers, Alexander left behind horses. They were larger than the Asian breeds and renowned for their raw speed and stamina, which made them ideal war horses, and they were soon in great demand. The citizens of Alexandria Eschate bred them up into valuable herds that they traded with the surrounding people.

That wasn't the only breeding they were doing. DNA evidence shows that Greeks and Qin were interbreeding, but ultimately it was the horse breeding and trading that was the Greeks undoing.

After the Qin Emperor died the Han dynasty took over and the Greeks from Alexandria Eschate officially entered Chinese history. By this time they'd grown rich and their wealth made them arrogant—and stupid. When the Emperor sent envoys to purchase horses, the good citizens of Alexandria Eschate took the Emperors money, killed one of his envoys, and kept the horses. That particular Emperor was very cultured, enlightened and just, but not a man to be trifled with. He launched the 'War of the Heavenly Horses' in 104 BCE, collected the horses he was owed and more or less ended Greek rule of the city, 225 years after it was founded. After all those years of interbreeding and a limited infusion of fresh Greek blood, there probably weren't many actual Greeks left anyway.

In the meantime, Greek mercenaries in the Qin army undoubtedly learned how to play tsu' chu as part of their training, so the game would have been played in Alexandria Eschate. The city was a part of the pan-Hellenic Empire where people could move about more-or-less freely from the Chinese borders to the Greek homeland, taking Chinese gold, exotic goods and new ideas with them.

When one such, Aristonicus of Carystus, returned to Athens he was given the singular honour of having a statue of himself erected in Athens and given the equivalent of the keys to the city—for his prowess in phaininda. Which is odd, because phaininda didn't occupy as prominent a position as, say, gymnastics or athletics in the Athenian world, so why was a returning soldier given such an honour? Perhaps he introduced tsu' chu, which, with a little adaptation, became Phaininda. Allowing for just a few years leeway in dates (it was a very long time ago) the time line fits remarkably well.

Alexander didn't live long enough to enjoy his Empire, he died of an infected wound in Babylon in 323 BCE at the age of just 32. After his death the Greek states began a slow decline and, through a series of treaties and military conquests, were eventually incorporated into the Roman Empire in 146 BCE. The Romans loved all things Greek and adopted them wherever they could, and their adoption of phaininda was one of the most enthusiastic. It must have been phaininda because, by the time the Romans arrived, Sparta was long gone and episyros along with it, so they probably never encountered the game. They replaced the soft linen ball with a small, hard one, probably upped the violence level, turned the Greek game into their own and took it across Europe.

The Britons picked it up and it came to be called cnapan and hurling, and probably several other names that've mostly been forgotten.

But what of the other forms of mob football?

Their ancestors came from an entirely different direction.

Anglo-Saxons and Vikings

After the Romans left Britain in the 5th C waves of Germanic people—mostly Angles, Saxons and Jutes, now collectively called the Anglo-Saxons—invaded from Northern Europe. The 5th C was a time of great upheaval in Europe and people were on the move everywhere, partly because of the power vacuum left by Rome's departure, but mostly because tribes like the Huns, Alans and Bulgars came out of the East and wrought havoc throughout Europe. The Anglo-Saxons were pushed westward and crowded into what is now the Netherlands and Denmark, then across the North Sea into Britain where they pushed the native Romano-Britons into Wales and Cornwall.

As I said, it's not recorded anywhere if the Anglo-Saxons played any sort of football, perhaps they did, but the next wave of invaders certainly did.

Vikings first came to prominence in Britain in 793 CE when they attacked an abbey at Lindisfarne in Northumbria. It was a bloody and brutal introduction and the start of a string of raids all around the coasts of the British Isles. Contrary to modern interpretation, the name Viking originally meant someone who travelled—regardless of whether it was exploring, fighting or trading—and intended to return home again. And they weren't specifically Scandinavian. The Vikings that raided Britain originally came from the bays and fiords of NW Norway, which were then a series of tiny independent Norse communities, but as they travelled they often swelled their numbers by picking up crew from other places.

The Norse soon began to settle onto the Scottish Islands and Ireland and intermarry with the locals. They also began raiding the settled parts of Scandinavia and upset its king, Harald Fair Hair, who reacted by invading the Norse communities and sending many of them fleeing across the seas to their relatives in Ireland and the Isles. But they continued to raid Scandinavia from there, so Harald followed them, forcing many to go to newly discovered Iceland.

About 70 years later, in 865 CE, the Great Heathen Army, a coalition of Scandinavian and Celtic states led by the sons of Ragnar, invaded England and established Danish (an English catch-all name for Scandinavians) rule there, called the Danelaw. That invasion led to the first post-Roman story about the beginnings of English football.

It was a simple story, it just said that the first game of football played in Britain was in the east of England, when locals kicked the severed head of a Danish prince they'd just defeated.

It was a small story, but so persistent that it was used as a defence nearly 1,000 years later by a group of 18th C youths who were taken to court for playing a particularly violent game. They claimed that townsmen of the area had once beaten off a Viking raid, captured the raider's captain, cut his head off and used it as a football.

The judge ruled that football was an 'immemorial custom' and acquitted them.

But an 18th C judge's probably tongue-in-cheek ruling does not mean the story's true. It's perfectly feasible and, in a way, logical and psychologically sound for people to vent their feelings on an enemy, and it must have been quite empowering for the average, powerless, person to get a good kick in. Also, at the time heads held a particular significance as the essence of the soul, so by kicking it they were delivering a particularly potent insult, but I suspect that that was all it was—just a good kicking.

Kicking the Dane's head was, allegedly, followed by a custom of kicking the heads of executed criminals. This persistent and tantalisingly gruesome story suggests a beginning for the game that really needs to be looked at properly.

Despite our impressions of those times, judicial executions were rare in the early medieval, at least when compared to later periods, and beheadings even rarer. But death was a very common feature of life and held none of the squeamishness that surrounds it today, and when it occurred, death by judicial execution was usually ritualized and surrounded by religious significance revolving around penitence and salvation.

Basically, if the condemned confessed their sins before their death their dying became their penitence and they would therefore go to heaven, regardless of what they'd done. Most confessed and, oddly, many seemed quite reconciled to their death—life was generally crap and they were getting a shortcut to heaven.

But not by beheading. There was a rather odd early Christian belief that the dead body retained some vestige of life, enough to enable it to be resurrected on judgement day when all the dead would rise and be judged. The only way to deprive a body of that vestige of life was to remove its head, a headless body was totally dead and therefore could not rise and the person was condemned to eternal hell. For that reason beheading was not for the penitent and was reserved for the worst offenders—heathens, traitors and heretics chief amongst them—and enemies that no one wanted to confront in the afterlife.

It's a belief that must have survived into the 17th century (and may even today, among some of the odder sects) and been an underlying reason for Oliver Cromwell, along with his close associates, being exhumed by Charles II and posthumously beheaded. It might also point to an unexpected magnanimity by Cromwell when he allowed Charles 1st's head to be sewn back on, thereby guaranteeing his resurrection.

Anyway, it's unlikely that heads would have been tossed to the crowd because, like Cromwell's, they were much too valuable put on a stake and displayed prominently as a warning to other would-be revolutionaries, traitors and serious miscreants.

If someone was deemed bad enough to be killed, they were normally hanged. Much more protracted and painful, but the torment made it a more significant penance and therefore enhanced the victim's chances of entry into heaven.

So, while kicking the severed head of a defeated Viking probably happened on occasions, kicking the heads of executed fellow Christians was much less likely, at least on a mass scale—although there was one occasion that appears to be verified.

Just prior to the English Civil War when religious tensions were running high, a Catholic priest was caught preaching and sentenced to be hung, drawn and quartered for treason. The local butcher was given the job (it seems to have been common for 'executioner' to be included in a butcher's job description) but he botched it. Eventually the priest was put out of his misery and his head cut off and, accidentally or deliberately, given to the crowd and a good couple of hours of 'football' ensued. When they got tired of the entertainment they stuck sticks in the eyes, ears, nose and mouth and buried it along with the body.

This story has a level of detail that makes it more likely than not to be true, but, on balance, I think it unlikely that football began in post Roman Britain with the kicking of severed heads. On the other hand, if the ancient Chinese could make kicking an enemy's stomach into a proper football game, who's to say that the English couldn't have done the same with a head?

Anyway, back to Vikings and football.

Football, of one sort or another, was played across the far north of Eurasia from Siberia to Norway, mostly using a ball made of leather stuffed with anything from feathers to sand (it was before animal bladders became popular). An example of these games was *kila,* played in Novgorod in northern Russia. It was a hard game normally played between villages with the simple aim of getting the ball into the opposition's village. The ball could be passed between players, kicked or thrown in any direction and players were allowed to tackle or knock each other over. Actually, it sounds quite a lot like Georgian lelo burti.

The Swedes, southern Norwegians and Danes had close links to Russia, so it's reasonable to assume that they played a similar game and took it to Britain with their Great Heathen Army, where it became mob football. Probably no one's head involved, just an invading army bringing their game with them, all very similar to the Chinese a thousand years earlier. The regions where mob football was played later fit nicely within the borders of the Danelaw, so the ancestry of mob football all looks pretty straight forward.

But that was the Great Heathen Army. What of the earlier Norse that Harald had driven out?

Well ... that's where the story gets interesting.

When Iceland was discovered in the late 9th C many of the people from the western islands, now a mix from generations of intermarriage of Scottish, Islanders, Irish and Norse, settled the new land and travel and commerce across the North Atlantic flourished. Although nominally subject to either Norway or Denmark, the Icelanders became a distinct culture with their own history, and thanks to their Irish side's love of literature, they were the first to write it down in the Icelandic Sagas.

They wrote about football and something called the 'Icelandic Game', which must have been unique to Iceland. But, while stories about the game and the exploits of the players abound, the old writers assumed that everyone knew the basics of the game and didn't bother to recap them.

And therein lies our problem. The Icelanders spoke about three ball games, *knattleikre, soppleikr* and *sköfuleikur,* and gave good reason to think that they were different, but the Sagas were there for a good yarn and, frankly, I suspect the old Icelandic commentators never let facts get in the way of a good story. Yes, they recorded history, but only the memorable and sensational parts of it. They were there to entertain on long winter evenings, so stories of great deeds and momentous events—like six men dying in a football match—were told, and the uninteresting things, like 30 men enjoying a good game and no-one was hurt', went unrecorded.

The media has evolved over the last 1,000 years, but has it changed?

All we really know is that there were three types of football played in Iceland, not if any were unique to Iceland, nor which was the Icelandic game.

Soppleikr, which translates to 'fungus game', probably refers to a game played with a ball carved from a big, hard, parasitic bracket fungus that grows on birch trees in the Northern Hemisphere. The Norse and the Sami, a people from western Russia right across to northern Norway, boiled them in ash lye to make them more elastic and used them as footballs. They wouldn't have been as resilient as leather balls, so soppleikr probably would have been more of a handling than a kicking game. But soppleikr was widely played well before Iceland was settled, so that can't have been the Icelandic game.

On the other hand, **sköfuleikur** could have been. The name translates to the 'scratch game', which is just about as much as I can find out about it, apart from that it was a ball game similar to knattleikre (I'll get to that), but without sticks. This meant it was a throwing/passing/kicking game rather than a hitting one. The name 'scratch game' doesn't really give us any clues as to its origins or play, except perhaps, the Orkney Islands ba' game came about because of a scratch from a tooth that killed Earl Sigurd.

A big leap of faith, I know, but the ba' game was introduced from Iceland and included aspects that were, as far as I know, not incorporated in any other game. The ball, for starters. It used a cork (fungus, as in soppleikr) inner encased in leather and was clearly designed to float, which reflected the game's goals, one of which was in the sea and the other on land.

And those goals suggest that the ba' game had links far to the west.

In the 10th C Erik the Red was banished from Iceland for three years for murder. For want of anything better to do, he sailed west to a land that had only been seen from a ship that had been blown off course as it sailed from Norway to Iceland. He explored the new land, laid claim to some of it for himself and, when his time was up, returned to Iceland to organise settlers. He called his new land 'Greenland' to make it sound more attractive, and the Icelandic sagas say that he left Iceland with 25 ships filled with gullible settlers in the year 985, but only 14 ships arrived. When they realised they'd been tricked it was too late and too dangerous to turn back, so they established a settlement and made the most of it.

About a hundred years later another group of migrants, the Inuit, crossed the narrow sea from North America to northern Greenland and met the Icelanders on one of their summer hunting expeditions to the north. The Inuit had a long journey to get there; starting in Central Asia they'd moved north and east through

Siberia before crossing the Bering Sea to Alaska sometime between 2000 and 6000 years ago. They'd occupied Canada north of the tree line, then Greenland around 1000 years ago.

The two groups met, intermingled and traded; the Inuit for artefacts such as iron tools and trinkets, the Icelanders for food, fur and walrus ivory which they traded to Europe.

The Norse also learned to play Inuit football, **aqsaqtuk**.

Aqsaqtuk was played on ice (as you would expect) with a ball made of hide held together with whale bones rather than stitching, and stuffed with caribou hair, moss, feathers, whatever was available. The ball probably evolved from a walrus head—there's a story about Inuit Ancestors playing an eternal game of aqsaqtuk under the northern lights using a walrus head as a ball, which means that the Inuit game was old when they arrived in Greenland.

Like all games at the time, there probably wasn't much in the way of a rule book, just two teams of indeterminate numbers lined up opposite each other and trying to get a ball passed the other team, then they all rushed forward to kick it into a goal. Teams were each named after something in the environment, usually a bird, and the name would determine which way the team played. If they were named after a water bird they played towards the water, if a land bird then toward the land.

And it's the land/water goals that link it to the ba' game. Actually, one goal a trough of water, one at a wall or some other structure, was a reasonably common theme in early football in the north and west of Britain.

As settlements go, Norse Greenland was not the most prosperous and, although more or less self-sufficient in food, it was dependant on Iceland and Norway for basics such as tools and timber, and the economy relied very heavily on walrus ivory. When African elephant and Russian mammoth ivory flooded the European market Greenland's economy collapsed. The settlements in Greenland were eventually abandoned in the first half of the 15th C because of a combination of climate change, economic downturn and Inuit hostility, but for most of their 400 year stay they'd enjoyed long periods of peace with their neighbours, give or take the odd massacre, and meetings seem to have been for the most part at friendly trading fairs and other gatherings.

Around the year 1,000 Eric the Red's son sailed west and discovered and settled America, but just how far those that came after him penetrated is debatable. The discovery of a 14th C Danish coin in Maine suggests that they went at least that far south, but abandoning Greenland would have sealed the fate of any American settlements. It's a long way from Canada to Iceland, too far for longships to go without a victualling stop. The colonists would have either seen the writing on the wall and got out while they could, or stayed and been absorbed into Native American culture.

Back in Iceland, or perhaps even Orkney, aqsaqtuk was adapted to suit the locals. Cork/fungus was borrowed from soppleikr, encased in leather to make it more durable and a new game invented, but whether that game was called sköfuleikur is very debatable, especially when it was described as a game similar to knattleikre.

Was sköfuleikur uniquely Icelandic? Maybe, but the Icelandic game was probably knattleikre.

Knattleikre games involved two opposing teams of indeterminate sizes, but probably no more than a few dozen players each, drawn from surrounding farm-steads. Each team had a captain, and players on each side appeared to have been paired with players on the opposition team according to size and strength, like forwards against forwards and wingers opposing wingers in rugby.

The field must have been defined and marked because the object was to get the ball over the opposition's goal line, and the ball could be put 'out of bounds' so there must have been side lines, but there's no indication of the size of the field. There was a referee—although what rules he enforced are uncertain—penalties, and possibly penalty boxes.

Games could go on for days and players were free to enter and leave the field at will. A passage in a medieval Icelandic book states that, because a man may leave the field whenever he wishes, he is responsible for his own welfare and any injuries he might sustain. In other words no one's making him play, he's put himself in harm's way so it's his own fault if he gets injured or killed.

But it wasn't really football. Knattleikre was played with a hard wooden ball about the size of a fist, and bats to hit the ball (or the opposition) with.

Teams lined up opposite one another and the game was started by a player hitting the ball into the opposition, one of whom caught it and ran with it toward the opposing goal line until he either passed it or hit it to another player, or was tackled and the ball wrestled from him. Wrestling (or all in brawling) seems to have been a major feature of the game and there are occasional mentions of weapons being used, but these incidents may have been more disgruntled and highly excited spectators taking the law into their own hands, rather than actual players. It was a spectator sport played on a defined field that provided ample opportunity for on-lookers. Tournaments drew huge crowds from all over Iceland (and possibly even from Greenland and Norway), and with so much celebration and alcohol the potential for spectator involvement was high—like the time when Egill ran up to a player with the ball and buried an axe in his head. Egill was only six at the time, so it's more likely that he was spectator than a player.

Knattleikre seems to be a lot like the ancient Celtic game of hurley, which isn't surprising given that Icelanders were at least half Irish. If they were the same game, which is likely, it would mean that knattleikre has a very ancient lineage. Celtic historians tell us that by the year 800 the Celts in Ireland, Scotland, Isle of Man, Wales, Cornwall and Brittany had been playing the ancient stick-and-ball game for hundreds, if not thousands of years, and called it variously *hurley* (Ireland), *shinty* (Scotland), *cammag* (Isle of Mann), *bando* (Wales) or *soule* (Cornwall). The origins of the game are cloudy, to say the least, but it was likely to have been brought to Britain with the migrating Celts somewhere between 600 and 1,000 BCE.

But there is another possibility. Tomb paintings from about 4,000 years ago show the Egyptians playing a stick-and-ball game with a painted leather ball stuffed with papyrus, and sticks bent at one end like hockey or hurley sticks. Similar games were also being played across the Eastern Mediterranean at that time.

But Ancient Mediterranean to Ancient Celts?

It sounds like a stretch of the imagination, but back in the Bronze Age the Celts, especially in Cornwall and Wales, were trading extensively and directly with the Eastern Mediterranean in tin and copper, rare and vital ingredients of bronze, and other metals. And where trade goes, so do traders, in this case probably the seafaring Phoenicians from modern day Lebanon which, back then, was part of the Egyptian Empire. And where traders go, so too do their games, so it's quite possible that the Celtic stick-and-ball games originated in Egypt.

Either way, it means that Gaelic football, and Australian rules for that matter, have very ancient ancestors.

It's not beyond the bounds of possibility that knattleikre was the origin of the native North American game, lacrosse, which has strong similarities to it. Lacrosse is thought to have originated in Eastern Canada at pretty much the same time as the Icelanders were there. Possibly a coincidence, but probably not.

But did knattleikre have anything to do with football?

Perhaps.

The sagas tell us that sköfuleikur was a game similar to knattleikre, but without sticks, and if you take the sticks out of knattleikre and replace the small, hard ball with a larger, softer one designed to be carried or kicked, you get a game that sounds quite a lot like rugby. Or Cornish hurling to goals and Irish caid.

And it makes sense that those games have Icelandic roots.

The Icelandic sagas frequently feature the Scottish Isles and there are mentions of the other Celtic lands, which suggests that the Icelanders had a strong presence on Britain's west coast, from the northern Isles down to Ireland, Cornwall and Brittany in the south—all the areas which had minimal influence from either the Anglo-Saxons or the Danes. Their relations with Vikings, probably

Icelanders, were known to be comparatively peaceful and preferred trade over warfare. Many of the Icelanders themselves were Celtic, or at least with considerable family ties to the Celts, and they treated them with kid gloves, even the less-than-welcoming Welsh.

Wales was comparatively peaceful during the 500 years of the Rome's rule, the locals and the legionaries probably played more than they fought and the Roman's influence on cnapan can be seen not just in the size, weight and hardness of the cnapan ball, but also in the direction of play. On the other hand, the consensus of history seems to be that the Vikings maintained an arms-length relationship with the Welsh. They mounted comparatively small raids, which were sometimes successful and sometimes beaten back, but for the most part they traded peacefully and never claimed any territory, established any settlements or any permanent presence. So it follows that their influence was minimal and cnapan probably remained true to its Roman roots.

In Brittany la soule showed a very confused ancestry that reflects its very confused early years. Roman rule was particularly harsh, and after they left the Bretons had to hold off invasions by the Germanic Franks while, at the same time, dealing with separate groups of sometimes friendly, sometimes not, Vikings.

In Ireland and Scotland there was no Roman influence, apart from that taken to and fro by traders, but the Norse from northern Norway and Iceland were there in big numbers, so caid and the ba game were either home grown or Norse inspired.

Cornwall was different. The Roman presence was lighter than in Wales and Brittany, and there appears to have been fewer troops stationed there. They undoubtedly exposed the Cornish to harpastum and its influence is clear in Cornish hurling to country, although sheathing the ball in silver adds a new dimension to its weight and hardness. Hurling to country differs from harpastum in one major way—the object of the game is to get the ball to a goal behind the opposition—which indicates an influence from the Icelanders and/or the Danes.

Cornish hurling-to-goals was a different matter. It could have been a Cornish invention, if it were not for a similar and unique game shared across the Irish Sea, and their only connection was the Norse who had settlements in both places.

Unlike the Welsh, the Cornish welcomed the Norse and apparently lived peacefully with them. In 838 they even formed a united army to fight the Saxon King Egbert at the Battle of Hingston Down. They lost, but the fact that they formed a combined army speaks volumes for the Cornish-Norse relationship. It's recorded that there were Viking raids in Cornwall, but they rowed up rivers to sack monasteries housing English (Saxon) monks, leaving far more exposed—and potentially richer—Cornish establishments alone.

Apart from family ties, this can all be put down to trade. It doesn't get much attention, but the Vikings used their sea-going skills at least as much for trade as for raiding, probably much more. The Norse would have needed Cornish tin and copper as much as anyone else and had possibly been trading with the Cornish for hundreds of years. After the Romans left they picked up the trade and carried it as far as Byzantium, and got wealthy from it. Many Vikings stayed on in the East and became mercenaries, forming the elite Byzantine Emperor's Varangian Guard, and got even richer from that.

They had everything to lose and very little to gain from attacking Cornwall.

It's even recorded that they swept Cornish seas for pirates, probably fellow Vikings among them, and thus kept the sea-lanes open—mostly for their own benefit.

There's a strong likelihood that many of the traders in Cornwall, especially in the main trade centre around the mines in the Tamar valley in the east, were Icelandic. There was probably a permanent Icelandic presence, even a settlement there.

And that just happened to be the exact place where hurling-to-goal was played.

Perhaps that was the real 'Icelandic Game.'

Epilogue
ORIGINS

We'll never know footballs origins for sure—as I said at the start, it's all like trying to see what's going on at the other end of the field in a fog with only half the lights working, but it looks like:

- Soccer is descended from mob football, which came from a Northern European game with roots in Central Asia, and with the suspicion of an input from China or Japan.
- Rugby and its derivatives are also descended from mob football, but with a strong input from an Icelandic game with roots in Celtic hurley, which was either brought to Britain with the Celts from Europe around 3,000 years ago, or been introduced from the Middle East sometime since.
- Australian Rules football came out of a blend of rugby, Irish caid, Irish hurley and Indigenous Australian marn grook. It also has possible roots in China and, through hurley, the Middle East or the Celtic homelands in Europe.
- Gaelic football came from a blend of rugby, soccer, Australian rules and Irish caid, with roots in Iceland and/or Northern Europe, and Irish hurley.
- American football was born out of rugby and soccer, with possibly a little bit of Italian calcio and Native American Pasuckuakohowog.

Football, in one form or another, has been developing in cultures right across the world for a very long time. It survived some very hard times and came through them all stronger than ever, until, over the space of a thousand years or so, a combination of wars, invasions and immigrations focused it all on a tiny group of islands off the west coast of Europe. There it spent another thousand years incubating, and when conditions were right it exploded and through wars, invasions, industrial expansion and colonial-inspired emigration, it travelled to the four corners of the Earth.

Football, whatever the code, became truly the World's Game.

ABOUT THE AUTHOR

Born in New Zealand, Graeme Dobson came to Australia when he was 17 'for the adventure'. After 6 months he found himself in Darwin, then north again on a rusty cargo boat to Singapore and beyond. He's been a traveller ever since, but Darwin became home.

Graeme graduated with a degree in Applied Science from the Northern Territory University when he was in his forties, followed by an MSc in aquaculture conducted in some of the most isolated locations on the Kimberley coast. He went on to establish a business developing aquaculture in remote Indigenous communities which won him two Prime Minister's Awards. Graeme was also awarded a Churchill Fellowship to further his studies in Europe, a prestigious Federal Fisheries Scholarship and contracts to develop village based aquaculture in Eastern Indonesia. In 2015 he was awarded a PhD from the Australian National University for his studies in the historic ties between North Australia and the islands of Eastern Indonesia.

He and his wife, Barbara, are now building a house on a hill overlooking Gympie.

www.graemedobson.com.au

UNDER THE BANYAN TREE

A puzzle and a quest take the reader far beyond Australia's borders and its conventional history. An adventurous tale as much about doing history as finding the answers.

Professor Campbell Macknight

The history of Australia's north coast is a story of ancient industry and international trade with tentacles that reached as far as China. It tells of travel to the far reaches of the world where an old, mid-19th century Groote Eylandt man, spoke of chasing huge fish across cold seas and hunting furred creatures on seas hard as stone.

It's a story of great, forgotten empires on Australia's doorstep and rich Sultans who claimed that Australia's north as their own long before Cook laid eyes on it.

It's a story very few Australians know about.

When marine biologist Graeme Dobson asked elders about the origins of a strange stone structure in the middle of a bay, off a tiny island, near the coast of Arnhem Land they replied 'Not ours', and so began a remarkable quest that became a mystery wrapped in an adventure, folded into history.

His research took him to the far corners of Arnhem Land and into the Seas and Islands to its north. It led him back through time, past missionaries, colonists, huge fishing fleets, Dutch map-makers, Portuguese explorers-come-slavers, unknown settlers and miners, and pearl cultivating tribesmen until he finally found the answer in another bay off another tiny island, this time in the remote Indonesian Aru Islands.

This is a mystery/adventure with a difference, plus fascinating insights into little discussed history of northern Australia.